# STALIN
## *As Warlord*

**1** *Overleaf.* Stalin in 1919 aged 39 years, successively Chief Commissar with the North Caucasus, South, Ukraine, Petrograd, South and South-West Fronts.

# STALIN
*As Warlord*

Albert Seaton

**B. T. BATSFORD LTD**
London

© Albert Seaton 1976
First published 1976

ISBN 0 7134 3078 8

Filmset by Servis Filmsetting Ltd, Manchester

Text printed in Great Britain by
Biddles Ltd, Guildford, Surrey
for the publishers
B. T. Batsford Ltd
4 Fitzhardinge Street, London W1H 0AH

# Contents

# List of Illustrations

*Maps*                                                    *page*

# Acknowledgments

Gratitude is expressed to the authors and publishers for kind permission to quote from the following books: *The Turn of the Tide 1939–1943* by Arthur Bryant – Collins, London; *Delo Vsei Zhizni* by Marshal of the Soviet Union A. M. Vasilevsky – Izdatel'stvo Politicheskoi Literatury, Moscow; *General'nyi Shtab v Gody Voiny (Kniga Vtoraia)* by General of the Army S. M. Shtemenko – Voennoe Izdatel'stvo Ministerstva Oborony SSSR, Moscow: and to the Imperial War Museum for permission to reproduce the photographs of Marshals of the Soviet Union Zhukov and Konev, and to the Radio Times Hulton Picture Library for the use of the 1920 photograph of the cavalry army military council.

# Notes on Sources and Style

Since there is sufficient Russian printed matter available on Stalin as a military commissar and commander to form the basis of a work covering several volumes, the problem in writing this book has been to condense, in narrative form and within a limit of 100,000 words, the dictator's military activities over a period of 35 years. Moreover, since this book is intended for the general reader as well as for the \ Russian and military specialist, it has been necessary to include some background information covering Russian history, the Imperial Russian Army and the Red Army which followed it. Limitations of space have precluded comment or assessment by the author, and this is, in any case, unnecessary, since the material is for the most part self-explanatory. The substance of this book has been extracted from a much fuller monograph.

Before the Second World War, information, other than that contained in the Soviet encyclopedia contributions, the *Grazhdanskaia Voina* and the popular *Stalin i Krasnaia Armiia*, certainly existed concerning Stalin's military activities from 1918 to 1920; but it was sparse and difficult to get. By 1938 Stalin had already been accorded great fame as a military leader and theorist, at least by Soviet authors, so much so that historians outside Russia tended to turn to Trotsky's writings as a palliative. But Trotsky's works, valuable though they are as commentaries, are based on recollections committed to paper many years after the event; and Trotsky, even in maturity, was still fascinated by a turn of phrase, by words rather than by their accuracy or import. Trotsky has supported his descriptions of Stalin by a skilful use of what has now become known as *The Trotsky Papers,* copies of official records removed by him from the Soviet archives prior to his banishment. *The Trotsky Papers,* although authentic, are by themselves unsuitable for a biography on Stalin since their subject matter is Trotsky, and they represent in any case merely a random selection of documents. Trotsky's account of the part played by Stalin in the Civil and Polish Wars is therefore largely uncorroborated, and his chronology – even such factual detail as the military appointments held by Stalin during the period – is contrary not only to the information contained in the fourth volume of Stalin's *Sochineniia* published in 1947, but also to that in the successive issues of Lenin's *Polnoe Sobranie Sochinenii* and in the *Leninskii Sbornik.*

Much new light has been thrown on the Soviet High Command and the course of Red Army operations during the Civil and Polish Wars from 1918 to 1920, by the publication in Moscow during the late sixties and early seventies of a mass of official documents, edited and annotated by Soviet archivists, comprising correspondence, military appreciations and orders, and teleprinter traffic. This is particularly informative on the roles played by Lenin, Trotsky and Stalin *vis à vis* those of their military specialists, and does much to discredit the versions given by both Trotsky and Stalin. It can of course be proved that numbers of important documents are missing from the published Moscow collections, but this does not necessarily detract from their value for they have impeccable communist origins and represent an authoritative though not a definitive source of great importance.

Few Soviet documents have yet been published covering the period of the Second World War and, if the Moscow academic press is to be believed, few Soviet historians are permitted unrestricted access to the official archives. In Stalin's lifetime the work of military historians was too superficial to throw much light on the true nature of the military leadership during this period. Indeed, one of the most revealing publications of the time was probably the 1950 *Stalin – Kratkaia Biografiia* (which, according to Khrushchev, was edited personally by the dictator), since this unwittingly shows how Stalin misunderstood German strategic aims between 1941 and 1943. After Stalin's death, and particularly during Khrushchev's ascendancy, a number of detailed official histories of the Second World War appeared, together with a flood of military studies, war memoirs and reminiscences. Khrushchev was mainly responsible for the denunciation of the Stalin personality cult and for the exposure of some of Stalin's crimes against humanity, the party and the state, and he decried Stalin's military ability and caused Soviet historians to do the same. Yet within a short space of time a second Tsaritsyn group of generals began to laud Khrushchev's military genius, and this was only stifled with Khrushchev's removal from power. For the next few years the Soviet military press was uncertain and lacked its earlier uniformity of pattern. Condemnation of Stalin continued, but by degrees criticism became more moderate, and on some aspects, notably the repressions, muted. For Khrushchev bequeathed to the new Soviet régime a number of problems, among them that of publicly reconciling Stalin's excesses with the infallibility of Lenin and the Communist Party. From 1968 onwards increasingly frequent mention has been made of Brezhnev's role in the Second World War, relatively modest though this was. But whereas Khrushchev has been relegated to obscurity, it is impossible to do this to Stalin; so the dictator continues to dominate, in literature as in life, the 30 years of the history of the Soviet Union following Lenin's death.

The Soviet generals who were once close to Stalin are sensitive about their reputations, and their accounts are, not unnaturally, sometimes coloured by animosity, jealousy and prejudice: but all are informative. Some of the Soviet military studies are particularly well written and admirably produced. Much of the content of the more important historical works of the post-Stalin era is probably true, but it is certainly not the whole truth, for, of that part which can be verified, some is palpably false. Yet from this great wealth of Soviet evidence there emerges an unequivocal picture of Stalin as a military commander in the Second World War, whether written by an admirer or by an enemy, under Khrushchev or under Brezhnev. Even the silences are eloquent – *Tacent quia periculum metuunt : etiamsi tacent, satis dicunt.*

Of the memoirs of those officers who worked directly under Stalin, Zhukov's *Vospominaniia i Razmyshleniia* is full and instructive but lacks clarity and consistency; Vasilevsky's *Delo Vsei Zhizni* on the other hand provides a particularly informative, well-ordered and balanced account; Shtemenko's two volumes on the

*General'nyi Shtab* is a well-presented work of great value, by one who remains Stalin's ardent admirer. Of the front commanders who were close to Stalin, Rokossovsky's *Soldatskii Dolg*, Meretskov's *Na Sluzhbe Narodu*, Bagramian's *Gorod-Voin na Dnepre* and *Tak Nachinalas' Voina* all give an insight into Stalin's mentality and military capabilities; in addition Konev, Golikov, Tiulenev and Khozin have written memoirs or contributed to the Soviet military press. The front commanders Eremenko and Malinovsky belonged to the new Tsaritsyn group and were once protégés of Khrushchev, as was the tank commander Rotmistrov, and this is apparent in their writings. Some of the chiefs of staff and army commanders, such as Leliushenko, met Stalin frequently; many others, Batov and Moskalenko among them, did not see the dictator until late in, or after, the war, but he frequently spoke to them on the telephone during the course of operations. The artillery, air and naval chiefs, Voronov, Novikov and Kuznetsov, and the armament officials and designers Vannikov, Iakovlev, Emelianov and Grabin are authors of most informative accounts. All these reminiscences, and a score of others, have been used in compiling this work, and have been compared with each other (bearing in mind the origin and date of publication), and with western and German evidence. Whenever available, original Russian language works have been used in preference to translations.

Notwithstanding the restriction of space, a brief description of the Soviet state and military teleprint, telephone and radio system has been included, because its failure was partly responsible for the defeat of the Red Army in 1920 and again in 1941. The communication system is, in any case, part of the Soviet High Command.

In transliterating Russian words the Library of Congress method has been followed except that *y* has been used instead of *ii* for the endings of Russian surnames and the designations of tsarist regiments. There are unavoidable inconsistencies in the spelling of some proper names, particularly in quotation. Geographical names are shown in accordance with *The Times Atlas* current between the two world wars even though this does not necessarily follow the Library of Congress method or the spelling used on modern Russian maps. Surnames have been shown without initials (except on first mention to distinguish between two of the same name), and without titles or ranks. These can be found by reference to the index.

Because this book contains a great amount of factual material hitherto unpublished outside the Soviet Union, it has been thought necessary to annotate the text to show sources for the benefit of the historian and specialist; the source references have, of necessity, been much abbreviated and should be used in conjunction with the bibliography. The general reader can happily ignore the note numeration. Only six general maps are included since it is obviously impracticable to produce campaign maps to illustrate a text which covers so wide a field.

An appendix has been included at the end of the book in the form of short notes describing the organization and the terminology of the Russian and the Red Armies, for the benefit of the general reader who is unacquainted with this subject. Such readers may find it convenient to read the appendix before embarking on the main body of the book.

All dates are in accordance with the Julian calendar until 21 February 1918 and thereafter in the new style of the Gregorian calendar.

# Foreword

The subject of this book covers a very wide field and the work could not have been completed without the assistance of a large number of people. To all of them I express my gratitude.

I should like in particular to thank my readers: Professor Dr Alexander Fischer of the Johann Wolfgang Goethe University, Frankfurt; Mr Jeremy Newton of Queen's College, Oxford; Mr Michael Parrish of Indiana University; and Professor Dr Peter Scheibert of the Philipps University, Marburg.

I am most grateful to the Governing Body and the librarians of St Antony's College, Oxford, for the use of their resources. My warm hearted thanks go, too, to the Librarian and staff of the School of Slavonic and East European Studies, London University, and to the Chief Librarian and the Librarian in charge of the Library's Historical Section of the British Ministry of Defence Library (Central and Army), for their generous loan of Russian, German and English printed material.

In addition I thankfully acknowledge the assistance of government departments, learned organizations, libraries and many people in England, Germany and the United States. In particular: the Keeper of the Public Records, London; the Director and the staff of the Bundes-Militärarchiv, Freiburg; the Librarian and staff of the Slavonic Section of the Bodleian Library; the Soviet Studies Centre and the Librarian and staff of the RMA, Sandhurst; the Librarian and staff of the Institute of Contemporary History and Wiener Library; and the Librarian and staff of the Royal United Services Institute for Defence Studies.

I am particularly grateful to: Professor Dr Andreas Hillgruber of Cologne University for his advice on reading; Dr David Kahn, formerly of St Antony's College, for information concerning cryptography; Mr B. Stagg of *The Post Office Electrical Engineers' Journal* for his technical comment on line systems; and Major J. K. Zieleznik MC and the staff of the Post Office Telecommunications Museum for their interest in, and advice on, telegraph equipment in use in the Soviet Union between 1918 and 1945, and for their kindness in setting up and operating Hughes and Baudôt teleprinter circuits, entirely for the benefit of this study.

Lastly I should like to thank my wife who has typed and retyped the script many times and, over the years, has shared with me the arduous research.

# I
# *Tsaritsyn*

Stalin was born at Gori in 1879, the son of a Georgian cobbler named Vissarion Djugashvili. In 1894 he entered the theological seminary in Tiflis, where, in cloistered seclusion, the monks attempted to instil into the future atheist, regicide and revolutionary, a reverence for God, the tsar and the church. Five years later he was expelled and became a professional revolutionary and a Bolshevik.

From 1902 onwards the young Djugashvili was imprisoned no fewer than six times. A fellow prisoner by name of Vereshchak described Djugashvili as a rude and unpleasing speaker with an outstanding memory, crude and lacking in principle, having little educational background or culture, with 'an aptitude for striking secretly by the hands of others while remaining in the background himself'.[1] Extracts of Vereshchak's account considered to be sufficiently laudatory to Stalin were later to be published in *Pravda*.[2]

The February 1917 revolution had caught the Bolsheviks by surprise and many of them were abroad or in Siberia. Djugashvili, who had taken the name of Stalin, had been exiled in 1913 for revolutionary activities; this had not exempted him, however, from military call-up in December 1916, but he had been returned to Achinsk, presumably as medically unfit due to obstetrical palsy, a birth injury to his left arm.[3] Stalin was among the first to arrive in Petrograd.

On 10 October 1917 the Central Committee of the Bolshevik Party resolved on armed insurrection against the *bourgeois* Provisional Government, Stalin voting with Lenin in favour of the motion. A bureau of seven members was set up to undertake on the spot policy decisions on behalf of the Central Committee, these being Lenin, Trotsky, Zinov'ev, Kamenev, Stalin, Sokol'nikov and Bubnov, and a few days later a party 'military centre' was created consisting of Sverdlov, Stalin, Bubnov, Uritsky and Dzerzhinsky.[4]

Trotsky, a Bolshevik and Central Committee member of only a few weeks' standing, had, however, already formed, on 12 October, a revolutionary military committee, an unofficial body within the Petrograd Soviet, which, under the guise of defending the revolution, was to organize the Bolshevik *coup*. This committee had 66 members, all Bolsheviks except for 14 Left Socialist Revolutionaries and four anarchists. Lenin had intended that the five members of the party 'military centre' should form a part of the Petrograd Soviet revolutionary military committee, but, said Trotsky, they did not do so, although four of the five 'sometimes undertook some military work'.[5] The fifth, Stalin, 'kept away altogether'. For, according to Trotsky, the 'military centre' was merely a paper organization; and Stalin, whom he once described as 'not devoid of courage but merely preferring to expend it economically', wanted to face both ways and remain uncommitted.[6] Stalin, for his part, did not deny that the insurrection had been entrusted to the revolutionary military committee of the Petrograd Soviet, but insisted that this committee was carrying out the decisions of the Central Committee, the moving spirit of which was the party 'military centre' headed by Stalin himself.[7]

The Bolsheviks had promised peace and land to the peasant and independence to the minorities; they had singled out the officer as the class-enemy of the soldier. The old army, recruited mainly from Russian and minority peasantry, disintegrated in a flood of desertion. Many officers went into hiding or began to make their way to the Ukraine or to the territory of the Don Cossacks, the most powerful and most conservative of the Cossack hosts, which, even under the tsars, had preserved a measure of autonomy; for during November it became clear that neither the *ataman* of the Don Cossacks, nor the Ukrainian nationalists, would recognize the authority of the Bolshevik centre. A number of generals, Alekseev and Denikin among them, escaped and set off south-eastwards,

SOUTHERN RUSSIA

0                    200
         Miles

Vyazma

Smolensk
Orsha                    Yukhnov

Borisov
Bialystok          MINSK  Mogilev

WARSAW        BELORUSSIA

POLAND     Brest-Litovsk        Rogachev    Bryansk

PRIPET  MARSHES

Lublin            R. Pripet    Mozyr      Gomel

R. Desna

Konotop

Priluki    Romny
Lvov                    KIEV

Fastov              Lokhvitsa
Berdichev      Skvir

Belaya
Tserkov                  Poltava
U  K  R  A  I  N  E
Kremenchug
Uman

Ekaterinoslav
(Dnepropetrovsk)
Zaporozhe
Iasi              Nikopol
Kishinev

Odessa    R. Dnieper
Taurida
RUMANIA            Perekop
Sea of
Azov
R. Danube
CRIMEA

Sevastopol
Yalta

Black    Sea

joining the throng of the aristocracy, the wealthy, the educated and
the conservative, towards what they hoped would be the security
of the established order. The Don was to prove the Vendée of the
Russian revolution.

———————

The main government organ of the new Bolshevik régime was the
Council of People's Commissars (*Sovnarkom*), theoretically
responsible to the Soviet and its executive the *Vtsik*; in fact the
real source of power lay in Lenin and the executive of the Central
Committee, later to be named the Politburo, consisting of Lenin,
Trotsky, Sverdlov and Stalin. Sverdlov and Stalin were little
known outside party circles, both being behind the scenes political
organizers; Stalin was, however, still in the ascendency, even
Trotsky admitting that Lenin was steadily 'advancing' him.[8] With
Sverdlov's premature death in 1919 it was inevitable that Stalin
must come into collision with Trotsky.

On 4 March 1918, immediately after the signing of the Treaty
of Brest-Litovsk with the Central Powers, a Higher Military
Council (VVS) was formed. Trotsky became the first Commissar
for Military Affairs and, on 18 March, the Chairman of the VVS
and Collegium, the other members being the Bolsheviks Podvoisky,
Mekhonoshin, Skliansky, Antonov-Ovseenko and the former naval
officers Al'tfater and Berens. Bonch-Bruevich, a former general of
the Litovsky Guard Regiment, joined the VVS as its military
director. In fact Bonch-Bruevich was responsible only for defence
against the Central Powers, as all interior fronts were directed by a
special department transferred from Moscow Military District to
the Commissariat when it moved from Petrograd to the new capital
on 10 March.[9] The military direction remained confused, particularly since orders were issued not only by these two operational
bodies, but also by numerous other directorates, some newly
created as part of the Red Army and some taken over from the old
imperial army. Not until 8 May were these reorganized as a single
executive body, the All-Russian Main Staff, with the former general
Stogov (who in October deserted to the Whites) and the commissars
Egorov and Bessonov at its head. Even this rationalization failed
to provide the necessary centralized control.

The infant Soviet state was threatened by counter-revolutionary
forces and Trotsky soon appreciated the urgent need to re-employ

former tsarist officers in the Red Army. The most experienced of the officers were of course those of the pre-war cadres. Some regular officers in the ministries, the larger headquarters and the defensive screens in West Russia, had already become part of the Bolshevik military organization without a break in their service. Others, already demobilized, Shaposhnikov among them, wrote in and volunteered.[10] Some, like Littauer, were courteously invited to return, and permitted to decline.[11] Those who entered the Red Army came from a wide variety of tsarist regiments, the general staff and the foot guards being well represented, but there were comparatively few from the guard cavalry or cavalry of the line. The cadre officers' motives for joining either the Reds or the Whites were probably personal and varied, for there are no apparent grounds to suggest that they were based on divisions of wealth or social origin. Contrary to popular belief, in Russia and elsewhere, the regular officers did not form an exclusive society drawn from the nobility (which in any case was merely a bureaucratic caste), for they came principally from the *petite bourgeoisie* and the *razno-chinets*, the landless intelligentsia.[12] This was largely true also of the officers of the cavalry of the line, most of whom, for all their foppish manners, had neither property nor means other than their army pay.[13]

The pre-war cadre officers filled the principal command and staff appointments in the Red Army, except in the cavalry. The regular officers were, however, in the minority, for large numbers of former emergency officers were recruited for the formations and units. The experience and standard of efficiency of the wartime officer appears to have varied widely, for most of them came from the tsarist reserve of sub-ensigns or *praporshchiki*, men who originally had no experience or training as officers but who, by virtue of their education, were regarded as officer potential. Some had become efficient commanders and some were loyal to the tsar. Others, less patriotic, less able or less politically conscious, went into the tsarist service armed with little but egalitarian sentiments which turned them into poor officers, for, as Knox, the head of the British military mission, said, they hated military life and were too lazy or too lacking in character to enforce discipline or trouble themselves about their men.[14] This new type of officer, according to Trotsky, 'could not even make up his mind to sock the soldier on the jaw'.[15]

Other sub-ensigns made good revolutionaries, for some had already been convicted of subversion prior to 1917; others were a cross-section of the politically active intelligentsia, reflecting the views of Socialist Revolutionaries or Social Democrats, out of sympathy with the monarchy, patriotic ideals or the imperial armed forces. Numbers of these *praporshchiki* later became marshals of the Soviet Union.

The recruiting of former officers was soon put on to a compulsory basis and all were required to register. According to Denikin those who did so, if they did not later pass over to the Whites, were eventually 'exterminated or sucked down into the Bolshevik mire wherein human depravity and real tragedy found oblivion'.[16] Trotsky regarded 'the idealistic officer' as an insignificant minority, 'the rest who remained with us being without principles or energy to go over to the Whites'. Lenin, although he later admitted that the Red Army could not have been created without the former officers, said that he was going to 'make use of our enemy – compel those who are opponents of communism to build it'.[17] Many may have joined through fear, for, on 29 July, Trotsky ordered that any who refused to serve should be sent to concentration camps, and, on 30 September, commanded the arrest of families of those who had deserted to the Whites; Lenin elaborated this further by directing 'shooting for evasion of mobilization' and the taking of hostages from the families of officers and the *bourgeoisie* as a safeguard against desertion and treason.[18] Officers and their families were murdered. Some of those who did register for service were immediately thrown into concentration camps or Cheka cells from which they were brought out from time to time for examination or torture. Some died; some rotted away in forced labour camps; some passed via the Cheka into the Red Army. Yet, during 1918, more than 22,000 former officers volunteered or were mobilized into the Red Army and between 1918 and 1920 this figure rose to 48,000.[19]

The use of political commissars in the armed forces to supervise the commanders was not, of course, a Bolshevik innovation; Napoleon had revolutionary commissars accredited to his Army in Italy; Kerensky's Provisional Government had used them since the previous summer. But the replacement of Kerensky's commissars by Bolsheviks and Left Socialist Revolutionaries appears to have been done in a haphazard manner, and it was not until after Trotsky had taken office that an attempt was made to remove from the regional soviets and local partisan organizations the control of military affairs and the appointment of commanders and commissars.

The election of commanders by the troops had been short lived, and the dictatorship of the proletariat was eventually applied by the dissolution of all soldiers' elected committees, replaced in name, but not in substance, by the Bolshevik revolutionary military councils at all front and army headquarters. Although the title of these councils was in harmony with the spirit of popular revolution, in fact they consisted of the military commander, not necessarily a former officer, and one or two political members nominated from the centre and usually approved by the Politburo. None of course was elected, and all members were jointly accountable for their actions to their superior headquarters. Commissars were eventually appointed down to regiments.

By the early summer of 1918 the military situation was developing unfavourably for the Bolsheviks. A Czecho-Slovak corps had gained control of the Trans-Siberian railway and formed, together with the Ural and Orenburg Cossacks, the nucleus of the new White Siberian Front, which, moving westwards, took Ufa and Simbirsk and, on 6 August, the Tatar city of Kazan where the imperial reserves of gold were stored.

The Don and Kuban Cossacks had at first not been unfriendly towards Bolshevism, since they assumed that the Cossack territories would be permitted to become completely autonomous republics. For this reason the arrival on the Don of the thousands of former Russian officers and other anti-Bolsheviks was an embarrassment to the *ataman*. The presence of a Volunteer Army of 4,000 aristocrats, officials, schoolboys, and officers who had elected to serve in the ranks, was indeed so unwelcome that it was prevailed upon to move south where the Kuban Cossacks, who were of Ukrainian stock, had already suffered from the arrogance and depredations of the mainly Russian city soviets. There the Volunteer Army began to recruit both Kuban Cossacks and Circassians. In spite of their lack of weapons they soon showed that they were of high fighting quality, and began to destroy, one by one, the Bolshevik strongholds in Caucasia. Their effectiveness was based largely on their mobility.

The indigenous Don Cossack herdsman and farmer had little affinity with the Great Russian except in language; he could have had nothing in common with the openly hostile Red Guards arriving from the northern industrial areas. The *ataman*, Krasnov, encouraged by the Austro-German occupation of the Ukraine which sealed his west flank from Bolshevik foray, eventually roused his host and began to expel the Red forces. From 8 May German troops occupied Rostov, Bataisk, and the Taman peninsula across the Kerch straits, together with part of the Donets Basin. Krasnov exchanged his grain with the Germans for captured stocks of Russian weapons, preparatory to re-equipping the Don host and its traditional ally the Kalmyk.[20]

Bolshevik Russia, though it still stretched from the Arctic to the Caucasus, was being rapidly compressed from west and east. Much of the southern part of this narrowing funnel was the territory of the Don Cossacks, reaching eastwards from the Ukraine border almost as far as Tsaritsyn. When Rostov was lost and Kazan threatened, the Moscow government had to rely on the railroad, which ran south-eastwards across the Don Cossack territories through Tsaritsyn and then on to Tikhoryetsk and Stavropol, for its communication with the Caspian, the Caucasus and the Black Sea littoral. The Don, the Caspian and the Caucasus had become of primary importance to the economy of European Russia, following the loss of the rich agricultural and industrial Ukraine to the Central Powers.

The Soviet State was threatened by extinction and all measures were geared to the fight for survival. Lenin himself remained in the capital and had sent members of the Politburo and Central Committee as party and personal representatives to the threatened sectors. Trotsky boarded the train which was to become his travelling headquarters for many months ahead, a train so heavy that it needed two locomotives to draw it, equipped with offices, library, printing press, radio and telegraph station, carrying its own motor vehicles and an armed escort, dressed in black leather uniforms to make them look, as Trotsky said, more imposing.

.On 29 May 1918 a telegram had been received in Moscow from the Soviet North Caucasus Military District, describing the unsatisfactory military situation there, and calling attention to the importance of Tsaritsyn as a base and as a river and railway communication centre.[21] A further report came from Ordzhonikidze, Lenin's Commissar Extraordinary, critical of the conditions in Tsaritsyn and of the flabbiness of the officials. Since the situation called for resolute measures, Lenin instructed Stalin, on 29 May, to go to Tsaritsyn to organize, in a civilian capacity, the food deliveries to Moscow and Petrograd. He was then to move on to the naval base of Novorossisk and to the Transcaucasus.[22]

Stalin arrived by train in Tsaritsyn on 6 June 1918, with two armoured cars and an escort of 400 Red Guards. As a member of the Politburo and Central Committee, the representative of both party and government, he had plenipotentiary powers, except in the field of military operations.

On 7 June Stalin reported to Lenin the 'bacchanalia of profiteering and speculation' in Tsaritsyn; he had abolished the many committees and appointed his own commissars, and he was going to declare 'a grain week'. The rest of the telegram concerned the uncertain news from the Caucasus, the latter-day published version concealing that Stalin was, at the time, ignorant that German troops had occupied Bataisk.[23] On 13 June Lenin ordered Stalin 'or Shliapnikov', to go to Novorossisk immediately to forestall the seizing of that base by the Germans. Four days later Lenin again demanded action.[24] Shliapnikov then went to Ekaterinodar to meet the naval delegates, who carried out the sinkings of the Black Sea Fleet on 19 June.

The Bolshevik troops in the south were under the command of the North Caucasus Military District, with its headquarters at Tsaritsyn; the military council consisted of Snesarev, a former general from 1 Ekaterinoslavsky Grenadier Regiment, and Zedin, a naval rating and old Bolshevik. Snesarev was theoretically responsible for the area of the Don, Kuban, Black Sea, Stavropol and Daghestan, stretching from the Voronezh *guberniia* southwards for 1,000 miles down to the Turkish border. In reality, however, the northern part of the district was Don Cossack territory, while much of that to the south-west was in the hands of the Kuban Cossack host and the Volunteer Army; in Caucasia, both Armenia and Azerbaijan had declared themselves independent, while Georgia had become a German protectorate; only in the country of the Terek Cossacks did the Bolsheviks have a decisive numerical advantage.[25] The number of Red Guards in Caucasia, estimated at 100,000, was in fact unknown, but in any case Snesarev's and Zedin's control over them was largely nominal since the Bolshevik troops and the Red Guards acknowledged prior allegiance to their own semi-independent soviet republics. The Red Army strength in the land-bridge between the Don and Volga was increasing rapidly, however, with the arrival of armed bands and refugees, calling themselves 3 and 5 Ukrainian Armies, who were retiring, under German and Ukrainian nationalist pressure, eastwards towards the haven of industrial Tsaritsyn.

On 14 June Snesarev divided his district into the Khoper, Tsaritsyn and Kuban Groups, each of only 1,000 men or so, and appointed one Krachovsky to the command of the Tsaritsyn Group.[26] Nine days later, either at the bidding of the VVS or at Stalin's prompting, he replaced Krachovsky by Voroshilov, an old Bolshevik well known to Lenin and Stalin, the new Group Voroshilov incorporating Krachovsky's command and 3 and 5 Ukrainian Armies.[27] Voroshilov had no previous military experience, for since 1914 he had been employed in what was, presumably, a reserved occupation, the ordnance factory in Tsaritsyn, where 'he cloaked his activities as a political agitator under the cover of leading the workers' choir'.[28] A 1917 photograph shows him as a diminutive and clerkly figure, dwarfed by 11 burly soldiers, the only civilian member of the military section of the Lugansk Soviet.[29]

On 25 June the railway from Central Russia through Tsaritsyn to the Black Sea and the Transcaucasus was cut near Tikhoryetsk by a northern detachment of Alekseev's Volunteer Army, thus separating Kalnin's Group Kuban from Voroshilov's Group Tsaritsyn.[30] Since the telegraph was also destroyed, the only southern communication link remaining to the Bolsheviks in Tsaritsyn were the pony messengers who had to run the gauntlet of Volunteer Army and Don Cossack patrols. The middle Volga shipping route was shortly to be stopped up by the White forces advancing from Siberia, leaving only the two railroads Tsaritsyn–Tula and Kamyshin–Tambov connecting Moscow with the Caspian. Supplies from Caucasia and Trans-Caspia had to be brought in by water and offloaded at the Tsaritsyn or Kamyshin riverports for railing inland.

Stalin wrote to Lenin on 7 July telling him that the railway to the south was still blocked and, if only the military specialists (he called them *sapozhniki* synonymous with blockheads in tsarist Russia) had not been sleeping, the line would not have been cut. Stalin insisted that the deteriorating situation demanded the presence of a plenipotentiary with military powers, and suggested that he himself might be appointed. He asked for an immediate answer on the direct line.[31]

Three days later Stalin penned an angry letter to Lenin, intemperate even by the uninhibited Bolshevik standards of the time, complaining of Trotsky's high-handed action in ignoring Snesarev and Zedin. Trotsky, said Stalin, had, without reference to Tsaritsyn, dealt directly with the Don, Kuban and Stavropol military organization. Lenin should hammer (*vdolbite*) into Trotsky's head that he should not make appointments without consulting the people on the spot. This outburst was coupled with an abrupt demand for aircraft, armoured cars and six-inch guns, 'without which the Tsaritsyn Front will not remain in being'.

To get things done I must have full military powers. I have already written to you about this but have received no answer. Very well. In that case I will, without formality, root out those commanders and commissars who are ruining everything. I am obliged to do this in the common interest and, in any case, the lack of a chit from Trotsky will not stop me.[32]

The next day Stalin sent another telegram, impatient to the point of rudeness, complaining about the dilatoriness of the Tsaritsyn headquarters and the military specialists. He had, he told Lenin, already assumed full military responsibility and he was removing commanders and officials as he thought fit.[33]

As a result of this correspondence Stalin was officially appointed on 19 July as the chairman of the military council of the North Caucasus Military District, with Minin, a Bolshevik writer and mayor of Tsaritsyn, as the second political member. Zedin was transferred to the Volga flotilla. On 22 July Stalin and Minin signed Tsaritsyn Order No. 1 giving notice that they comprised the new military council 'together with such military commanders as they might appoint'.[34] Snesarev was not a signatory.

Trotsky has made light of Stalin's military activity in the south and has said 'that he headed only one of twenty armies', that is to say Voroshilov's Group Tsaritsyn.[35] This version has been generally accepted in the west.[36] Yet, on 24 July, Trotsky signed an order detailing the responsibilities of the North Caucasus Military District, reaffirming that it was to command not merely Group Tsaritsyn but all military and partisan activity from the borders of Voronezh to Baku. Stalin's angry outburst a fortnight earlier had presumably struck home, for Trotsky's signal was most deferential to the new chairman.[37]

Budenny, a Don *inogorodnii* uitlander and former sergeant of 18 Seversky Dragoons, was second in command of *vakhmistr* Dumenko's 1 Socialist Cavalry Regiment when he attended a political mass meeting near Tsaritsyn. Stalin, described by Budenny as 'a swarthy, thin man of medium height', was present there, and from this encounter began the life-long association between the two men.[38]

Snesarev signed his last order at Tsaritsyn on 16 July and was put on a train for Moscow. From 22 July onwards orders were issued daily over the signature of the military council, mostly concerned with the defence of the city of Tsaritsyn, mobilizing the 1896 and 1897 classes and covering such tactical detail as the movement of a Serb battalion, together with a company of the Peasant Regiment, an artillery section and eight machine-guns. On 26 and again on 29 July, the military council was pleading to the VVS for help, asking for an attack from the Voronezh *raion* on the enemy's northern flank to take the pressure away from Tsaritsyn; for unless help was forthcoming the North Caucasus Military District would be lost 'with consequences so vital to Russia'.[39]

Stalin said that he travelled widely in the region of Tsaritsyn, but apparently not into Caucasia or the Don Cossack territory. Voroshilov, who commanded only the Group Tsaritsyn, began to accompany Stalin on his tours. At the beginning of August, at Stalin's suggestion to the VVS, Voroshilov's name was added to the district military council. Henceforth orders lost their tsarist general staff format and took on the appearance of minutes of a political meeting, for Stalin appears to have conducted military affairs much as he wished. Or, as Voroshilov expressed it, 'a group of old Bolsheviks and revolutionary workers rallied round Comrade Stalin and, in place of the helpless staff, a Red, Bolshevik stonghold grew up in the south'.[40]

Stalin had described the military specialists to Lenin as 'psychologically unfitted . . . in general they feel themselves to be strangers, guests'; and he spoke the truth. For numbers of officers had been shot, and many of his specialists, including those newly dispatched from Moscow, were guests of the Cheka. Voroshilov has quoted with approval the account of Nosovich, a former colonel appointed in May by Trotsky as chief of staff to the district:

> Stalin's order was brief, 'Shoot them!' . . . a large number of officers, some belonging to the [counter-revolutionary] organization while others were merely suspected of being accomplices, were seized by the Cheka and immediately shot without trial.

Nosovich described Stalin's attitude to Trotsky's orders from the centre:

> Trotsky . . . sent a telegram that the headquarter military staff must be left alone to get on with their work. Stalin wrote across the telegram a categorical and significant order 'Take no notice'.[41]

Of the three principal military specialists on the district headquarters, Nosovich, arrested by Voroshilov, fled to the Whites; another was shot.[42] Stalin made no secret of his views in his letters to Lenin, for, on 4 August, he wrote of 'the inertia of the former commander [Snesarev] and the conspiracy of certain persons brought in by him' and he gave himself the credit for the 'timely removal of the so-called specialists'.[43] Over 30 years later Stalin was still congratulating himself on 'ruthlessly breaking down the resistance of the counter-revolutionary military experts appointed and supported by Trotsky'.[44]

With the removal of the specialists, Stalin's council was military only in name. Minin, the writer, was the regional representative. Voroshilov, described by Trotsky as 'a hearty and impudent fellow, not overly intellectual but shrewd and unscrupulous', was himself dependent on the advice of the non-commissioned officers, comrades like Dumenko and Budenny, and on that of the remaining military specialist, a former captain Sokolov. Trotsky subsequently characterized Voroshilov as 'a military know-nothing, half-guerilla, half-party man hanging on to his job for dear life . . . very indulgent with the chiefs of his divisions'. But Trotsky liked the ring of these words and applied them to other of his enemies, and his latter-day account is not always supported by what he said at the time. For on 27 October 1918 Trotsky praised Voroshilov as 'a conscientious worker with a pretty firm hand (*dovol'no tverdaia ruka*) over his indisciplined subordinates'; and of Voroshilov's military specialist, whom Trotsky subsequently described as a weak and pliant alcoholic unlikely to expose Voroshilov's ignorance, Trotsky wrote 'he is an able worker with an excellent understanding of the organization of 10 Army'.[45] The North Caucasus Military District had no designated military commander, but as Stalin was a political figure of almost unlimited power, described in the 1957 *Grazhdanskaia Voina* as bringing to the councils 'his enormous experience of party work and of the revolutionary struggle', Stalin decided military as well as political problems.[46] It is doubtful whether anyone in Tsaritsyn would have contradicted him.

On 4 August Stalin told Lenin that Cossack partisans upstream of Tsaritsyn were attempting to block the link with Kamyshin and had already cut the Tsaritsyn-Moscow railway. Troops would be thinned out from Tsaritsyn to thrust up the Don to the Khoper river, clearing the railway and disorganizing the enemy rear areas. This would take all his efforts. Matters did not stand well in the Caucasus, said Stalin, where there was widespread fighting against the Kuban and Terek Cossacks. The Group Kuban was apparently in the process of final disintegration – 'I say "apparently" because reliable intelligence about Kalnin has been impossible to get'.[47] Stalin's fears were justified for, a fortnight before, Kalnin's headquarters had been overrun; the deputy commander, a former colonel of the general staff, had committed suicide together with his wife rather than fall into the hands of the Whites, while the bareheaded Kalnin, a Latvian old Bolshevik, was last seen running for his life down the railway track.[48]

Voroshilov's popular account has described Tsaritsyn as threatened from the east by Astrakhan and Ural Cossacks, from the

2 Stalin's manuscript report to Lenin from Vyatka dated 5 January 1919 describing the Perm defeat (see page 42 ).

**3** *Above left*. Vatsetis, a Latvian tsarist colonel and the first Red Army C in C from 1918–19. He was purged in 1938.

**4** *Above right*. S. S. Kamenev *(right)* a tsarist colonel and Red Army C in C from 1919–24 (died 1936), together with his chief of staff Lebedev, a former tsarist major-general (died 1933).

**5** *Below left*. Egorov, a tsarist colonel and Commander of the Red Army South and South-West Fronts. From 1931 he was Chief of General Staff (purged 1939).

**6** *Below right*. Tukhachevsky, a tsarist second-lieutenant and Commander of the North Caucasus and West Fronts. From 1925 he was Chief of Staff of the Red Army (purged 1937).

west by Don Cossacks, while the Volunteer Army stood near at hand at Kotelnikovo. In reality the only threat to Tsaritsyn during the summer of 1918 came from Krasnov. The terrible atrocities of the Red Guards on Don Cossack soil had caused an uprising on the middle Don and the Khoper, and had enabled the *ataman* to mobilize ten classes, so raising the military strength of the host to 40,000 men. But Krasnov was unable to deploy the whole of this force against Tsaritsyn, for much of the Cossack territory was still in turmoil and he was also waging war against the Bolshevik forces in the Voronezh *guberniia*.

The Don Cossack, although ethnically Great Russian, had, over the centuries, acquired a passion for liberty, free speech and for meetings. Although he had more dash and initiative, he lacked the discipline and stamina of the Russian from the north. His loyalty lay with the host and he suffered from Cossack sickness, the reluctance to leave his paternal *stanitsa*; he co-operated only grudgingly with the *khokhol*, the Ukrainian Kuban Cossack. The Don Cossack excelled as a scout and raider, a lancer and swords-man; he was a dangerous adversary in close combat, a *beau sabreur* unfitted by temperament, military organization or training to fight pitched battles.[49] The Don Cossack's lack of dismounted troops and infantry experience resulted in a defective command and a serious fault in the structure of Krasnov's force, for the predominantly mounted element, supported only by horse artillery three-inch guns, could not hold ground. These military and personal deficiencies resulted, in Denikin's words, in extraordinary fluctuations – from lightning success to total collapse.[50]

At the end of July a Don Cossack force under Mamontov drove in Voroshilov's levies west of the Don near the Chir bridge, and crossed the shallow and slow moving river. Raiding patrols came whooping eastwards over the steppe, penetrating almost to the city outskirts, while others, under Fitskhelaurov, struck north towards Kamyshin. If Budenny is to be believed, the Red armoured trains and cavalry were used offensively, the fighting taking the form of forced marches and scattered raids, the struggle being fierce and pitiless, wounded and prisoners being done to death by both sides.

On 11 August Stalin, Minin and Voroshilov signed an order covering the shortening of the front and regrouping, all commanders being ordered to form independent companies directly under their own command 'for the struggle against deserters', a euphemism for the shooting down of broken units. Two days later Stalin declared a state of siege throughout the *guberniia*, and, on 14 August, the *bourgeoisie* were mobilized to dig the defensive trench works around the city. On 15 August the poet Minin sent a graphic and staccato telegram to Lenin:

> Varying fortunes ... our forces took *stanitsa* Voroponov capturing seven machine-guns ... order in the town ... send every cartridge cartridge cartridge [*sic*] ... Tsaritsyn key to southeast and source of corn ... demands urgent help.[51]

Stalin continued to concern himself with minor detail, although his orders for 16 August, besides appointing Shchadenko as a military commissar, showed an unexpected interest in Zhloba's Steel Division in the North Caucasus Republic, for he nominated Zhloba, a former miner, as 'the representative in the south of the military council'. On 22 August an order signed by 'the military council', no names being given, presumably in case it should fall into White hands, was sent by overland messenger to Sorokin, a former Kuban Cossack medical assistant who, following the routing of Kalnin's headquarters, commanded the Red troops in the area between Kotelnikovo and Vladikavkaz. Sorokin was ordered to instruct Zhloba to report to Tsaritsyn in person.[52] The messenger did not, however, reach Sorokin until 2 September. Meanwhile the danger to Tsaritsyn had receded, for Mamontov had broken off his attacks and fallen back 40 miles to the west. By early September Voroshilov was able to reoccupy and restore the positions on the bank of the Don.

On 31 August two dispatches were sent to the capital. The first was a cheerful and friendly personal letter to Lenin, following the unsuccessful attempt on the party leader's life, in which Stalin said that the Cossack enemy was finally breaking up. He asked that Artem should be directed to send some light torpedo-boats and two submarines down the Volga to the Caspian, which area, Stalin assured Lenin, was to be had for the asking, leading 'without doubt' to the freeing of Baku, Turkestan and the North Caucasus. Subsequent events failed to justify this optimism. The second was the telegram to Sverdlov, signed by both Stalin and Voroshilov, congratulating on his escape, 'the greatest revolutionary in the world, the tried leader and mentor of the proletariat, Comrade Lenin' and urging him to reply 'to this low-down attempt from round the corner, by the organizing of a public, massive, systematic terror against the *bourgeoisie* and its agents'.[53]

On 6 September, Stalin sent a telegram as *Narkom,* for he was the only signatory, detailing a number of localities reoccupied, and ending once again on a buoyant note 'the enemy is crushed and withdraws beyond the Don'.[54] This, too, was premature.

---

During the first weeks of July the Central Committee decided that the outcome of the revolution 'lies on the Volga and the Urals' and by the end of the month Lenin was to add 'that its fate rests on one map'.[55] The military situation continued to worsen during August, the Bolshevik weakness lying in the lack of a proper machinery for centralized military control, a defect pointed out in a paper by Egorov urging the appointment of a supreme military commander. Egorov's suggestions were accepted by Lenin and Trotsky, and the former colonel Vatsetis was appointed Commander-in-Chief.[56] The VVS was abolished, its functions being assumed by a Revolutionary Military Council of the Republic (RVSR) set up on 2 September, consisting of Trotsky as chairman, Vatsetis, Danishevsky, Kobozev, Mekhonoshin, Raskol'nikov, Rozengolts and Smirnov; later Aralov, Podvoisky, Skliansky and Iurenev were added. All, except Vatsetis, were Bolsheviks. The executive of the RVSR was the *shtab,* known from 11 October as the *polevoi shtab* (field headquarters). Vatsetis's post as the Commander of the East Front was taken by S. S. Kamenev, a former general staff officer and colonel of 30 Poltava Regiment. From this time onwards the Red Army began to be organized in established military fashion, further fronts being formed and the many screens, groups and detachments being concentrated into armies; these did not have a corps organization and at first consisted of only a few thousand men.

On 18 September a new South Front was created to replace the North Caucasus Military District and Stalin was appointed as chairman of its military council, the other political member being Minin, with Voroshilov as the district deputy military commander, all three retaining in addition their appointments on the military council of Group Voroshilov (later 10 Army) in Tsaritsyn.[57] On 28 September Stalin presided over what he called the first meeting of the council, to reorganize, on paper at least, the Red forces on the Don and in the Caucasus into the four groupings of 8 (Voronezh), 9 (Povorinsk), 10 (Tsaritsyn), 11 (Vladikavkaz) and 12 (Terek) Armies.[58]

Meanwhile, on or about 13 September, an unknown military specialist at Balashov wrote a paper on the proposed tasks and organization of the new South Front. The writer viewed the operations against Alekseev as separate from those against Krasnov and he was critical of the way the battle against Krasnov was being fought, for there was little co-ordination between the forces at Tsaritsyn and those north of the Don bend. Krasnov could only be destroyed, thought the writer, if a single command were to be set up in the area of the north Don directing the operations of 9 Army facing south, and 10 Army facing west, the junction point between the two being at Kamyshin. The writer suggested that Egorov should take command of 9 Army – which he later did; Voroshilov, however, was apparently unknown to, or little regarded by, the writer, for he believed the command of 10 Army to be vacant.[59] This paper may have influenced Trotsky in his decision to order the move of the South Front headquarters to Kozlov, a railway town about 400 miles north of Tsaritsyn. Shortly afterwards he appointed to the South Front a military specialist commander, a former general of artillery and chief of staff of the Rumanian Front, named Sytin. Sytin went to Kozlov while the other members of the military council remained at Tsaritsyn.

On 22 September Sytin complained to Vatsetis about the difficulty of working with Tsaritsyn since he received no replies to his signals; two days later he protested once more when he became aware that Stalin, Minin and Voroshilov had, without consulting him, issued an order to Sorokin covering the task and organization of the troops in the North Caucasus.[60] Vatsetis had the order cancelled.

Meanwhile Krasnov's Don Cossack cavalry had begun their second offensive and were again driving Voroshilov's troops eastwards. On 27 September Stalin's council, in a state of alarm, sent another order to Sorokin, commanding him to send Zhloba's

Steel Division, at that time 400 miles away, post-haste to Tsaritsyn; and, to give the order fitting legality, they instructed the former captain Sokolov to append his name to the ladder of signatures. That same night the council sent a situation report to the RVSR, written in Stalin's inimitable style:

> Situation deteriorating from 20 September. *Ataman* Krasnov has thrown twenty regiments, mostly horsed, against our front with some elements of Alekseev's Volunteer Army. Front broken . . . Something could still be done from the north sector of the South Front, but this sector is absolutely supine (*vialyi*) and the commander Sytin, in some stange way, is not interested in the matter . . . moreover, to our repeated enquiries as to the situation on the north sector he has, up to now, made no reply.

The signal ended in another demand for a large quantity of munitions, including 30,000 three-line Russian rifles, 150 Maxims and 50 three-inch guns, adding that 'unless this minimum is delivered immediately we shall have to retire to the left bank of the Volga'.[61]

The RVSR instructed Sytin to go to Stalin, armed with a written brief detailing his functions and accompanied by the RVSR member Mekhonoshin, a former Bolshevik student. On 30 September, the day after his visit, and as soon as he had got away from Tsaritsyn, Sytin telegraphed his report to the centre. The South Front military council had met at 2200 hours the previous night, Stalin, Mekhonoshin, Sytin, Minin and Voroshilov being present. Minin, not Stalin, took the chair. Sytin pointed out that Tsaritsyn was to the flank, even to the rear, of operations, remote from the centre and relying on a single railway line through Saratov, often out of action for days on end because of storm damage. He and Mekhonoshin wanted the headquarters to be at Kozlov or Balashov. Minin and Stalin insisted on Tsaritsyn. There was disagreement, too, as to the competence of the council to nominate military commanders and conduct operations, and Stalin, Minin and Voroshilov passed their own resolution 'finding themselves unable to recognize Sytin's full jurisdiction (*polnaia vlast'*) or the legality of his brief'.[62]

Trotsky has described his difficulties with the Tsaritsyn group that summer; 'in the early autumn Voroshilov began to disregard the orders from his superior South Front Headquarters, leaving unanswered its questions and ignoring its rebukes'. Trotsky said that he fumed against Voroshilov and he blamed Stalin for over-leniency in failing to make him carry out orders. It never entered Trotsky's head, so he subsequently said, that Stalin was the actual instigator of Voroshilov's insubordination, for Stalin, busy at work behind the scenes, 'bore himself so that at any moment, he would be able to jump back, his skirts clear'. This is Trotsky's explanation of what Rotmistrov called the weakness of the Central Committee 'in tolerating a conflict wherein Stalin and Voroshilov ignored the requirements of the RVSR'.[63] But Trotsky's inability to discern what was afoot in Tsaritsyn was due to his own deficien-cies and his attempt to keep abreast of military operations from a moving train. As soon as a High Command was brought into being with professionally trained commanders, it was inevitable that Stalin would be found out. For a study of the teleprinter traffic between the RVSR and Tsaritsyn indicates that Vatsetis and Sytin had no doubt where the responsibility lay.

Stalin associated himself with the activity of only one of his armies – that in Tsaritsyn – for he, too, lacked professional guidance. Trotsky, for his part, appears to have forgotten, or has concealed, that the military council of 10 Army also formed, with the addition of Sytin, the military council of the South Front. According to an account published during Stalin's lifetime, the military council of the South Front was empowered to select its own front headquarters' location, and, in the event of Sytin not proving suitable, to recommend his replacement within a week.[64] In the event, it was Stalin who was replaced.

The Latvian colonel Vatsetis was not one of those military specialists described by Stalin as 'strangers or guests' with the Red Army. He identified himself with the revolution, although he might have been a little less confident if he had seen Lenin's draft of 30 August (afterwards amended) containing the random and wanton suggestion that Vatsetis should be shot *pour encourager les autres*.[65] Vatsetis's sympathies were presumably those of a minority separatist, since he was not a Bolshevik and was to remain outside the Communist Party until the day he was liquidated in 1938. He was probably a man of mediocre ability – said to be better with troops than on the staff – for he had failed to qualify for the general staff on completing the 1909 course at the General Staff Academy. At the time of the revolution he commanded, at the age of 44, 5 Zemgalsky Latvian Rifle Regiment. Trotsky called him 'stubborn, cranky and capricious'.

The South Front continued to be commanded by two military councils, with Sytin and Mekhonoshin at Kozlov, and Stalin, Minin and Voroshilov at Tsaritsyn. On 2 October Stalin and Minin signed a signal to the RVSR, with personal copies to Lenin, Sverdlov and Vatsetis, but not to Sytin:

> Situation on South Front unsteady due to lack of armament and the failure to send submarines. With munitions we could have cleared the Povorino railway, driven back the Cossacks and sent detachments to Baku and Astrakhan. Since the RVSR has not given us what we requested, we feel it necessary to put the following questions:
> 1. Do you consider it necessary to hold the south?
> 2. If yes, can you provide the means?
> 3. If you cannot supply, should we not make a timely withdrawal to prevent the front disintegrating?
> 4. If you do not think it necessary to hold the south, then say so outright.[66]

A second, more temperate, signal the same day emphasized that the need was for weapons, clothes and supplies, not for men who were to be had in plenty since they could draw on the Don *inogorodnie* and the populations of the North Caucasus.[67]

The Central Committee sat on 2 October to consider the in-subordination of party workers to the decisions of the centre; on that day Sverdlov telegraphed Tsaritsyn chiding the council and reminding it that all decrees of the RVSR were binding on the fronts.[68] Vatsetis's replies were more direct. His first signal of 3 October to Tsaritsyn was a categorical order that there was to be no regrouping of any units without the approval of Sytin. The second summarized the situation as it was seen in Arzamas:

> It is noted by your telegrams that Sytin did not take part in the meetings of the military council. . . . You have centred your main attention on the Tsaritsyn sector at the expense of

others. . . . It has been proposed repeatedly that you should move from Tsaritsyn to Kozlov in order to join its commander, but up to now . . . you have continued to operate independently. Such a disregard of orders. . . . I consider to be intolerable . . .[69]

That same day Vatsetis appealed to Trotsky, who was then at Tambov, against 'Stalin's order No. 118 which must be cancelled', for Stalin's actions, said Vatsetis, were disrupting all the Commander-in-Chief's plans.[70] Stalin and Voroshilov, in their turn, so Stalin said, sent a telegram to Lenin demanding that the Central Committee should examine the actions of Trotsky, which threatened the destruction of the South Front.[71] On 4 October Trotsky signalled Sverdlov, with a copy to Lenin, insisting on Stalin's recall; and unless Voroshilov and Minin submitted to the orders of Sytin, Trotsky proposed to commit them for trial, for as long as Stalin and Minin remained in Tsaritsyn they were, according to the constitution of the RVSR, merely members of the military council of 10 Army.[72] Lenin supported Trotsky, and Stalin was removed from the South Front appointment. Stalin was recalled to Moscow on 6 October, returning to Tsaritsyn five days later, to remain there until 19 October when he finally gave up his additional post as the political member with 10 Army. Trotsky reconstituted the South Front council on 5 October and Voroshilov and Minin were excluded. Yet although Lenin had sided with Trotsky, Stalin had not fallen from grace, and the party leader went to some pains to emphasize this publicly by appointing him on 8 October to the membership of the RVSR and returning him to Tsaritsyn to conclude his business.

Meanwhile the raids and counter-raids continued on the Don–Volga land-bridge, and Stalin and his council signed their daily operation orders, often concerning only the movement of a cavalry squadron or an infantry battalion. The broad situation was well summed up, however, in a report prepared by Vatsetis for Lenin and Sverdlov and dated 7 October. Vatsetis put Krasnov's Don Cossack strength at no higher than 11 cavalry and two and a half infantry divisions, the latter being made up of dismounted cavalry and peasant levies; these were opposed by Iakir's 8 Army on the line of the Khoper, Egorov's 9 Army between the Khoper and Kamyshin, and Voroshilov's 10 Army covering Tsaritsyn. The

Volunteer Army, which Vatsetis estimated at 80,000 strong, was not immediately involved in the fighting since it was still in the Caucasus.[73]

The pressure against Tsaritsyn became increasingly acute and Vatsetis allocated his few available reserves, mainly reliable Latvian regiments, to Sytin. On or about 8 October Vatsetis himself visited Kozlov. By 15 October the situation inside Tsaritsyn was critical and Stalin, Minin and Voroshilov were thoroughly alarmed, for they sent a constant flow of telegrams to Lenin, Vatsetis and Sytin, appealing for help. Vatsetis's reply that same day was characteristically robust:

> From today's telegrams direct to me I see that the defence of Tsaritsyn has been brought by you to a catastrophic state. . . . You alone are responsible for the chaotic situation. . . . In view of the serious state of Tsaritsyn I am now sending reserves there. . . . Under no circumstances is Tsaritsyn to be given up.

Vatsetis followed by a signal to Sytin: 'I agree entirely with your decision to go over to the offensive but I beg you to push home the attack with such vigour and purpose that it really deals effectively with the Cossack troops operating against Tsaritsyn'.[74] Meanwhile Lenin and Sverdlov were demanding from Vatsetis the most urgent measures for the relief of the city.

At nightfall on 15 October, Minin was telegraphing Sytin in gloomy terms, saying that the evacuation of Tsaritsyn had begun and that there was a great need of everything 'which you have promised but have not sent'. On the following night at 2200 hours Minin spoke to Sytin once more, saying that the position was very bad and would have been worse if Zhloba's Steel Division, consisting of eight infantry and two cavalry regiments, had not arrived the previous night with its artillery. The division had gone straight into action and had already inflicted 1,500 casualties on the enemy. If it had not been for this division, said Minin, it was possible that Tsaritsyn might have been lost the next day. Vatsetis should be told that the position was worsening every hour.[75]

There is still much difference of opinion in present day Soviet military literature regarding the responsibility for the movement of Zhloba's division out of the North Caucasus. It is said that Zhloba left on the long march even before receiving Stalin's order dated 27 September, which he may have done, since it is over 300 miles in a direct line from Stavropol to Tsaritsyn. Because of this action Zhloba was outlawed as a deserter by a 12 October decree of the RVS of the North Caucasus Republic, for Armavir and Stavropol fell to the Volunteer Army shortly afterwards.[76] Zhloba's surprise attack into the rear of the Cossack forces barely 12 miles from the centre of Tsaritsyn, saved the city for the moment. But the fighting continued during the remainder of October and early November, until Cossack troops were drawn away northwards to face 8 and 9 Armies. By then other Red Army levies had been moved by Vatsetis into Tsaritsyn from Kamyshin, Astrakhan, Saratov, Nizhnii Novgorod and Moscow.

Tsaritsyn was saved, according to Voroshilov, 'by Stalin's indomitable will to victory, in spite of the almost hopeless situation'. At a later date Tsaritsyn was to be renamed as Stalingrad in honour of its defender.

---

On 23 October Stalin joined Lenin in Moscow and showed himself to be co-operative and almost contrite; for he much desired, he told Lenin, to work closely together with Trotsky, and he agreed to fit in with Sytin and Mekhonoshin on the South Front military council. Lenin telegraphed Stalin's case to Trotsky that same night.[77] Stalin did not return to the South Front, however, for shortly afterwards came the sudden collapse of the Central Powers, followed, on 13 November, by the Moscow repudiation of the Treaty of Brest–Litovsk. Civil war broke out in the Ukraine between the forces of the German puppet *hetman* Skoropadsky, Ukrainian nationalists, Bolsheviks, greens (armed deserters), anarchists and banditry.

On 17 November Stalin was appointed to the Ukraine Front in the area of Kursk, which had been given the mission of reoccupying the Ukraine, the other members of the military council being Antonov-Ovseenko and Zatonsky.[78] Troops were allocated to the new front by Vatsetis, and five military specialists joined it from Kozlov, together with Voroshilov, Shchadenko and 20 party workers from 10 Army 'who were placed at Comrade Stalin's disposal'.[79] Their tasks appear to have been political as well as military for, according to the 1 December issue of *Zhizn' Nat-*

*sional'nostei,* Voroshilov and Sergeev (Artem) had arrived in Kursk as members of 'the provisional government of the Ukraine'.[80] The Kursk group began operations near Kharkov but it appears to have achieved little while Stalin was with it. But the party workers continued to complain to Stalin, even after he had returned to Moscow, about Vatsetis's 'wrongful acts and omissions', his lack of interest in the Ukraine and his sabotaging of their work.[81]

On 30 November, Lenin appointed Stalin, together with Trotsky, Sverdlov, Krasin, Nevsky and Briukhanov, to the newly formed Council of Defence which sat under Lenin's chairmanship to co-ordinate and control all measures for the prosecution of the war. A latter-day Trotsky said that Stalin did little there, merely regarding its membership as an additional title; a much older Stalin was to style himself as the deputy chairman of that council.

# 2
# From Perm to Rostov

Towards the end of 1918 the right wing of Kolchak's White forces in Siberia began a westwards offensive, scattering Lashevich's 3 Army and taking the city of Perm together with 30,000 prisoners and a great store of booty. Although the axis of this offensive was in the general direction of Moscow, it was also intended to link up with the Archangel White troops to the north of Kotlas, about 500 miles away.

In the second week of December 1918, Lenin, much alarmed, had sent two telegrams to Trotsky's train, telling him 'to put pressure on Vatsetis' to reinforce the Urals.[1] A week later he described to Trotsky 'the catastrophic state of 3 Army and its drunkenness'. Lashevich, an old Bolshevik and former sergeant, was 'drinking and in no fit state to restore order'. Lenin had considered sending Stalin there, and he asked Trotsky to telegraph his opinion and go to the East Front himself. Trotsky did not go but he signalled his agreement that Stalin should journey to Perm and 'restore order, purge the commissar personnel and severely punish the offenders'.[2] On the first day of the New Year, Stalin, together with the Pole Dzerzhinsky, the head of the Cheka, set out to investigate.

On 5 January Stalin sent a preliminary report to Lenin in his own handwriting, emphasizing the material weakness of 3 Army; it had been reduced from 30,000 to 11,000 men, and reinforcements were urgently required. For the units sent by Vatsetis, said Stalin, were so unreliable that they were even hostile to the Bolshevik cause. It was *absolutely* essential to *rush* three *completely* reliable regiments to the area (Stalin's italics): otherwise 'Vyatka is threatened with the fate of Perm'.[3] In reply Lenin told Stalin to remain with 3 Army and to signal his proposals by priority cipher.[4] Eight days later Stalin sent a further dispatch, giving some of the causes of the defeat. The language and content were to the point, Stalin blaming exhaustion, lack of reserves, mismanagement on the part of the army commander, the isolation of the commanders from the troops and the instability of the rear; for, said Stalin, the Soviet and party organizations behind the front were hopelessly incompetent. Stalin condemned 'the downright criminal (*prestupnyi*) method' of directing operations by the RVSR in sowing confusion with contradictory orders.[5] In acknowledgement Lenin authorized Stalin to take all necessary measures on the spot.[6]

Stalin's and Dzerzhinsky's final report, signed in Moscow on 31 January, was a comprehensive work, the result of a detailed investigation into operational, tactical and administrative matters. Stalin paraphrased Kamenev's evidence in this fashion:

A directive was received [from the RVSR] saying that 2 Army ... was to be ready for another assignment on another front, without saying where this was likely to be. In these circumstances 2 Army could not be committed in case it might be impossible to extricate it. . . . Then suddenly Shorin, the Commander of 2 Army, was called to Serpukhov, thus paralysing 2 Army (things being what they were), and a further five days were lost. At Serpukhov, Kostiaev [a former engineer and general staff officer] . . . merely wanted to know whether Shorin had belonged to the general staff – which he had not . . . Kostiaev said that he 'would think about it'.[7]

The report continued, in Stalin's own words:

Gusev . . . the front political member . . . received three telegrams in succession, each giving a different main axis for the East Front. . . . One may easily judge how light-hearted are the attitudes of the RVSR and the Commander-in-Chief to their own directives.

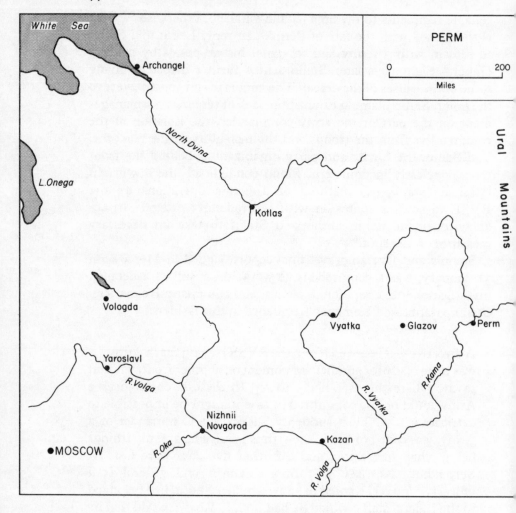

Nor did Stalin spare 3 Army:

> The military council consists of two: Lashevich, who commands; as for the other, Trifonov [the political member], I have not succeeded in ascertaining what his role or function is . . . it looks as if he does nothing . . . the headquarters is entirely divorced from the scene of operations, having no liaison officers at the divisions or brigades to watch and inform . . . and army headquarters is satisfied with formal written (and often imprecise) reports. The army is completely in the hands of subordinate formations, the commanders of which behave like feudal princes . . . lack of centralized control and the everlasting screams of protest about the weakness of junction points and boundaries. And it is a fact that while 3 Army was shedding its blood the neighbouring 2 Army was marking time and doing nothing for a fortnight.

Stalin had something of the quartermaster-general about him in his insistence on statistics – a trait out of keeping with the military methods of the time, for it was part of the Russian character to make grandiose plans without first ascertaining whether the means were available to carry them out. Stalin set out his figures in pedantic detail, noting that 3 Army had lost 248 of its 571 machine-guns, and, between August and December, had received 13,153 men, 3,388 bayonets, 134 machine-guns, 22 guns and 977 horses; holdings and losses of warlike materials were listed; butter, fats, aluminium and steel rails, were similarly itemized by weight, length or cubic capacity.[8]

Voroshilov's panegyric has made bold claims for Stalin's three week stay in Perm.[9] But his version is contrary to both White and British contemporary accounts and is not supported in modern Soviet works.[10]

In March Stalin was present during the Eighth Party Congress, where one of the main points discussed was the future organization of the High Command and the Red Army. Many of the delegates arriving from the fronts were seething with anger against Trotsky, but Trotsky himself did not attend. Although Stalin had instigated the resistance of the Tsaritsyn group only six months before, and continued, in private, to denounce the military specialists and the

RVSR, he did not publicly identify himself with what was to become known as 'the military opposition'. So when the absent Trotsky came under attack 'for his dictatorial manners, for his scornful attitude to the front workers and his unwillingness to listen to them, for his adoration of the specialists, and for his torrent of ill-considered telegrams sent over the heads of commanders and staffs, changing directives and causing endless confusion', Stalin spoke with Lenin against the opposition, prominent among whom were Voroshilov and Minin.[11]

At the closed session, on 21 March 1919, Lenin refuted the contention that a feudal army was being raised based on serfdom and a system of rank, and that the *Narkomvoen* and RVSR duplicated each other; and Lenin defended Trotsky against the charge of not carrying out the policy of the Central Committee. Lenin pointed out that 'the Politburo decides all questions of strategy and the movement of reserves, discussing these questions almost daily'.

> We have of course . . . made our mistakes. . . When Stalin carried out his Tsaritsyn shootings I thought . . . that the shootings were wrong. Those documents which Comrade Voroshilov has quoted to illustrate the mass heroism of 10 Army – and in part of Comrade Voroshilov himself – disclose our mistakes. . . . There were disagreements between Stalin and myself . . . but there was no question that the policy of the Central Committee was carried out by the military.

Lenin continued:

> Comrade Voroshilov has said that we had no military specialists at Tsaritsyn and we had 60,000 losses. But that is dreadful . . . and to say 'We managed without specialists' – is *that* really defending the party line?[12]

In May 1919 the Red forces were driven out of Latvia, while, further to the south, Vilna had been taken by the Poles, who then began to force the Bolsheviks eastwards. On 13 May Rodzianko's 5,000 strong White Russian corps crossed into Russia and was redesignated as the North-West Army, under the overall command of Iudenich, the White Commander-in-Chief Baltic. When Rodzianko began his march on Petrograd, he was opposed by part of 7 Soviet Army, which, although it totalled 15,000 men and 160 guns, was extended over a 400 mile front and was already under attack by White Finnish forces.

Trotsky took no part in repulsing this offensive, but he did play an important role in October of the same year when Iudenich made his second march on the former capital. Iudenich got closer to Petrograd in October than he did in the previous June, but whether this justifies Trotsky's description of Iudenich's first campaign as 'passing practically unnoticed by the party', is to be questioned.[13] Rodzianko's success was in fact rapid and by taking deserting Red Army units into his ranks he increased his numbers three-fold, Soviet historians putting the White strength at over 15,500 men.[14] On 12 June the Bolshevik garrisons of the coastal forts of Krasnaia Gorka and Seraia Loshad', in the Red rear, mutinied and declared for Rodzianko.

On 17 May Lenin had sent Stalin to Petrograd with plenipotentiary powers to organize the defence in the north-west. Four days later Petrograd was declared to be 'one of the most important fronts', and on 10 June the Central Committee formally resolved that the Petrograd front was 'the most important front of the republic'.[15]

Lenin had always followed the course of day-to-day military operations closely and, since Trotsky was rarely in the capital, dealt directly with the RVSR. Skliansky, as its secretary, had the duty of relaying to him daily, sometimes hourly, the most important military developments, together with requests for decisions.[16] An ageing Stalin once said that Lenin had had no military knowledge and had confessed to being too old to learn, so he had encouraged his younger colleagues, Stalin among them, to study military affairs and act in his stead.[17] Stalin's assertion is contradicted by the volume of evidence available. Trotsky, on the other hand, maintained that Lenin 'remained in Moscow with all the threads concentrated in his hands', giving judgement on military questions 'which were new to all of us' on the basis of information which came, for the most part, from party representatives with the fronts.[18] Lenin lent a ready ear to complaints against the RVSR made verbally or by ciphered telegram, and his lack of military knowledge

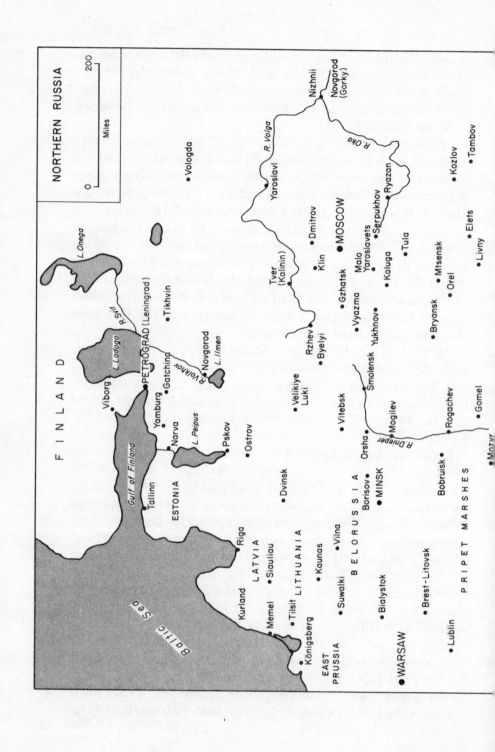

NORTHERN RUSSIA

0    200
Miles

FINLAND

Baltic Sea

EAST PRUSSIA

Königsberg
Memel
Tilsit
Kurland
Siauliau
LATVIA
Riga
LITHUANIA
Kaunas
Vilna
Suwalki
Bialystok
Brest-Litovsk
Lublin
WARSAW

Tallinn
ESTONIA
Dvinsk
Borisov
MINSK
BELORUSSIA
Bobruisk
PRIPET MARSHES
Mozyr

Viborg
PETROGRAD (Leningrad)
Gatchina
Yamburg
Narva
L. Peipus
Pskov
Ostrov
Velikie Luki
Vitebsk
Orsha
Mogilev
Rogachev
Gomel
R. Dnieper

Gulf of Finland

L. Ladoga
R. Svir
L. Onega

Novgorod
L. Ilmen
R. Volkhov
Tikhvin

Vologda

Smolensk
Yukhnov
Vyazma
Byelyi
Rzhev
Gzhatsk
Malo Yaroslavets
Kaluga
Bryansk
Orel
Mtsensk
Tula
Serpukhov
Ryazan

Tver (Kalinin)
Klin
Dmitrov
Yaroslavl
MOSCOW

R. Volga

R. Oka

Nizhnii Novgorod (Gorky)

Kozlov
Elets
Livny
Tambov

did not inhibit him from controlling the RVSR and interfering with the lower echelons, sending a daily stream of notes and signals to Skliansky, Trotsky and the front councils, in emphatic and often violent terms, urging, chiding and threatening. He was constantly 'surprised', 'alarmed' or 'shocked' at the lack of information from, or success of, the fronts, describing the conduct of his close party colleagues as 'monstrous' and 'criminal'.

On 20 May Lenin sent a telegram to Stalin at the Smolny, 'trusting that the general mobilization of Peterburgers will result in offensive operations and not just sitting about in barracks'.[19] On 27 May he warned Stalin that the rapid White advance obliged him to assume treachery; a few days later Lenin dispatched the following signal:

It is said (1) that the Petersburg units are more demoralized than the reinforcements from the provinces which deteriorate under their influence (2) that in spite of their numbers they are not fit for the offensive (3) that the military have already decided on evacuation (4) that the Commander of 7 Army [Remezov] is not at his post but has turned himself into Zinov'ev's adjutant. Inform me of the position in cipher.[20]

On 2 June Lenin was again instructing Stalin to keep him informed of developments; the next day he was demanding from Stalin an early, strong and decisive offensive.[21] On 8 June Lenin ordered the emergency transfer of troops to Petrograd from other fronts; two days later he was berating Skliansky for being misled by someone 'playing down the disaster' at Petrograd, Lenin calling Skliansky's tardiness 'an act of treason'.[22] Meanwhile the defence of Petrograd had been removed from the control of the RVSR and placed directly under the Committee of Defence and the Central Committee, Stalin becoming 'the Extraordinary Commissioner in command of the Petrograd area and other regions of the West Front'.[23]

On arrival in Petrograd Stalin had held a meeting with Vatsetis, and Nadezhny and Remezov, the commanders respectively of the West Front and 7 Army. On 20 May he was at the headquarters of the West Front at Staraya Russa, then going on to Gatchina and Kronstadt. On 9 June Stalin signalled Lenin to say that he was siting his second line of defence on the old Peterhof-Gatchina fortifications once used against Kerensky; he wanted further reinforcements and he complained yet again about the unreliability of those already dispatched by the All-Russian Main Staff.[24] On 16 June, the two coastal forts were reoccupied by Bolshevik troops, Stalin, so he said, personally directing the attack on Krasnaia Gorka 'from the firing line'.[25] That day Stalin sent the telegram described by Trotsky as 'overbrimming with provocative braggadocio'. 'The naval specialists assure me,' said Stalin, 'that the capture of Krasnaia Gorka from the sea counters all naval science. I can only deplore this so-called science. Its swift capture was due to the rudest interference in the operations by me. . . .' On the telegram Lenin wrote 'But Krasnaia Gorka was taken from the land!'.[26] Among the West Front directives is one, dated 14 June, requiring the fleet to concentrate against Krasnaia Gorka, and the guns of Kronstadt to bombard it from a range of 15 miles; from this it would seem that Stalin was not the only director of operations.[27]

Voroshilov's cartographic account of Rodzianko's repulse shows a large red banner marked 'Stalin' flying over the Smolny, while 7 Army near Gatchina deployed 6 and 2 Rifle Divisions in defence of Petrograd. Success, denoted by the broad red arrows, went to 6 Division.[28] Again the military directives throw a different light on the affair. On 14 June the headquarters of West Front had moved to Smolensk, and Nadezhny, a tsarist corps commander originally from 14 Georgian Grenadier Regiment, would appear to have been directing the Petrograd battle from there, strengthening 7 Army by removing formations from his other armies. On 17 June he had a teleprint conversation with Remezov (a former general staff officer from 117 Yaroslavsky Regiment) and suggested that 7 Army should envelop Rodzianko from the south by thrusting on Veimarn or Yamburg. Remezov replied that he had already drawn up his plan and proposed to make his envelopment closer than that suggested by Nadezhny, deploying eleven regiments in the south and six regiments (of 6 and 19 Rifle Divisions) in the north between the main road and the coast. Meanwhile 7 Rifle Division would be held in reserve in the area of Gatchina. Nadezhny was not content with Remezov's plan, which resembled, he said, a frontal attack (*lobovoi udar*), much of it through wood and swamp. He wanted

7 Army to adopt the West Front solution and commit the newly arriving reserves further to the south.[29] Remezov had, therefore, elements of five rifle divisions in this sector, and some of these appear to have been converted to the 1918 establishment of nine regiments to the division. Whatever was finally settled, the main attack certainly did not come, as Voroshilov said, from 6 Rifle Division on the extreme right against the Gulf of Finland.

At the time of Stalin's arrival in Petrograd 6 Rifle Division covered the main south-west approaches to the city, and this formation appears to have captured his attention. Stalin's reports to Lenin were in the first person, for he had apparently begun to regard Remezov and Nadezhny as interlopers. The Commissioner continued to stress the lack of support from Moscow, for on 22 June he signalled Lenin 'our attack began yesterday, although we have not received the promised reinforcement . . . our offensive goes well . . . we have secured the line Kernovo–Kaskovo [in front of 6 Division] and have taken prisoners and two or more [*sic*] guns'. He ended 'send quickly two million cartridges at my disposal for 6 Division'.[30]

Some of Stalin's political and military assessments at this time were Lenin's views, relayed back to the capital. Lenin had suggested treason and Stalin had not been slow to unearth it. A search of the foreign consulates had brought to light what Stalin claimed to be a counter-revolutionary conspiracy, and the Cheka began to work on and embroider the evidence. Trotsky believed that Stalin's revelations were inspired by hostility to himself, a not improbable hypothesis; yet the Cheka's quarry appears to have been the RVSR, military specialists in general and perhaps those who had offended Stalin. For, according to Stalin, it was evident that the All-Russian Main Staff and the field headquarters of the RVSR, headed, Stalin reminded Lenin, by Kostiaev, 'were all working for the Whites'; he conjectured that both organizations were responsible for certain mass desertions, which he named. He added a goad, so clumsily worded as to be offensive: 'The whole question now is that the Central Committee should summon up the courage to draw the proper conclusions – but has the Central Committee sufficient character and resolution?'.[31]

At the beginning of June Okulov, the political member with the West Front, had complained to the Central Committee about

Stalin, saying 'that 7 Army is being divorced from the West Front and is receiving reinforcements and equipment through parallel lines of supply'. Okulov wanted 7 Army either returned to the West Front or put directly under the RVSR. Lenin asked for Stalin's views.[32] This complaint by Okulov, an old Bolshevik who was hostile to the Tsaritsyn group, drew from Stalin the reply that it was his 'profound conviction that Nadezhny is not a commander, or capable of commanding, and will finally wreck the West Front', while 'party workers such as Okulov who urge the military specialists against our commissars . . . are harmful and demoralize the vital core of our army'.[33] The Central Committee acceded to Stalin's demand that Okulov be removed.

Trotsky subsequently charged Stalin and Voroshilov with 'merging both of Iudenich's campaigns into one so that the famous defence of Petrograd is represented as Stalin's handiwork'.[34] In fact Stalin took no credit for the October battle but merely repaid Trotsky in his own coin, by ignoring operations other than those in which he was personally involved. Stalinists have since improved on these methods by imputing to both Trotsky and Zinov'ev plans 'to let the enemy into Petrograd'.[35]

On 5 July, following the repulse of Rodzianko, Stalin was appointed as the political member of the West Front military council, together with a new commander, Gittis, who was, in due course, to replace Nadezhny. From 9 July to 26 September Stalin was at Smolensk.

On 18 July Stalin sent a personal telegram to Lenin outlining the position as he saw it on the Polish sector. The situation in the area of Minsk was poor; at Dvinsk – no better; at Lubents it was even worse. The Red units were in tatters and the enemy would not wait. Stalin believed that the front could do much, however, if Lenin would give it one suitable division. But he feared, he said, that Lenin would not do so, and then later, in a month's time, three divisions would not be enough. It was no use standing where they were; therefore they had decided to attack, scraping up and sticking together units as they went. Something might come of it. Stalin ended by condemning 'the military commander [Nadezhny], who is no use, for he only ruins everything'.[36] Stalin's brave intentions were not realized, however, for the enemy began his own offensive. By 1 August Lenin, fearful for Petrograd, was again harrying Stalin, ending; 'Ought you not personally to be taking heroic measures there?'.[37]

By 11 August Stalin had returned to his well-worn theme, describing the situation to Lenin in gloomy terms and heaping reproaches on the military centre. The Polish enemy was prising loose 16 Army so that the flanking armies would have to close up to stop him, using not one army but the whole front. It was apparent, he said, that the West Front was in the same position as the East Front the previous year, 'when Vatsetis and Kostiaev needlessly messed up operations'. He had already warned Lenin that the West Front was a ramshackle affair (*loskutnyi dvor*) which needed immediate reserves. Stalin ended: 'Now decide yourself; will you let us have a division . . . or will you allow the enemy to destroy the already crumbling 16 Army; but decide immediately, for each hour is precious'.[38]

---

Kamenev, the Commander of the East Front, was easy to get on with, and the political members Smilga, Lashevich and Gusev, spoke highly of him. Gusev lived *en famille* with the Kamenevs. Trotsky and Vatsetis, however, were hostile to Kamenev, and Kamenev's daughter has described a Trotsky visit to Simbirsk, when, dressed in black from head to toe, armed with a parabellum pistol and accompanied by a retinue, he burst into Kamenev's office, shouting threats in a highly excited state.[39] Vatsetis did not want the East Front to pursue Kolchak beyond the line of the Urals. Kamenev was in favour of doing so. Trotsky supported the Commander-in-Chief and, on 5 May, at Vatsetis's urging he summarily dismissed Kamenev, sending him on indefinite leave.

Having been advised by Gusev to put his case to Skliansky, Kamenev set out for Moscow where he lived with his family in a railway coach at the Kazan terminus. Meanwhile the East Front military council protested to Lenin against Kamenev's removal. Lenin interviewed Kamenev on 15 May, requiring from him a briefing, and then told him to return to his old command.[40]

Trotsky knew nothing of this – he was not aware of Kamenev's whereabouts, and he first heard of the reappointment on 21 May, Lenin explaining that he had reinstated Kamenev 'as a consequence of the signal' from Smilga, Gusev and Lashevich.[41] Trotsky was losing influence with Lenin, possibly because his military judgement was being called into question; his conduct had alienated military as well as political workers, and Vatsetis's personality had served to sharpen this conflict, for his correspondence shows him as an arrogant pedant. Lenin, having sided with Kamenev against Trotsky and Vatsetis, privately told Smilga, Lashevich and Gusev to let him have, by ciphered telegram, details of any future disagreements between Kamenev and Vatsetis.[42]

On 6 June Kamenev prepared a plan for the continuation of the advance into Siberia; Vatsetis vetoed it. The military council of the East Front protested to Lenin, and Smilga and Gusev were called to Moscow for consultation. On 14 June a meeting of six members of the Central Committee was held in Petrograd, at which Stalin was present, and a plenary meeting followed in Moscow the next day. These meetings sided against Vatsetis and, in consequence, Trotsky, according to Gusev, 'exasperated by his setback in the Central Committee vented his rage on the East Front'.

Matters finally came to a head at the Central Committee meeting of 3 July, for everyone voted against Vatsetis. Trotsky stormed out and wanted to resign all his offices, an offer which was declined. It was decided that Kamenev should be appointed as Commander-in-Chief, bringing in Lebedev, a former general staff officer of the Moskovsky Guard Regiment, who was Kamenev's chief of staff, to replace Kostiaev. The RVSR was to be reconstituted to include only Trotsky, Skliansky, Rykov, Kamenev, Smilga and Gusev, a council consisting largely of former members of the East Front, who were not kindly disposed towards Trotsky.[43] Trotsky, smarting under his reverse, remained for the rest of the summer with the South Front at Kozlov, his absence and estrangement from the RVSR serving, in Kamenev's view, to bring the organization closer under Lenin's control.

Stalin supported Smilga and Gusev against Vatsetis. A few days later his ally Dzerzhinsky brought to light the results of a Cheka investigation, implicating Vatsetis in suspected treason.[44] Vatsetis was arrested, subsequently released, and then, since the Central Committee felt itself to be in his debt, appointed to an academic post as an instructor.

Although Kolchak and Iudenich had retreated and the authority of the White government in Archangel was on the wane, a new and greater threat was looming in the south. The British had prevailed upon Krasnov to resign as *ataman* of the Don Cossacks, because the White generals refused to co-operate with him; as Alekseev was dead, Denikin had taken over the supreme command of all the White and Cossack forces, and was already receiving British support in weapons and supplies.

Denikin's force consisted of three armies: on the right, Wrangel's Caucasians on the Manych; in the centre, Sidorin's Don Cossacks in the Don bend; and on the left, Mai-Maevsky's Volunteer Army to the north of Rostov. The White strength in the south rose between May and October 1919 from 64,000 to 160,000 men.[45] Opposing Denikin was Egor'ev's South Front, stretching from the middle Dnieper to the lower Volga, and consisting, from west to east, of 14, 13, 8, 9 and 10 Armies, totalling in July about 178,000 men.[46] Denikin's principal aim, so he said, was to strike north and take Moscow, but in fact his formations fanned out across the Ukraine and South Russia, apparently intent on recovering territory and material resources and on protecting the Ukraine from the Poles. By the middle of August the larger part of the Ukraine had been taken, including the cities of Kharkov and Belgorod; in the east Wrangel had advanced beyond Tsaritsyn, nearly half-way to Saratov. The momentum of the offensive showed no signs of falling off.

Denikin's rapid successes caused a split in the views of the Bolshevik Government and its military command, a conflict of ideas which continued to be ventilated in the world press generations after the event. Expressed in simple terms, it was whether to counter-attack Denikin in the flank, on an axis running roughly from east to west, or in the centre by a thrust running from north to south. The east-west axis from the lower Volga to Rostov was aimed at overrunning the territories of the Don Cossacks, Denikin's principal supporters; but this advance had to be made over the open steppe with few roads and rail links, against an implacable enemy. When put to the test of battle it failed. The main axis was then changed to the north-south direction down the Donets Basin, traversing an industrial area inhabited by workers whose sympathies lay with the communists. This virtually destroyed

Denikin's forces. Subsequently, both Trotsky and Stalin claimed to be the author of the victorious plan, imputing to the other the unsuccessful course of action.[47]

Trotsky has used documents in an attempt to prove that the successful plan, based on a shrewd appreciation of geographical, economic and political factors, was his own, and he has convinced both Souvarine and Deutscher that this was so.[48] Yet all that can in fact be deduced with certainty from his papers is that Vatsetis and Kamenev disagreed on the strategy to be adopted by the East Front.

On 27 July Trotsky, who was with the South Front, reported to Moscow that its commander Egor'ev considered 'Kamenev's plan of operations *incorrect*' (Trotsky's italics); Trotsky suggested that Egor'ev be replaced by someone 'who acknowledges the operational authority of Kamenev and agrees with his plan', almost intimating that such a commander might be hard to find.[49] In his writings Trotsky discusses this incident, immediately following his description of the disagreement on the axis to be used against Denikin, so that the reader might assume by this juxtaposition that the Egor'ev affair was part of the same controversy. Yet an examination of the correspondence between Kamenev and Egor'ev indicates that the disagreement was based on entirely different objections.

Egor'ev, a former general of artillery, had sent to Kamenev on 24 July a detailed appreciation fully accepting Kamenev's first strategic plan, to strike the main blow on the east-west axis across the Don Steppe. The Don Cossack population admittedly, said Egor'ev, would not take kindly to Soviet power, and the rail communications were more plentiful west of the line Voronezh-Rostov than to the east; but there were numerous roads and earth tracks over the plain, excellent for summer use, and the *balki* gullies and rivers were no obstacle; on the Don itself there were fordable shallows every eight versts. It was true, continued Egor'ev, that the steppe could be used to advantage by the Cossack cavalry, but it also gave excellent fields of fire to the Red motorized machine-guns. Egor'ev did bring to Kamenev's notice the possibility that Denikin might counter-manoeuvre by striking due northwards from Kharkov; he imagined that Kamenev had taken this contingency into consideration and held reserves to deal with it, for Egor'ev's troops there, 'Ukrainian formations in a chaotic state

[14 Army commanded by Voroshilov], would be unable to stop it'.[50]

The next day, however, Egor'ev received a further teleprinted order from Kamenev, altering the original concept, in that 14 Army was required not merely to pin the enemy opposing it but was to advance southwards and secure such far-flung objectives as Kharkov and Ekaterinoslav, this being additional to the main blow to be struck westwards across the Don Steppe. Egor'ev's angry reply of 25 July demanded that Kamenev should change his orders or find a new commander for the South Front.[51]

Trotsky was determined to disagree with Kamenev, and his signals met with a sharp rebuttal from Lenin and the Central Committee.[52] The plan which Trotsky later claimed as his own would appear to have been based on an imprecise paper, written by Vatsetis on 22 June 1919, in which geographical, economic or political considerations were not mentioned. Vatsetis came to a conclusion, not a logical deduction to be drawn from his preamble, that the decisive blow against Denikin should be made 'by 8, 13 and 14 Armies of the South Front striking due south' while '10 and 9 Armies maintained pressure from the Volga to the Don to restrict the enemy withdrawal'.[53] This was the Vatsetis plan, the authorship of which appears to have been subsequently assumed by Trotsky.

The first Kamenev plan was based on the immediate use of those reserves made available by the south flank of the East Front, since these could be quickly transferred to 10 and 9 Armies in the area of the lower Volga north of Tsaritsyn. These two armies, which formed a single group under the command of Shorin, were to make the main thrust in mid August, westwards across the Don Steppe.[54] The Central Committee had accepted this concept in preference to that of Vatsetis, because the plan reflected the position of Red Army troops on the ground and because Lenin was opposed to delaying a counter-offensive while extensive redeployment took place.[55]

Shorin's August offensive was successful only insofar as it made some ground towards Tsaritsyn and the line of the Khoper. The South Front's subsidiary pressure by 8 and 13 Armies, forming a group under the former general Selivachev, failed entirely, since it was attacked by Denikin on 12 August; 8, 13 and 14 Armies of the South Front were herded off to the north. In the west, Kiev fell to the Whites at the end of August and Kursk was lost shortly afterwards. By the beginning of October the Volunteer Army stood at Orel, Voronezh having been taken by Sidorin's Cossacks. A raiding force of about 8,000 Don Cossack cavalry under Mamontov broke deep into the Bolshevik rear, seizing Tambov on 18 August and then Kozlov, the headquarters of South Front, forcing Trotsky to flee for his life.[56]

Denikin's advance on Moscow and the bitter resistance of the Don Cossacks raised serious doubts in Kamenev's mind regarding his own strategy; for at some time between 21 and 26 September he wrote an undated appreciation which attempted to justify his earlier choice of the main east-west axis from the lower Volga flank. It was still necessary as a primary task, he believed, to separate Denikin from the Cossacks who were his main support; but he now wondered whether this could not be done by making political concessions to the Cossack peoples. If the Shorin offensive from the Volga were to be continued, the enemy 'might penetrate even further to the north'; and it was easier to reinforce the area south of Moscow with formations railed from the West Front, than to send them to far-away Tsaritsyn. So he offered the Central Committee the alternative of concentrating all reserves to the south of Moscow, primarily as a defensive measure. Political, economic and geographical factors were not even hinted by Kamenev.[57]

Lenin and the Central Committee, after considering this document, ordered Kamenev 'not to consider himself bound by his former recommendations, or by any previous decisions of the Central Committee', and they gave him 'full powers as a military specialist to take what measures he thought fit'.[58] This instruction would appear to reveal the extent to which the Central Committee relied on Kamenev's judgement, and tends to support Denikin's contemptuous dismissal of the generalship of Trotsky 'and other commissars' as being 'at first quite fictitious'.[59]

---

Where Stalin stood during this dispute is easier to determine. Between 3 July and 9 September 1919 he voted with Lenin against Trotsky and in support of Kamenev. By the second half of September when Kamenev changed his mind, Stalin as well as Trotsky would have known the contents of the Commander-in-Chief's new appreciation.

Following the two plenary sessions of the Central Committee on 21 and 26 September decreeing that 'the best workers and commanders should be sent to the south, the South Front being the main front of the republic', it was decided on 27 September to reinforce the southern approaches to Moscow. On this day, too, the South Front was split, throwing off Shorin's group which was redesignated as a new South-East Front. Egorov, a former lieutenant-colonel of 132 Bendersky Regiment commissioned in 1905 from the Kazan military school, replaced Egor'ev at the South Front. Trotsky had been present with the South Front during a long period of defeat, and the Central Committee decided to move Stalin there. By mid-October the South Front stood at 119,000 troops and 600 guns while Shorin's South-East Front mustered 58,000 men and 285 guns.[60]

Stalin did not arrive at the South Front headquarters at Sergievskoe until 3 October, where he found Trotsky well esconced. Both of them went to Moscow to attend a Politburo meeting on 15 October, during which it was decided that Trotsky should go to Petrograd, which was again threatened by Iudenich.[61] Stalin, according to his *Kratkaia Biografiia*, then set to work 'rooting out Trotsky's placemen', and he 'scrapped the old criminal plan' replacing it by one of his own 'which was a stroke of strategic genius'.[62]

At about this time Stalin was supposed to have written the letter to Lenin, sneering at the obstinacy of Kamenev for adhering to the plan to attack Denikin from the east. It was necessary right away, said Stalin, 'to throw over this discredited plan and launch an attack on Rostov from the Voronezh area by way of Kharkov and the Donets Basin'. He then marshalled a number of pertinent political, economic and military factors in favour of his newly found strategy – a friendly population, coal and good communications; and he ended his otherwise logical and well-reasoned letter with an emotional flourish:

> Without this change of strategy my work . . . will be pointless, criminal and superfluous, giving me the right, indeed making it my duty, to go anywhere, even to the devil. . . .[63]

This letter was originally published in *Pravda* in 1929 and was undated, an omission noted by Souvarine. There are a number of doubts as to its timing, relevance and purpose, particularly since subsequent Stalinist accounts dated the letter as 15 October and placed its authorship at Serpukhov.

It is certain that Stalin attended the Politburo meeting in Moscow on 15 October. Serpukhov is on the railway 70 miles south of Moscow, and Stalin might have returned to Serpukhov the same day. But Stalin does not appear to have been a signatory to the front orders of 14, 15 or 16 October.[64] The concentration of Red Army formations immediately south of the capital was already well under way when, on 15 October, the Politburo meeting, attended by Stalin, had decided to switch the South-East Front to the defensive and so release more troops for the protection of Moscow. Moreover, the opening words of Stalin's letter '*two months ago* the Commander-in-Chief raised no objection to an offensive through the Donets Basin' give some ground for believing that the missive, whatever the true form of its content, was written nearer the middle of November.

Why Stalin should have written this letter at all, even in November, may be partially explained by the jealousy which existed between the fronts over the allocation of resources. Smilga, Shorin's political member, wrote to the Central Committee on 3 November insisting that the South-East Front remained 'the main and decisive theatre'.[65] Meanwhile Stalin and Egorov were keeping up a constant pressure on Kamenev for reinforcements, on 29 October demanding 83,000, and hinting on 12 November that they might have to withdraw if they did not get them.[66] Between 5 and 12 November Stalin countered Smilga by sending to the Central Committee two angry and discourteous demands for reinforcements, together with an ultimatum that 'either Gusev and the headquarters of the Commander-in-Chief should go, or the military council of South Front should be replaced'. For this demand Stalin was rebuked by the 14 November session of the Politburo.[67]

Voroshilov's account describing Stalin as the architect of the strategy which crushed Denikin is at variance with the documentary evidence which indicates that there were three strategic plans, the first belonging to Vatsetis and the other two to Kamenev. Stalin may indeed have written his complaint to Lenin elaborating on the advantages, which were by then self-evident, of a strategy based on the main blow being made by his own South Front; but he probably did this when his battle was almost won, between 12 and

14 November, in order to forestall the reinforcement of the rival South-East Front. By subsequently antedating the letter by about a month Stalin attempted to endow himself with strategic foresight.

Rotmistrov, writing at the time of Khrushchev's ascendancy, has said that Kamenev's first and unsuccessful plan 'corresponded with the conditions of the political and military situation and the grouping of the forces of the South Front at the time', and that 'the final strategic plan of the main thrust from the area of Orel and Voronezh was not determined personally by Stalin, as was put out in military literature during the time of the Stalin personality cult, but was worked out collectively between the Central Committee and the military command, the object being to defeat those enemy forces south of Moscow. . . .'[68] On the basis of the documentary evidence so far made available, Rotmistrov's conclusions are not improbable.

Stalin remained at the South Front, redesignated on 10 January 1920 as the South-West Front, from 3 October 1919 until 23 March 1920, and it was his subsequent boast that during this period when Denikin was finally defeated, victory was achieved 'without the presence of Comrade Trotsky'. Nor did Trotsky visit the front during this time.

Among the documents of this period of the South Front offensive are a number of operational directives, signed by Egorov and Stalin. It is impossible to estimate Stalin's personal contribution. On occasion he took action on his own account, for, on 25 October, he was on the teleprinter to Ordzhonikidze, the political member with 14 Army, discussing the temporary loss of Kromsk. Stalin told Ordzhonikidze 'to fight – it was simply a question of fighting *(ibo rech' idet ob istreblenii)* for Kromsk could easily be regained. Under no circumstances,' continued Stalin, 'should counter-attacking regiments be committed to battle piecemeal, but the enemy should be smashed by one massive concentration on a single predetermined axis'.[69] Stalin did not hesitate to bring to Lenin's attention trivial matters, such as the unauthorized drawing of equipment by other formations, what Stalin called 'the plundering of South Front's engineer stores at the Ryazan dump', demanding that the culprit, Kornev, 'be made answerable for his actions'.[70] Whatever his military value, Stalin, together with Trotsky, on 27 November was awarded the Order of the Red Banner, according to Stalin's own citation, 'for his services in the defence of Petrograd and for his self-sacrificing work at the South Front'.

Budenny's cavalry, by then part of the South Front, included a number of commanders who subsequently occupied senior posts during the Second World War, among them Voroshilov, Shchadenko, Kulik, Timoshenko, Apanasenko, Tiulenev, Meretskov, Kharitonov, Kostenko, Khrulev, Cherevichenko, Lopatin and Leliushenko. None of them was a former cavalry officer. Budenny himself was an extended-service equitation instructor, well decorated for bravery, a man of limited education who appears to have been a difficult subordinate; like Voroshilov, he was a shrewd intriguer. Budenny pressed Stalin and Kalinin to expand his cavalry corps and he recommended that a cavalry army should be formed by uniting his own 1 Cavalry Corps and Dumenko's 1 Composite Cavalry Corps, with Budenny himself as army commander. According to Voroshilov, Stalin 'recognized the power of massed cavalry, although the past could provide no precedent for such an original experiment as the formation of a cavalry army. . . .'[71] Trotsky, according to Stalin, opposed the idea.[72] Budenny's proposal was not acted upon, however, for his corps of three cavalry divisions, together with its infantry formations, numbering in all only 9,200 men and 26 guns, was merely redesignated, on 19 November, as a cavalry army. It had no corps organization, but, since it had been raised to the status of army, it was provided with a military council, the newly joining political members being Voroshilov and Shchadenko.[73] The renaming of a cavalry corps as a cavalry army is still regarded in Soviet military literature as 'a new phenomenon of the military art'.[74]

After a 40-day advance Budenny reached the Sea of Azov on 7 January 1920, splitting the enemy between the Crimea and the Caucasus. Three days later Egorov's South Front was redesignated as the South-West Front, and it became responsible for operations against the Crimea. That same day Shorin's South-East Front took over Budenny's 1 Cavalry Army and Sokol'nikov's 8 Army, to add to its own three armies, and, on 16 January, it was renamed the Caucasus Front.

Stalin was in the forward area only once during the South Front advance.[75] According to Trotsky, Stalin was incapable of 'appearing under the open sky before a regiment' or of 'appealing to the hearts of soldiers and commanders' by a personal address.[76] Yet Trotsky was not necessarily a reliable judge for, although he rated highly his own ability to address troops, impressing this on Lenin and on the Russian and foreign press, in the company of soldiers he himself appeared, according to Budenny, as a foreign and rather ludicrous figure, ignorant of traditional military procedures and with so little understanding of the intelligence and education of the rank and file that his address gave rise to angry and audible mutterings among the men.[77] A reliable non-communist witness, present on such an occasion, has described how the soldiers found Trotsky's harangue incomprehensible and irritating.[78]

Stalin retained his own personal connections with the former Tsaritsyn group transferred to the Caucasus Front. Budenny and Voroshilov had earned a name among the Whites for cruelty and atrocity, and stories of the cavalry army's indiscipline and drunkenness had reached Lenin's ears. It was unpopular, too, with other Red commanders and staffs. Budenny, Voroshilov and Shchadenko looked about for allies, sending letters and telegrams to Lenin, Stalin, and even Trotsky; they begged Stalin to intercede for them and to present their most humble greetings to Vladimir Il'ich. Budenny wanted to be rid of Shorin and Sokol'nikov; he would have liked to expand his command and he still coveted Dumenko's cavalry corps. On 3 February, according to Budenny, Stalin was on the direct line to Ordzhonikidze, the newly appointed political member for the Caucasus Front, saying that he had arranged to have Shorin and Sokol'nikov dismissed shortly 'for adopting an attitude of mistrust and enmity towards the cavalry army'. Stalin continued: 'I am completely convinced that your new *Komfront* [designate Tukhachevsky] should . . . use the right flank to some purpose, and put Dumenko's corps into the cavalry army . . . for flank operations'.[79] It was soon brought home to Tukhachevsky, a 26 year old former second-lieutenant of the Semenovsky Guard Regiment, who, according to the version accredited to Ordzhonikidze, 'was ill-disposed to the cavalry army and to Budenny in particular', that Budenny, Voroshilov and Shchadenko had a powerful ally.

Shorin had been commissioned in 1892, he was neither staff trained nor qualified, and in 1914, at the age of 44, he was a captain. As a Red front commander he suffered a severe check at the beginning of February 1920 when the Cossacks rallied temporarily and defeated Budenny's and Dumenko's cavalry. On 3 February Lenin and Trotsky jointly signed a telegram to Stalin appointing him to the Caucasus Front – in addition to the posts he already held – and instructed him to transfer troops from the South-West Front after first journeying out to see Shorin. Stalin replied sharply that it was his profound conviction that journeys by individuals were not needed; what was wanted was 'the transfer of cavalry reserves – the South-West Front being without them'. He continued, 'Budenny and Ordzhonikidze consider . . . Shorin the reason for our failures. I am not entirely well and ask the Central Committee not to insist on the journey'.[80]

Lenin did not insist. On 19 February Stalin telegraphed the Politburo expressing his disagreement with an order from Kamenev withdrawing formations from 'the Ukrainian Army of Labour'; on this telegram Lenin wrote 'he is just cavilling, the Commander-in-Chief is absolutely right'.[81] The next day Lenin signed a telegram, written in Lebedev's handwriting, instructing Stalin to speed up the transfer of troops to the Caucasus Front. Stalin's reply to Lenin, dated 20 February, said that he was not clear why the matter should be Stalin's responsibility since the reinforcement of the Caucasus Front was entirely the concern of the RVSR, the members of which according to his information were in good health, and not that of Stalin, who was overburdened with work anyway. This brought a mild reproof from Lenin.[82] These documents, including Lenin's reply, have since been published in Moscow, except, apparently, Stalin's 20 February signal. Instead, Stalin is said to have replied that same day – possibly in answer to the reproof – 'you may be assured that everything possible will be done'.[83]

Stalin, however, regarded his work as finished. He had, for the time being, lost interest in military matters and he wanted to return to the capital. Even the Polish capture of Mozyr was of little concern to him. Finally, on 23 March, he set out for Moscow and severed his connection with the South-West Front.

# 3
# Poland

The Polish relationship with Denikin had been cool since Warsaw feared that the Whites, if victorious, would be unlikely to permit Polish troops to remain on Belorussian or Ukrainian soil. Warsaw feared and distrusted the Bolsheviks. The Polish aim was to push its own frontiers eastwards, and their armies in Belorussia continued to edge towards Smolensk, reaching, by January 1920, the area of Polotsk and Borisov. In the south Warsaw intended to weaken its powerful and troublesome neighbour by detaching from it, as part of the process of self-determination, its subject Ukrainian peoples.

Before April 1919 Lenin had favoured war with Poland, but the threat from the south forced him to advocate peace; indeed, from the Trotsky-Markhlevsky correspondence it can be deduced that there was a secret understanding between Warsaw and Moscow.[1] But no sooner had Denikin been defeated than Trotsky began to threaten, in *L'Internationale Communiste,* to overrun Poland. Warsaw, for its part, had been evasive to Bolshevik requests for an armistice, and Lenin came to the conclusion that a new Polish offensive was to be expected.[2] Yet Russia needed peace with Poland for, although most of Caucasia was in Red hands by the end of March 1920, there had been a new build up of White forces in the Crimea under Wrangel, Denikin's successor, where 20,000 men of the Volunteer Army and 10,000 Cossacks were being reorganized and re-equipped.

On 25 April three Polish armies attacked the Soviet South-West Front, which had 12 and 14 Armies deployed facing west, and 13

65

Army to the south opposite the Crimea. By May the Poles were in Kiev and over the Dnieper.

The Russo–Polish War of 1920 was fought in two theatres, separated by the great barrier of the Pripet Marshes, nearly 300 miles in length from east to west. The Soviet High Command decided as a preliminary measure to draw off the Polish pressure against the South-West Front by attacking in the north in Belorussia, and Gittis was replaced by Tukhachevsky in command of the West Front. The offensive would then be taken up by Egorov's South-West Front. The military situation was somewhat altered, however, when on 25 May Wrangel launched an attack against 13 Army, capturing 8,000 prisoners and occupying the rich Taurida littoral to the north of the Crimea. The Central Committee concluded that Egorov, even when joined by Budenny's 1 Cavalry Army, would not be strong enough to defeat both Wrangel and the Poles in the Ukraine. Priority was to be given to driving out the Polish invaders and, as the South-West Front objected to this decision, the Central Committee on 26 May detailed Stalin to rejoin the front. He arrived at Kharkov by special train the next day.

On 29 May Stalin sent a personal signal to Lenin saying that he had visited the Crimean area, 'the situation there giving rise to great anxiety', and had had the Commander of 13 Army, a Latvian former colonel Pauka, replaced. Stalin had a number of requirements, mostly of a trivial military nature; Lenin, in a ciphered reproof, told him 'to address all military communications to Trotsky as well'.[3]

Egorov's offensive against the Poles, beginning on 26 May, was at first unsuccessful, and Stalin asked for a further two divisions to be allocated to the South-West Front. On 2 June Lenin replied, explaining that Tukhachevsky, too, was in difficulties; he reminded Stalin that the South-West Front was bound by the Politburo decision not to attack in the Crimea for the time being.[4] Stalin's unreferenced reply to Lenin of the same day read:

> I understand your telegram to signify that the Central Committee refuses the two divisions, notwithstanding my warning; it has therefore released me from responsibility for the undesirable consequences which will probably result. Well, so be it. I recall

the decision of the Poliburo, but Wrangel is disregarding that decision. . . .[5]

The following day, Stalin requested the Politburo to secure a cease-fire with Wrangel; should this be impossible, he asked for permission to attack the Crimea. Stalin wanted 'a quick and clear answer'; the Poles, he said, would not wait. On this signal Lenin noted, 'This is pure Utopia'.[6] Stalin had not yet given up, for on 4 June he told Lenin that he had 'just found some information from various sources' that Wrangel planned to envelop Odessa on 10 June.[7] He failed, however, to convince Lenin, and the Politburo adhered to its original decision.

On 2 June Kamenev instructed the South-West Front that the cavalry army should break through towards Belaya Tserkov–Fastov–Skvir to outflank the enemy grouping at Kiev from the south; Egorov and Stalin conformed in an order to Budenny the next day, giving the line as Novo Fastov–Pustarovka.[8] It was this order which was later described by Voroshilov to the Eighteenth Party Congress as 'the child of Stalin's military genius'.

On 4 June Stalin had a teleprinter conversation with Kamenev querying the role of the cavalry army. Stalin's message was formal and polite, but military terminology was not Stalin's forte at that time, for he became uncertain, even diffident. Kamenev's replies, though no less polite, showed signs of impatience. But he had, he said, discussed all this with Egorov two days before. Stalin assured Kamenev that Egorov was by his side and that he was talking with Egorov's agreement. Could Budenny first take Berdichev 'before turning to the right – for that would suit us very well?'.[9] The outcome appears to have been an exercise in deceit intended to impress the party leader with Stalin's sagacity, for he wrote that same day to Lenin, saying what was untrue, that he had 'altered the old [*Glavkom* and *Komfront*] plan . . . to a new, less deep and more realistic envelopment in the *raion* Fastov'.[10]

Budenny's four cavalry divisions attacked on 5 June; a week later all the Polish forces south of the Pripet were withdrawing rapidly westwards to escape encirclement. In Belorussia Tukhachevsky's West Front launched a new offensive on 4 July. Once again the Polish enemy began to retreat. By the end of the month the Red Army entered north Poland where, at Bialystok, the so-called

Provisional Polish Government was set up under the chairmanship of Dzerzhinsky. By the first week in August Tukhachevsky's
four armies were lining the Vistula and stretching more than 100
miles to the west of Warsaw.

Kamenev visited Smolensk on 22 July and confirmed Tukhachevsky's plan. Warsaw was to be outflanked from the north and
west and taken by 12 August. The great Lublin gap on the left
between Tukhachevsky and the Pripet Marshes, which now lay
much to the east, was to be covered by the Mozyr group of only
5,000 men. Basing its course of action on the optimistic appraisal
received from Kamenev, the South-West Front suggested on 22
July that its own front axis should be moved from Lublin further
to the south through Lvov. Kamenev agreed the next day and the
new front orders were issued over Egorov's and Stalin's signatures
and a copy was sent to Kamenev.[11] Budenny subsequently said
that Egorov told him that the West Front was already victorious
and did not need the cavalry army's close support.[12]

During July Stalin had reported to Lenin and Kamenev further
losses by 13 Army in operations against Wrangel.[13] Wrangel had
also made landings across the Sea of Azov and, on 29 July, a White
raiding force of 5,000 men crossed the Kerch Straits into the
Kuban.

Tukhachevsky had apparently persuaded Kamenev that the
West Front should eventually command all the armies fighting the
Poles, with the reservation that this should not be done until the
armies had left the Pripet behind them. On 28 July Kamenev told
Egorov that 12 Army, 'and then perhaps 14 Army', would be
transferred to the West Front, and Trotsky, in his minute to the
Politburo on 2 August, said that the South-West and West Fronts
were to be merged.[14] But in Trotsky's view Wrangel was such a
threat 'that Comrade Stalin should be charged with forming a
new [front] military council with Egorov or Frunze as commander,
by agreement between the Commander-in-Chief and Stalin'.
Lenin told Stalin that day that the Politburo had discussed the
reorganization of the fronts in order that Stalin should be able to
devote himself entirely to the problem of Wrangel. The Wrangel
threat, said Lenin, was becoming so enormous that inside the
Central Committee a tendency was growing to make peace with
Poland straightaway. Lenin wanted Stalin's views. On 3 August,

Kamenev issued the premature order uniting the West and South-West Fronts.

Meanwhile Stalin had sent off his reply to Lenin. How the fronts should be split was not, said Stalin, the business of the Politburo, which should not concern itself with details. He blamed Kamenev, and he said that he could not help pointing out that Soviet diplomacy sometimes wrecked, most successfully, the results of Soviet military victories. Lenin, taken aback by this reply, asked for clarification.[15]

On 3 August, a calmer Stalin described the organizational problems involved:

The decree of the Central Committee . . . is not clear in the parts concerning 'the forming' of the South Front military council and the joining 'of the South-West and West Fronts' . . . it is necessary to point out that it is not merely a question of joining up two fronts but more particularly one of sorting out and reallocating headquarters, command machinery and resources.

Stalin went on to explain that the handing over of the armies to the West Front would also involve the transfer of commitments to that front, commitments for which Stalin's old South-West (or new South) Front would no longer be responsible. For:

The South-West Front is not being broken up and shared out but will remain intact, with a view to . . . renaming as the new South Front, while those armies transferred from the South-West to the West Front would be maintained where they are at present by arrangements made by the headquarters of West Front.[16]

This reply seems to have mollified, even impressed, Lenin, for he asked for Stalin's military appreciation of the Lvov and Crimean sectors to place before the plenum of the Central Committee, 'for on your views may depend the weightiest political decisions'. Stalin answered that Lvov would be taken 'after some delay'; Poland, he thought, was becoming enfeebled; Wrangel would be defeated in the near future – by the beginning of the autumn if the Commander-in-Chief would send cavalry.[17] The plenum of the Central Committee accepted Stalin's recommendations in its protocol No. 35/5. Yet it is doubtful whether the Politburo and RVSR really understood the implications of Stalin's signal of 3 August, since they apparently took no action to follow it up.

On 4 August Egorov and Stalin signed a directive to 1 Cavalry and 12 Armies ordering them to establish their own communications with the West Front in Minsk through the Mozyr group. On 6 August Kamenev sent a warning order to the South-West and West Fronts, saying that 14 Army, in addition to 1 Cavalry and 12 Armies, was to be transferred to Tukhachevsky; the West Front was to establish its own signal link with 14 Army.[18] There, for the moment, the matter was left.

Meanwhile the cavalry army had exhausted itself in attacking towards Lvov and, on 4 August, its council, Budenny, Voroshilov and Minin, signalled Egorov and Kamenev that they had, on their own responsibility, gone over to the defensive. Kamenev replied on 6 August transferring 1 Cavalry Army to reserve 'for a rest, pending a new assignment'; Egorov and Stalin acted on Kamenev's directive and ordered 1 Cavalry Army into *front* reserve from 2359 hours on 8 August.[19]

On 7 August Tukhachevsky signalled Kamenev saying that he was unwilling to accept the three armies from his neighbour without 'four points first being met', among which were the transfer of all supply installations and the signal organization serving those armies, and the establishing near the South-West Front field headquarters of an 'operative point' or signal centre to maintain telegraph communication with the three armies, until a direct link could be established between them and Minsk; to set up this direct link, said Tukhachevsky, might take from 10–14 days.[20] According to Budenny's uncorroborated account, Kamenev told Tukhachevsky that the immediate transfer of the armies did not appear necessary.[21] The South-West Front, in its reply to Kamenev, could not accept Tukhachevsky's four points, as they would lead to the breakdown in the command of the new South Front. Instead, it suggested that the transfer of the armies should be timed to coincide with the establishing of an operative point, 'using the West Front's own equipment – for the South-West has none'.[22] The signal was signed by both Egorov and Stalin, but the wording and style were Stalin's.

On 10 August Voroshilov learned from Egorov that the cavalry army would be transferred to the West Front, but that while it remained subordinate to the South-West Front it should hold itself in readiness to attack Lvov. This conversation was apparently unpleasing to Budenny and Voroshilov, for, according to Budenny, they sent a telegram direct to Moscow asking Kamenev to take the cavalry army into GHQ reserve.[23] Meanwhile they reported information to the South-West Front, gleaned from Timoshenko's skirmishers, that the enemy in the area of Lvov was thinning out and sending troops northwards.

Lenin had come to the conclusion that Polish resistance was near its end. On 11 August he sent a hasty signal to Stalin announcing a victory which would be even greater if Wrangel could be smashed. He told Stalin to do his utmost, no matter what, to seize the whole of the Crimea with an immediate offensive. Everything depended on it.[24]

The politicians appear to have been at variance with the military. In the early hours of 11 August Kamenev told Tukhachevsky that the West Front's centre of gravity was too far to the north of Warsaw; 1 Cavalry and 12 Armies might be brought in, he thought, to fill the gap near Lublin in the south. At three o'clock that same morning the RVSR sent a signal, signed by Kamenev, Klim and Shaposhnikov, to the South-West Front, ordering 'the timely breaking-off of the Lvov operation', and directed 'as large a force as possible towards Lublin . . . to assist Tukhachevsky's left flank'. The command of 12 and 1 Cavalry Army should be transferred as quickly as possible to the West Front. Kamenev ended this strangely worded order with, 'I ask for your conclusions in this matter'. Nine hours later the Commander-in-Chief, believing that the Poles were in full retreat, sent another signal, timed at 1305 hours 11 August, urging 12 Army to begin its advance on Lublin immediately.[25]

There is no apparent reason why Kamenev's two telegrams should not have been deciphered by the early afternoon of 11 August, since teleprinter messages over the Baudôt and Hughes telegraph were received instantaneously at their destinations as they were being typed in Moscow. If they had in fact been speedily deciphered, Stalin might have dismissed them as being out of date and irrelevant, for the battle for Warsaw appeared to have been won, and Lenin's pressing personal signal had demanded the immediate reduction of Wrangel. Moreover the South-West Front had an interest in retaining the cavalry army and, according to Budenny, 'Stalin and Egorov were counting on using it against the Crimea'.[26]

On 12 August 1 Cavalry Army was ordered by the South-West Front to take Lvov. Budenny, writing in 1965, described the order as irregular since, again according to his uncorroborated account, the army was in GHQ reserve; yet this objection had not in truth prevented him from making the necessary offensive preparations on 11 August, the previous day.[27] The South-West Front continued to ignore, or act in ignorance of, the contents of Kamenev's two signals of 11 August, and, on 12 August, it addressed an untimed telegram to Kamenev, following up Lenin's signal of the previous day, and suggested that 1 Cavalry Army should be withdrawn to Proskurov, still in front reserve, where it would be available for use against the Crimea.[28]

This last message stirred Kamenev to issue clear orders, timed at 0310 hours on 13 August and countersigned by Kursky and Lebedev. Both 12 and 1 Cavalry Armies were to come under the command of the West Front from midday on 14 August. The West Front was to establish a command and signals centre at Kiev, but until this was done Tukhachevsky was to transmit his orders through the South-West Front signal network. The terms of this order could brook no delay and the South-West Front had either to comply or refuse. On 13 August Stalin telegraphed to the Commander-in-Chief, again an untimed signal, saying that the two RVSR telegrams of 11 August had 'just been received and deciphered – cause of delay to be investigated'. Stalin continued: 'The armies of the South-West Front are engaged in clearing the area of Lvov . . . a change . . . I consider to be impossible'.[29] Yet, as Budenny noted, on 12 August, the same day as Stalin had committed the cavalry army to battle, the South-West Front had suggested to Kamenev that the cavalry army should be railed off towards the Crimea. The ease of disengagement apparently depended on the direction in which the cavalry army was to be sent.

Egorov, however, felt compelled to comply with Kamenev's order, for the demands from the centre were being reinforced by threats, presumably from Trotsky. Stalin angrily refused to sign the draft: instead, he sent a telegram to the RVSR, full of reproaches. Kamenev's last order, he said, was completely ruining the South-West Front. Berzin, the second political member, feared to append his signature when a Politburo member had refused to do so. He asked Trotsky for instructions and was told in forceful terms to sign the order immediately. A faithful repetition of Kamenev's last order was issued at six o'clock in the evening of 13 August, signed by Egorov, Berzin and the former engineer officer Petin, merely transferring the command of the two armies to Tukhachevsky.[30] No action was taken by the South-West Front on Kamenev's signals of 11 August, laying down the new axes and tasks for these armies; and so the cavalry army continued to fight for Lvov.

On the evening of 15 August Tukhachevsky sent an order to Budenny telling him to quit Lvov and proceed to Vladimir-Volynsky; the order was countersigned by Butkevich, the commissar for the front headquarters, and was therefore valid. But, during the transmitting through the South-West Front signal network, Butkevich's signature was somewhere omitted, enabling Budenny to refer the order back to Minsk, the next evening, for authentication.[31] Technically Budenny was justified in doing so, although he should at the same time have put in hand preparations to disengage. In fact, military orders not bearing a commissar's countersignature were not infrequent, Vatsetis and Kamenev being common offenders, and in practice these orders were normally acted upon.

Tukhachevsky had begun his offensive on Warsaw three days before, making a steady but slow advance against bitter resistance when, on 16 August, his left flanking army and the Mozyr Group were shattered by a Polish striking force concentrated in the Lublin gap. In attempting to outflank the Poles from the north-west, three of Tukhachevsky's armies had been enveloped from the south-east. On 17 August Tukhachevsky sent another signal to Budenny. That same day Kamenev told Tukhachevsky by tele-print that no action had yet been taken by Budenny to regroup his army 'because of some very unpleasant events'; 'and', continued Kamenev, 'there is no surety that regrouping will start tomorrow since the cavalry army received your directive with only one

signature'.[32] Tukhachevsky's answer clearly showed his amazement and concern.

The Central Committee recalled Stalin from the South-West
Front on 17 August, after his refusal to sign the front order, Lenin
remarking, according to Trotsky, 'Stalin again caught in the act'.
Budenny, Voroshilov and Minin continued to disobey the orders
which they received from the West Front on 16, 17 and 19 August.
Instead, Budenny sent two long signals to the West Front exaggerat-
ing the enemy strength he claimed to be pinning and setting out the
reasons why he could not move. Egorov continued to side with
Budenny, and, even as late as 21 August, he had a teleprinter
conversation with Tukhachevsky, begging that the cavalry army
be allowed to complete the capture of Lvov.[33]

At the Politburo meeting of 19 August, attended by Stalin, the
members were still not aware that the West Front was about to be
crushed. Lenin's attention was rivetted on Wrangel, and Stalin
and Kamenev were bickering about cavalry for the Crimea. After
'having heard the military reports of Comrades Trotsky and Stalin'
the Politburo decided that the Crimea should be regarded as the
main front and that Timoshenko's cavalry division should be
diverted from Budenny to 13 Army.[34]

With the virtual destruction of Tukhachevsky's West Front,
Poland won the war. Lenin declined to allocate blame for what he
called 'this military defeat', and was content that the analysis
should be left to future historians. But Lenin's personal intervention had not been limited to his signal to Stalin on 11 August,
for the next day he had been enthusiastic about Stalin's proposal
to move the cavalry army against Wrangel, and had thought that
Tukhachevsky could procure the help he needed simply 'by calling
up all the adults' in his area.[35] Lenin's political and military judgement was not without fault.

Current Soviet military literature usually ignores the existence
of Trotsky, attributing actions initiated by him to his deputy
Skliansky. According to his public utterances at the time, Trotsky
does not appear to have been so averse to the Polish adventure as
he subsequently maintained. During the campaign he was subordinate to Lenin's military control and was obliged to conform to
the methods of Kamenev's organization within the RVSR.
Whatever he might have said later, Trotsky's papers show that at

the time he had, like Lenin, a high opinion of Stalin's ability as a military organizer for, on 11 May 1920, anxious about the cavalry army, he had considered it essential that Stalin should go there and put it aright. A latter-day Trotsky considered Stalin's strange behaviour with the South-West Front to have been the manifestation of a vainglorious desire to take Lvov at the time when Tukhachevsky was taking Warsaw. This may have been the case. But Trotsky was not reluctant to pass judgement, even when he was not in possession of the facts or was confused by them. For Trotsky has made no mention of Lenin's interference and he has translated the Berzin incident to Egorov's South Front in 1919; nor could he distinguish R. I. Berzin from Ia. A. Berzin.[36]

At the time, it was accepted in Red Army circles that one of the principal reasons for the Russian defeat was the delay in the movement of the cavalry army into the Lublin gap. Tukhachevsky tactfully touched on this point during his 1923 lectures to the Moscow Military Academy.[37] Shaposhnikov thought that it was a war that should have been won.[38] By 1929, however, Egorov made a half-hearted attempt to deny 'the legend of the disastrous role of the South-West Front', and by 1935 Rabinovich's history concluded that Trotsky's 'basically incorrect directive' forced 1 Cavalry Army to abandon the capture of Lvov. Later, at the Eighteenth Party Congress, Voroshilov described Trotsky's orders as treasonable. But by 1963 Todorsky's eulogy of Tukhachevsky ascribed the fault to the South-West Front, 'principally of its political member J. V. Stalin'; Rotmistrov and other writers under Khrushchev supported this opinion.[39] Stalin himself of course had no compunction, even as early as the Tenth Party Congress in March 1921, in blaming Smilga and Shvarts, the political member and chief of staff of the West Front, for exercising an unduly optimistic influence over Tukhachevsky, a view which Budenny was still ventilating in 1965.

The Soviet High Command and field organization had been unsatisfactory in that the South-West Front was responsible for operations in both Galicia and the Crimea. Because of the Pripet barrier, two separate fronts were certainly required in the west, but with a closer co-ordination than that exercised by Kamenev. Nor does Shaposhnikov escape censure for the drafting of the directive of 11 August. On reaching the Bug, the West and South-West

Fronts could have been merged, but only if the signal and supply facilities had permitted it. Whether Tukhachevsky could in fact have commanded seven armies and several independent corps over a 300 mile front is doubtful, and whether the transfer of armies should have been made at the crucial moment when the outcome of the war was about to be decided, is certainly to be questioned. Lacking reliable long range radio and telephone equipment, the RVSR in the area of Moscow was too removed to co-ordinate the two fronts.

Lenin's system of military control was defective in that Kamenev, although he enjoyed Lenin's support, was unable to overcome the indiscipline of members of the Central Committee forming part of the military councils of the fronts. Few men were more ruthless than Lenin; once, hearing of the lack of productivity in the Omsk engine sheds, he said he was 'surprised that Smirnov did not punish, by shooting, the sabotage of the railway workers'; on another occasion he approved the paying of a bounty of 100,000 rubles for each Polish priest or landowner hanged.[40] Yet Lenin was very indulgent with his closest associates, particularly with Stalin.

The Tsaritsyn group, apparently abetted by Egorov, continued to resist the orders from the West Front, even after Stalin's departure, this giving some indication of the lack of authority of the centre. Budenny himself had a long record of indiscipline. In tsarist days he had, as a sergeant, knocked down his sergeant-major in front of his troop and, on his own admission, had forced his men to give false evidence that the sergeant-major had been kicked by a horse. When Wrangel had taken Tsaritsyn in 1919, Budenny had refused to call off his corps counter-attack on the pretext that the verbal cancellation had been given only by the 10 Army political member, the military specialist not being present; many years afterwards he recounted – with evident pleasure – how he had told the commissar to 'clear off'.

The extent to which Stalin's refusal or delay in the carrying out of orders was indirectly responsible for the defeat of the West Front and the consequent loss of the Russo-Polish War is a question which can only be examined by considering the Russo-Polish War as a whole. Many other factors contributed to the defeat: political misjudgement, military misdirection, poor training and organization, indiscipline in the West as well as the South-West Front, over-confident and inexpert commanders and inadequate signal communications. It seems probable, however, that if 1 Cavalry and 12 Armies had moved off to the north when ordered to do so, Tukhachevsky might have been saved from so overwhelming a defeat.

# 4
# *Towards the Greatest Army*

After the death of Sverdlov, the Politburo had consisted of Lenin, Trotsky, Stalin, L. V. Kamenev and Bukharin, later increased to seven members by the addition of Zinov'ev and Tomsky. But it was Stalin who began to assume a plurality of functions. As a member of the subordinate *Orgburo*, he alone was concerned with the detail of the party machinery, besides being the commissar of *Rabkrin*, a body formed at Lenin's suggestion to inspect all branches of the government administration. Stalin was, moreover, the Politburo representative of the GPU (after it had absorbed the Cheka in 1922). Then, on 3 April 1922, he was appointed, again on Lenin's initiative, as General Secretary to the Central Committee, a newly created post which was to prove the most influential in the party and, by extension, in the government. Stalin became the executive for all the main party appointments and was to assume a directing role in the Central Control Commission, an inquisitorial body parallel to *Rabkrin*. The new General Secretary appointed and advanced those members who best served his, as well as party, interests.

Bazhanov, who had been selected in 1923 as Stalin's personal secretary and as secretary of the Politburo, has told how Lenin admired Stalin for his fist, not for his brain, and he quoted Lenin as once saying 'we don't need an intelligent man there – let us send Stalin'. Lenin, said Bazhanov, was unwilling to share his power with anyone, and he could not have been ignorant of the effect of centralizing so many activities under the hand of one man. But the party leader considered that Stalin, Molotov and Mikhailov, the three party secretaries, were entirely loyal to him, and that

Stalin was the obvious choice for the many key posts since he was unlikely to be a rival on account of his poor education.[1]

Bazhanov portrayed Stalin as a rough Caucasian, lacking in originality, with little understanding of politics, economics or finance, who read virtually nothing beyond 10–15 documents a year, a poor and boring speaker with a deliberate, dry and humourless style. Stalin's main characteristics were cunning, malevolence, political ambition and a pathological desire for power; he entrusted to no man his inner thoughts and was strangely out of place in a land where everyone talked too much. When he spoke he used words to conceal his thoughts; one could not know by his words whether he had thoughts or not. He was sly, the simple down-to-earth mentality of the peasant taking the place of intelligence. He had neither the critical faculty of the philosopher nor the dispassionate mentality of the sage, yet he was independent and obstinate. Stalin never generalized – he was not capable of it – for he had to have concrete facts. Given a question, he had an eye only for the practical solution; he solved positive, uncomplicated problems logically and with perspicacity, and he had the good sense to leave alone anything which was beyond his powers.[2] Stalin was vindictive, said Bazhanov, and the forgiveness of a slight was foreign to his nature. If it was in his interest he would sell anyone. Scornful of friendship and displaying an unbelievable cynicism in his personal relationships, he was treacherous and credited others with his own dark motives. He respected only those who stood up to him, though this would not save them. To Bazhanov is owed the well known description of Stalin living in the servants' quarters of the Kremlin eking out the existence of a state employee; in the presence of his family he maintained a contemptuous silence. He was not interested in money, possessions, sport or women, and art, music and literature meant nothing to him. The legend of the decisive Stalin was untrue, Bazhanov said, for he had seldom seen so mistrustful and cautious a man.[3] His dialectic was based on a constantly reiterated demand for facts.[4]

When Lenin was on his sickbed Kamenev, Zinov'ev and Stalin together formed the conspiratorial *troika* against Trotsky, rehearsing their parts prior to the meetings of the Politburo. Only Stalin greeted Trotsky cordially, shaking him warmly by the hand. While the Politburo was in discussion, Stalin would leave his chair, walking up and down the room with his waddling gait, his hands clasped behind his back, puffing at his pipe, a description to be repeated countlessly over the next 30 years. Stalin would make no comment until the discussion was finished, and then would summarize the majority view as if it originated from himself – and this was the decision usually adopted. Later, when his ascendancy was assured, he disdained to do even this, but merely left Bukharin to do the talking. Stalin rarely interrupted, but when he did so, his intervention was decisive and the other members hastened to agree with him.[5]

Bazhanov thought that Trotsky towered intellectually over Stalin and Zinov'ev, as a man who liked to shine but who attached more importance to the form than to the content, and was more concerned in how he spoke than in what he said – more of an actor than a politician, for politics were for him a stage.[6] Molotov and Voroshilov were steadily coming to the fore during these early years. Bazhanov saw Molotov as Stalin's creature, a stutterer and slow-thinker who never had an opinion of his own, but an industrious and thorough worker withal; and Voroshilov was 'quite a man, full of himself', yet in reality only Stalin's pliant puppet; Dzerzhinsky was an emotional, excitable neuropath; Budenny was ignorant and limited, a man without pretensions who, said Bazhanov, when asked by his subordinate for direction on a particularly important military question, replied 'Do what you want. My speciality is to sabre them down'.[7]

At some time after Lenin had returned to his office, he became aware of a situation similar to that which had faced Plekhanov 20 years before, except that Stalin had assumed the role of the young Lenin. Stalin tried to isolate the party leader from events, for that December he struck, somewhat prematurely, at Krupskaia, Lenin's link with the outside world, using, so it is said, vile abuse and threats, and promising to have her expelled from the party by his own Central Control Commission.[8]

Lenin had already recorded in his testament his fears concerning the concentration of so much power in the hands of the General Secretary and, on 5 March 1923, having heard of the Krupskaia incident, he wrote to Stalin that he had no intention of forgetting what was done against him. Four days later Lenin had his third and final stroke. The party at large knew nothing of these dissensions.

At one time Trotsky had professed to believe that the new Red Army should be based on a territorial militia, a part-time army centred on the industrial areas, drawing only a proportion of its troops, mainly private soldiers, from the agricultural periphery. Commanders were to come not from the regular army but from industrial management, the trade unions and the shop floor.[9] This concept found no support from his own military specialist staffs and little from the party ranks.[10]

Frunze, Voroshilov and Gusev pressed for the unified doctrine presented in Frunze's Ukrainian theses, to identify the Red Army with the new social system. But Trotsky denied that the Bolsheviks had invented a new concept of waging war, reminding his listeners that the White troops had been inferior in numbers but superior in military skill, and that the use of cavalry and manoeuvre was not a Red Army innovation but had been learned from Mamontov's Cossacks. War, he said, was a practical art, a skill, a trade; and to learn it, one did not have to be a Marxist, for the military specialists did it well enough. Meanwhile he advised the doctrinaire writers to confine themselves to the mundane but no less necessary tasks of teaching the soldier to shoot, oil his rifle and grease his boots.[11] Although this talk came strangely from the advocate of a militia to be officered by factory managers, Trotsky could be clear-sighted in criticism of his opponents' proposals. In the following year, in his condemnation of functionarism in the army, he said that according to Red Army history there were only heroes in its ranks, that every soldier burned with a desire to fight and that the enemy was always superior in numbers. This censure is still pertinent to much Soviet literature today.

Trotsky's remaining allies were being detached from him, Skliansky to be replaced by Frunze and Antonov-Ovseenko giving way to Bubnov. Muralov, the Commander of Moscow Military District, was replaced by Voroshilov. In June 1923 the Central Control Commission set up a military inquiry and its report was an indictment of Trotsky.[12] On 11 March 1924, as part of a far-reaching reorganization, the post of Commander-in-Chief was abolished and the Red Army High Command, though it still retained its tsarist pattern, was broken down into a central staff, an inspectorate and separate directorates (*upravleniia*) for each of the armed forces, all subordinate to the RVS. Frunze became the chief of staff with Tukhachevsky and Shaposhnikov as his assistants. Finally, in January 1925, Trotsky was replaced as Commissar for Military and Naval Affairs by Frunze.[13] The party disagreements concerning the cadre and militia systems were settled by a compromise whereby the Red Army was to be made up of both cadre and territorial divisions, so that by 1 October 1925 the new Red Army numbered twenty-five regular cadre and thirty-six territorial militia divisions.[14]

Frunze's championship of the military commander and one man command (*edinonachalie*) brought him under suspicion, if Bazhanov is to be believed, of wishing to bind the Red Army to himself. By the direction of the Central Committee, Frunze was forced, against his wish, to undergo minor surgery for an ulcer, and he died under the operation. His wife committed suicide immediately afterwards. Voroshilov felt obliged, or was directed, to write an apologia in *Pravda* defending the Central Committee decision.[15] Voroshilov then became the new Commissar for Military and Naval Affairs, an appointment which he was to hold until 1940. By July 1926, when Trotsky and Zinov'ev had been removed from the Politburo, the Red Army already belonged to Stalin.

Stalin's earlier writings give little guidance as to his military or indeed his political philosophy, for he preferred to rule through others, concealing the nature and extent of his power not only from the outside world but also from the population of the Soviet Union. Unlike Lenin, he was never the chairman of his own committees. It is true that the dictator sometimes posed, particularly abroad, as a moderate, subjected to extremist pressures from a hard-line element within the Politburo and party. Radek, however, put the situation in perspective when he said, in what was assumed at the time to be an inspired leak, that Litvinov only represented the man above him, a man endowed with a firm will who was hard, cautious and distrustful.[16]

In a speech made in 1925 to a plenary session of the Central Committee, Stalin, prefacing each argument with the word 'fact', had opposed the conversion of the whole of the Red Army to a militia. In the event of war, the Soviet Union could rely, he thought, only on its own might and not on foreign revolutionary movements.[17] In the main, however, Stalin appears to have used Voroshilov as his spokesman on military matters; and, according to Barmine, Voroshilov consulted Stalin on the smallest detail.[18] Voroshilov welcomed Russo-German military co-operation and was to extol the creation of a Soviet industrial armaments base.[19] Foreign weapons were bought for trials and research, and arms experts were hired on contract from abroad. State industrialization and the several five year plans, the effect of which was described by Chamberlin as early as 1934 as 'a vast undertaking with new industrial growth in the Urals and Western Siberia stretching from Magnitogorsk to Berezniky, 1,200 to 2,000 miles away from the western frontier', were to have a profound effect on military re-equipping.[20]

Von Manstein, during official liaison visits to the Soviet Union in 1931 and 1932, had talks with the principal Red Army commanders. Voroshilov seemed 'a not unsympathetic personality, but more of a politician than a soldier'; Budenny was *ein primitiver Haudegen*, entirely natural and uninhibited in his coarseness, and, unlike other senior commanders, was careless of the presence of commissars or secret police. Tukhachevsky gave the impression of being clever and devious, and was enthusiastic about Russo-German co-operation, insofar, said von Manstein, as this meant taking everything and giving as little as possible in return. The Germans also met Egorov, newly appointed Chief of the *Shtab RKKA*, but the elegant French speaking actress introduced to them as his wife made more impression than did Egorov. The visitors did not fail to notice that the woman presented to them in Kiev as Tukhachevsky's wife, was not she who had been introduced as Tukhachevskaia at an earlier reception in Moscow.[21]

It has been said that the Red Army military theory of this period was based on that of the imperial Russian school of the early twentieth century.[22] That there was a connection could hardly have been otherwise, for the revolutionaries relied on the teachings of Svechin and Novitsky, two former generals of artillery in the Bolshevik service, and their contemporaries, some of whom had been military theorists under Nicholas II. Sokolovsky lays a special emphasis on this continuity and considers that 'Russian military theory of the early twentieth century . . . far surpassed that of other countries'.[23] Such a chauvinistic view would have found no support from Shaposhnikov, who attended the 1909 course of the General Staff Academy; for there was, according to him, no national Russian doctrine, but 'just complete disorder in strategy and tactics' which was eventually dispelled by the use of direct translations from works by German military writers, so that Russian professors and students became disciples of the German precept 'with its crude insistence on the offensive'.[24] This German doctrine was carried forward into the twenties and the thirties. In 1931, Köstring, the German military attaché, reported that German influence could be seen in all aspects of the Red Army, and that 'German views and methods go through theirs like a red thread'.[25]

In tsarist times interest had also been shown in French military thought, and the Red Army continued to take note of French organization and methods. Tukhachevsky, who had had no staff training and little military service in the tsarist army, gave von Manstein the impression in 1931 that he was French oriented. Stalin, too, had a high opinion of the fighting ability of the French Army.[26]

At the beginning of the thirties the concept of 'the battle in depth' became popular, this being applied to both the offensive and defensive phases of operations, in the strategic as well as the operative field, Voroshilov stressing in 1931 that future war would be waged on the territory of the attacking enemy. Three years later Stalin adopted the slogan that the Red Army must be stronger than any possible combination against it, and drove the point home in his address to the Red Army Academy when he emphasized the need to cut the production of consumer goods in favour of armament and the needs of heavy industry.[27]

Until 1934 there were two committees responsible for defence, the Defence Commission headed by Molotov and formed within the Council of the People's Commissars (SNK), and Voroshilov's Revolutionary Military Council (RVS) which was part of the People's Commissariat for Military and Naval Affairs. Since these two committees tended to duplicate each other, the RVS was disbanded in June 1934, three months after the collegiate (military council) principle had been done away with at district and independent army level and Voroshilov's commissariat had been renamed the Commissariat for Defence (NKO). In September 1935 the *Shtab RKKA*, still headed by Egorov, became the Red Army general staff. In April 1937, the Defence Commission was reformed as a Committee of Defence, Molotov remaining as chairman, and it included among its members Stalin as well as Voroshilov. Eleven months later the RVS was revived as the Main Military Council RKKA consisting of Voroshilov as chairman and Stalin as one of its members. A similar council dealt with matters for the Soviet Navy, but Stalin did not sit on the naval council.

In view of the resurgence and rearmament of Germany, Moscow had decided in 1935 gradually to convert the Red Army from its mixed cadre territorial organization to a standing regular army based on a two year conscription period, so that by January 1938 only 35 of the existing 106 divisions should remain on a militia basis. The 1933 standing army strength of 885,000 was to be increased to 1,513,000 in the same period.[28] At the end of 1935 many of the former tsarist officer designations had been taken into use once more, and the constitution of the following year made service obligatory for all the population, irrespective of race, religion, social origin or former class.

In May 1937 the military commissars were restored to a level of command equality with the commanders, and the old system of military councils was reintroduced at military districts, fleets and independent ground armies.[29] This tightening of political control coincided with the purge of the army and the fleet. In August 1936 Zinov'ev, L. V. Kamenev, and five other party leaders had been put on trial and executed; in January 1937 the principal defendants in a second major trial were Radek, Piatokov, Muralov, Serebriakov and Sokol'nikov. The arrest and shooting of Tukhachevsky, Iakir, Uborevich, Eideman, Kork, Primakov and Putna was followed by the massive purge which, during the next two years, cost the Red Army three of its five marshals, all the heads of districts and the deputy commissars for defence, the chief of the political directorate (PUR) and tens of thousands of its commanders. There appears to have been no clear design for the arrests which covered the whole spectrum of Soviet life, and it is impossible to establish even a general pattern within the armed forces. It is certain, however, that Shchadenko and Mekhlis, the new head of the PUR, were responsible for many of the military casualties, particularly in the Ukraine and the Far East.

---

When Kuznetsov assumed his duties as People's Commissar for

the Navy, in place of the purged Smirnov, he said that 'in his ignorance' he took all important naval questions to Molotov, who was chairman both of the Council of People's Commissars and of the Committee of Defence. Molotov, however, merely referred him to Stalin. Stalin, according to Kuznetsov, devoted much attention to all naval affairs, and no one ventured to act without his approval.[30] Kuznetsov's account is supported by Hilger, who was part of the German Ambassador's staff. Hilger considered that Molotov had no creative mind or personal initiative, for he kept strictly to the rules laid down for him by Stalin. At meetings, Stalin, who held no government post, would ask Molotov to take the chair and it was one of the rules of the game when important issues were at stake, said Hilger, that Molotov would decline. Stalin's manner was simple and unpretentious, but the paternal benevolence used to disarm Germans would turn into icy coldness when he rapped out short orders to People's Commissars. Hilger had, he said, noted the submissive attitude of Shaposhnikov, successor to the purged Egorov as Chief of General Staff, when Stalin was in conversation with him. Hilger was, however, surprised by the assurance with which Stalin made decisions on a wide variety of subjects, and in particular by the extent of his technical knowledge when he chaired a meeting of German and Russian naval experts, discussing the ordnance specifications of the turrets for a cruiser which Germany was delivering to the Soviet Union. Without Stalin's express permission it was impossible to obtain any Soviet agreement.[31]

The Main Military Council RKKA appears to have been conducted in much the same way. Its chairman, Voroshilov, preferred to deal with people rather than with intricate military problems, but in any case the onus of decision did not rest with him. Meretskov, who acted as the council secretary, has described how the council met two or three times a week; Stalin often attended but whether he did or not, the minutes were forwarded to his office in the form of recommendations, to approve or reject as he thought fit. Stalin was, according to the secretary, well informed about the military commanders and on army life in general, and he would frequently have supper with the council and senior district staffs and continue his talks into the night.[32]

The designer Grabin has said that Stalin took a close interest in artillery development, for he attended the artillery proving trials in 1935, together with Molotov and Voroshilov, and questioned the staff on the characteristics and performance of the guns. He was particularly interested in the F22 project for a new 76 mm gun, and he directed the designers to criticize each other's inventions. The F22 was accepted for further development. But some time later Grabin was called to a Kremlin meeting, chaired by Molotov; Stalin said nothing, merely walked up and down. An artillery engineer, unknown to Grabin, then read a paper describing how the F22 had failed its test, and until the artillery engineer had begun to speak, Grabin had no idea of the business to be discussed.[33] In 1937 Voronov, as head of the artillery, had held firmly to his own view on the acceptability of the 1936 pattern 76 mm gun, behaviour which was described, even in 1969, as courageous. In this particular instance, so said Voronov, Stalin accepted his criticism, saying that it was better to listen to the user, 'for guns, unlike soap, could not be melted down again should they prove to be useless'.[34]

Soviet writers are agreed that Stalin took a personal and directing role in the development of army equipment.[35] Indeed, according to Zhukov, no single pattern of armament could be adopted or discarded without Stalin's approval, 'a measure which certainly cramped the initiative of the Commissar for Defence'.[36] Notwithstanding the practical nature of Stalin's direction, his knowledge was probably uneven, to be expected in one who had received no military training or scientific instruction. Vannikov, the Commissar for Armament, has told how, in early 1941, Stalin had favoured the 107 mm gun as the main armament for tanks and he had surprised Vannikov when he said that it was a good weapon 'for he knew it from the Civil War'.[37] Vannikov was undoubtedly right in advocating the 85 mm anti-aircraft gun for the purpose; yet Stalin, perhaps fortuitously, was not entirely wrong. For the 1910 pattern 107 mm gun, with the 1930 recoil modification, was still in service in 1940, and, although it was designed as a field gun, its anti-tank performance was much superior to any other weapon in service.[38] An incident similar to that recounted by Vannikov occurred later that year when Stalin told Hopkins, who was not always a reliable source on military technicalities, that he needed a million or more American rifles but not the ammunition since, 'if the calibre was the same as that used by the Red Army, he had plenty'.[39]

Vannikov complained that a sudden idea or casual comment often settled an issue, and Kuznetsov confirmed that it was easier to talk to Stalin alone than in committee, where a decision, sometimes rashly given, was final. Emelianov, a metallurgist, has illustrated this in his description of a 1939 meeting in Stalin's office in the early hours of the morning, to discuss one Nikolaev's paper on double-skinned tank armour, a proposal which had already been judged as valueless by Emelianov. Nikolaev described his armour as 'active instead of passive, for in being destroyed it protects'. This catchword, said Emelianov, fascinated Stalin and appeared to convince him. Stalin asked Nikolaev what had been the reactions of 'the representatives of industry'. When Nikolaev replied, using Emelianov's own words, 'that there are no miracles in this world', the dictator became angry, wanting to know *who* had said this. Nikolaev, confused, and trying to protect Emelianov, said he could not remember. '*Such* people should be remembered', Stalin replied. Emelianov, who described himself as sick with fear, sat silent, although he knew that the experiment must fail.

In 1940, Emelianov attended another meeting to discuss the use of cast instead of pressed and welded turrets for the T34 tank. Stalin wanted to know the tactical, as opposed to the technical, advantages. When Emelianov asked permission to speak Stalin rounded on him, with, 'What are you, a military man?'. Undeterred, Emelianov provided the required answer, but since he unwittingly addressed the dictator using his forename and patronymic instead of 'Comrade Stalin', he earned in thanks a scowl. Stalin turned back to the designer and the generals. 'How would the centre of gravity be changed by the new turret?' and, 'What was the difference in load on the front axle?'. The designer's reply of 'slight' angered him, for slight, he said, was not an engineering term. Emelianov again knew the answer, but his upraised hand was ignored. The proposal was rejected as inadequately prepared and Stalin ordered a new commission to handle it, the members to be the armoured general Fedorenko and 'him', Stalin pointed to Akopov, and 'him', with a jerk of the thumb towards Emelianov.[40]

Vershinin said in 1948 that Stalin alone made the final decisions in aircraft development, and this is supported by the air designer

Iakovlev's account written in 1966.[41] In 1940 Iakovlev was sent to Germany to inspect and purchase military aircraft, cabling his recommendations direct to Stalin. Yet Stalin also sought opinions from outside his immediate circle of advisers, according to Iakovlev even accepting impractical plans sent direct and unsolicited by junior designers, simply because they caught his fancy.[42]

By the end of the second five year plan 15,000 tanks were with the army, the main armoured formation being the corps, each of 400 tanks. In 1939, following the experience of the fighting in Spain, it was concluded that the primary role of armour was to support infantry, and the large tank formations were broken up. In the air arm the air brigade comprised three squadrons and totalled about 100 aircraft; three brigades made an air corps, and two or more air corps formed an air army.[43] The average annual production of aircraft from 1935 to 1937 was 3,500, of which 1,200 were fighters and 500 bombers.[44]

In July 1938 fighting had broken out against the Japanese in the area of Lake Khasan and, in the following May, there began a series of actions near Khalkhin Gol. But it had already been accepted in Moscow that, in the event of general war, the Red Army Far Eastern and West European establishments could not be interdependent due to the impossibility of reinforcing one from the other.[45] So when, on 3 September 1939, von Ribbentrop invited the Soviet Union to occupy those Polish areas previously agreed by the secret protocol of the Russo-German Pact as the Soviet sphere of interest, action was delayed for a fortnight until the signing, on 16 September, of the truce with Japan. The Red Army was ordered across the Polish frontier the next day. The troops involved were four armies of Kovalev's Belorussian Military District and three armies of Timoshenko's Kiev Military District. Two weeks before, on 1 September, the conscription age had been lowered from 21 to 19 years of age, and the two additional age groups were called up during October and November. This was to increase the size of the Soviet armed forces to over 4,200,000 men.

At the end of June 1939 Stalin had ordered Meretskov, the Commander of the Leningrad Military District, to draw up plans for 'a counter-offensive blow against Finland', which had to be won within a space of three weeks. Meanwhile other planning groups were working independently on the same problem, each taking their separate solutions to Stalin. Eventually Meretskov's plan was accepted in preference to Shaposhnikov's, since the Chief of General Staff was inhibited by the conviction that the Finnish resistance would take several months to overcome.[46] Meretskov said that in making his own preparations he consulted directly with Stalin.

At the beginning of the four months' Finnish Winter War 20 Red Army divisions were deployed against 15 of the enemy, but poor leadership and inadequate training, the lack of a centralized field command and the exceptionally bitter weather resulted in heavy Red Army casualties and repeated failures.[47] Stalin was sensitive to foreign press comment on the poor quality of the Red Army and, fearing armed intervention by Sweden, France and Britain, he became irritated by the delays. Meretskov was repeatedly called back to Moscow to report, the last occasion being at the beginning of January when he was required to brief Stalin in the presence of Molotov, Voroshilov, Timoshenko and Voronov. On 7 January Stalin transformed Leningrad Military District into the North-West Front commanded by Timoshenko. Meanwhile Mekhlis had been sent to the area to dismiss, arrest, and recommend the shooting of divisional commanders.[48] The final and successful offensive began on 11 February and lasted for four weeks; numbers of Red Army commanders who distinguished themselves were earmarked for promotion and important appointments, among them Timoshenko, Voronov, Meretskov, Pavlov and Kirponos.

At a meeting of the Main Military Council on 17 April 1940 Stalin said that it was necessary to bring the Red Army up to date, and that he believed that the cult of revolutionary tradition and the experience of the Civil War were proving to be obstacles to that aim.[49] On 8 May 1940 Timoshenko replaced Voroshilov as the Commissar for Defence. Generals' and admirals' ranks replaced the former revolutionary designations of *komarm, komkor* and *komdiv*, and the contemporary military press praised German military discipline of the First World War. On 12 August the single-command principle was reintroduced, the commissar again becoming subordinate to the commander and, by the disciplinary code of 12 October 1940, commanders became liable for court martial if, in cases of necessity, they did not use their personal arms to enforce obedience.[50]

During the summer of 1940 Meretskov became head of military training while Voronov was appointed as deputy to Kulik in the main artillery directorate (GAU). Pavlov, who had tank experience in Spain, took command of the Belorussian Military District, while Kirponos was given the Leningrad Military District. Zhukov was recalled from the Far East in May 1940, prior to taking command of the Kiev Military District, Stalin and the Politburo requiring from him a personal briefing on the Japanese Army, together with a report on Soviet strengths and weaknesses.[51]

By May 1940 the tank force had been broken down to 35 medium and four heavy tank brigades. In addition there were 98 tank battalions with the rifle and cavalry divisions, totalling in all about 13,000 armoured fighting vehicles.[52] Following the defeat of the French Army by a German force with an inferior number of tanks, the Red Army armour was hurriedly reorganized on the German pattern, the largest mobile formation being the mechanized corps consisting of two tank divisions and one motorized infantry division, in all over 1,000 tanks, of which 120 were heavy KV and 420 the new medium T34.[53] The Red Army command was still floundering, however, and there remained a wide difference of opinion as to the role of armour. Even Timoshenko and Meretskov were unable to find common ground.

During that summer Stalin continued to hold the late night military discussions in his *dacha*. According to Voronov, the dictator was rarely satisfied with second-hand briefings or reported opinion, and, in consequence, the Kremlin conferences and defence committees appear to have formed only part of the method by which he controlled the armed forces; he often saw Timoshenko, Voroshilov, Shaposhnikov, Budenny, Kulik, Meretskov and Golikov, the head of army intelligence (GUR), individually and privately in his own office. Beria, the head of the NKVD and secret police, Mekhlis and Shchadenko were other informants.

At one such meeting Stalin directed Shaposhnikov to write a general staff paper on the likely German plans to attack the Soviet Union, and this Shaposhnikov appreciation was presented, in the absence of its author, to the Politburo during September 1940.

Stalin would not agree, however, even on the premise and basis of the presentation, for Shaposhnikov had believed, rightly as it transpired, that the Germans would make their primary effort between the Pripet and the Baltic coast, the main force deploying north of the mouth of the San.[54] Stalin rejected this on economic grounds, for he considered that the underlying theme of German strategy must rest on seizing Ukrainian corn, Donets coal and Caucasian oil.

In August Stalin replaced Shaposhnikov by Meretskov as Chief of General Staff. According to what Shaposhnikov told Vasilevsky at the time, Stalin was pleasant and respectful (*uvazhitel'nyi*) when he gave Shaposhnikov his *congé*; Stalin said that the time had come 'to show the world that there had been a complete change in the military leadership since the Finnish War'; this might also, he thought, 'lessen international tension'.[55] Stalin privately told Meretskov that Shaposhnikov had been frequently unwell of late and that a younger man was needed.[56] Shaposhnikov remained a deputy commissar for defence and took over the responsibility for military engineering and fortifications.

Shaposhnikov's departure was, apparently, much regretted by the general staff. The son of a minor civil servant, he had been commissioned in 1903 into 1 Turkestan Rifles, qualifying at the General Staff Academy in 1910. He was a man of education, dry and reserved, and had, according to Vasilevsky, a keen and analytical brain, being outstanding in the operative sphere.[57] Golikov was impressed by what he described as Shaposhnikov's mental capacity and breadth of education, his mastery of both strategy and operations, his retentive memory and meticulous attention to detail, his clear thought and expression, his dignified bearing, and by his politeness and tact. He was, said Golikov, a man of discipline, integrity, modesty, benevolence, humanity and decency, an excellent speaker with an exceptional ability of getting things done on a personal plane. Yet he was exacting and demanding, in spite of his urbane and old-fashioned forms of address such as 'I beg you' and 'old fellow' (*golubchik*).[58] This opinion appears to have been generally shared by other members of the general staff, and by Knox, who knew him during the First World War.[59]

Meretskov was a child of the revolution who had entered the Red Army through the Red Guards. Largely self-educated, he was, according to Vasilevsky, a simpler and more expansive personality than Shaposhnikov, and was endowed with a marked sense of humour and much native cunning.[60] His writings show him to have been somewhat brash and insensitive. He had, according to Khrushchev, been arrested during the purges.

The first of Meretskov's war games was held in Belorussia in the late summer of 1940 and was conducted by Vatutin, then head of the operations department, since Stalin would not allow Timoshenko or Meretskov to go near the border for fear of provoking the Germans. The report was approved by Stalin.[61]

The second war game, held after the end of the annual conference on 29 December 1940, proved to be Meretskov's undoing. His address had given offence to Timoshenko and stirred some of his listeners to anger. Shortly afterwards all the participants received an unexpected summons to the Kremlin, where Stalin, members of the Politburo and the Main Military Council, wished to hear the conclusions. Meretskov was unable to summarize the salient points, and Stalin would not allow Vatutin to help him out. Stalin dismissed as propaganda the Soviet field regulations, quoted by Meretskov in working out the relative fire power of German and Red Army divisions, 'for here among ourselves we have to talk in terms of our real capabilities'. Future war, Stalin concluded, would be one of manoeuvre, and victory would go to the side which had the preponderance of tanks and motorized forces, a numerical superiority of two or three to one.[62] On 1 February 1941 Meretskov was replaced as Chief of General Staff by Zhukov.

Zhukov had been a tsarist non-commissioned officer in 10 Novgorodsky Dragoons and, like Meretskov, was self-educated. Although he had attended a senior commanders' course in 1929 he does not appear to have been staff trained or to have ever served in any staff appointment except as part of Budenny's cavalry inspectorate in 1930. Other than a short period as a deputy commander of the Belorussian Military District in 1938, the whole of his service in the Red Army had been in command of horse cavalry units and formations. At Khalkhin Gol in 1939, probably his first experience in commanding armour, only two tank and three motorized brigades were deployed. Zhukov apparently owed his appointment to Timoshenko, who asked Stalin for him. Zhukov's command at Kiev Military District was given to Kirponos.

By February 1941, therefore, most of the principal actors in the opening stages of the Russo-German War had already taken their places. Kirponos, Pavlov and F. I. Kuznetsov commanded the border districts. Timoshenko was the Commissar for Defence with Budenny as his first deputy, in charge of intendance, medical, veterinary and finance; Kulik was responsible for the GAU, the provision of all armament other than vehicles, and for chemical warfare; Rychagov headed the air force, part of the Red Army; Meretskov continued to be responsible for military training, and Shaposhnikov for engineering and fortifications; Zaporozhets was charged with political propaganda within the Red Army. All ranked as deputy commissars for defence but, other than Timoshenko, only Budenny, Kulik and Shaposhnikov were marshals of the Soviet Union. Shchadenko, who headed the main directorate for personnel and was shortly to take over the newly organized *Glavupraform,* was also a deputy commissar and held the army rank of Army Commissar 1st Class, equivalent to that of general; an important main directorate responsible directly to Timoshenko was that of armoured troops under Fedorenko. Zhukov was a deputy commissar and Chief of General Staff with Vatutin as his first deputy; Malandin was the head of the operations directorate with Vasilevsky as his first deputy; N. G. Kuznetsov was the Commissar for the Navy, Isakov being his chief of staff and Rogov heading the main directorate for naval political propaganda. Army Commissar 1st Class Mekhlis, the Commissar for State Control, remained with the PUR, independent of the Commissars for Defence and for the Navy.

During the late autumn of 1940, Zhdanov had told Admiral Kuznetsov that Germany and Britain were bogged down with the war in the west and that this gave the Soviet Union a chance to go about its business undisturbed. What this meant was revealed on 12 November, when Molotov relayed Stalin's territorial aspirations to von Ribbentrop.[63] The following February Zhdanov did not speak with the same assurance, but he continued to maintain that Germany was incapable of fighting a war on two fronts and he explained to Kuznetsov that the violations of Soviet air space, the intelligence preparations and the concentrations of German troops were merely 'precautionary measures on Hitler's part or a means of exerting psychological pressure'.[64]

On 20 March 1941, Golikov presented an intelligence appreciation to Stalin in which he set out the evidence of German activity in the border areas. But, according to Zhukov, Golikov's paper was nullified by its conclusions that a German attack was unlikely while the war was being fought in the west; Golikov professed to believe that the evidence in his paper originated from English or German intelligence services.[65] On 6 May Kuznetsov sent a similar memorandum to Stalin briefing him on information received from Vorontsov, the naval attaché in Berlin, about the imminence of war. He, too, added to the report his opinion that the information was false and fed to both the Soviet and German Governments by an outside agency.[66]

Stalin, presumably taking his precedents from the time of the German Empire and the period immediately after the First World War, appears to have entertained some strange notions as to the political power exercised by the German generals in the Third Reich. In September 1939 he had surprised Köstring by his question as to whether the German military leaders would obey Berlin's order to hand over occupied Polish territory to the Red Army. According to Khrushchev, Tiulenev and Voronov, his suspicion had ripened by the spring of 1941 into a conviction that the German military intelligence organization, manipulated by the generals, had an interest in fabricating evidence and staging provocations which would precipitate a war against the Soviet Union. He continued to persist in this belief after the invasion had taken place.[67]

During May and June Stalin, so Kuznetsov has said, became irritable and unnerved by the persistence of the intelligence reports concerning the imminence of war, and he brushed facts and arguments aside more and more abruptly. A pronouncement by Stalin, continued Kuznetsov, precluded any further discussion, it being unwise to express any other view, even privately to one's subordinates.[68] Zhukov's 1969 account criticizes Golikov and Kuznetsov for failing to add more honest conclusions to their reports. Yet at the time, according to Voronov, Zhukov did not stray a hair's breadth from Stalin's orders. Khrushchev's subsequent summing up of the situation was that any intelligence on Russo-German relations, however palatably presented, could only be forwarded to Stalin 'in fear and trepidation'.[69]

On 6 May Stalin publicly assumed the office of Chairman of the Council of People's Commissars, presumably to impress on Berlin the seriousness of the times. The significance was lost, however, on the German Ambassador, who associated the move with what he believed to be Molotov's decline.

In mid March Timoshenko had asked Stalin for permission to bring the infantry divisions up to war establishment by calling up the reserves. Stalin agreed, apparently with some reluctance, but of the total of 303 infantry, tank and motorized divisions, 81 were said to be still in skeleton form.[70] Timoshenko and Zhukov pressed in vain, so Zhukov has said, for the raising of further mechanized corps.[71]

Stalin's actions were dictated, according to Zhukov, by the desire to avoid war and he appeared confident that he would succeed in doing so. Although Stalin considered hostilities improbable, he still believed that if Germany attacked the Soviet Union the main enemy thrust would be made in the Ukraine.[72] For this reason the weight of the Soviet defence was sited to the south of the Pripet Marshes; and, said Zhukov, 'as Stalin was the greatest authority for us all no one at that time doubted his judgement'. Neither Timoshenko nor the general staff had ever thought it possible, continued Zhukov, that the Germans would concentrate such powerful tank forces against the Soviet Union and launch them on the first day in such strategic depth.[73] Although the present day Soviet press blames Kulik, Shchadenko and Mekhlis for the siting of the bulk of the *matériel* so close to the frontier, Stalin must have given his agreement.[74] For stress was laid on linear defence, with Soviet territory being held inviolate, this forming the basis of the orders of 5 May demanding that the rifle formations should hold their ground, any enemy penetration being destroyed by the mechanized corps and air forces in reserve.

There are some apparent contradictions in Stalin's political and military actions at this time. According to Khrushchev, when Kirponos asked Stalin for permission to fortify the border as a defensive zone, the dictator forbade such action as a provocative act.[75] Yet, on 18 April, five days after the signing of the Soviet-Japanese Pact, Stalin felt sufficiently secure to menace the Reich, surprising though this may seem, for he directed Kirponos to close up his formations nearer to the frontier; this order, which had a

**7** The cavalry army military council 1920, the commander Budenny flanked by his commissars, Voroshilov and Shchadenko.

8 *Above left*. Voroshilov, who had no military experience before 1918, was successively an army commander and commissar in the Civil War. From 1925–40 he was Commissar for Defence.

9 *Above right*. Mekhlis, formerly Stalin's secretary, until 1942 an Army Commissar 1st Class and head of the main political directorate of the armed forces.

10 *Below left*. Timoshenko, a Bessarabian Ukrainian and tsarist cavalry NCO, Commissar for Defence from 1940–41, and thereafter a theatre and front commander.

11 *Below right*. Budenny, a tsarist cavalry leader, later a theatre and front commander.

purely political significance, made no sense militarily and was described by Kirponos as 'passive defence'.[76] But the unexpectedly rapid overrunning of Yugo-Slavia and Greece by the Axis subdued Stalin once more.[77] In the purely military field Stalin had for many years abetted the theory of wars on enemy territory, wars which were to be won quickly with few Soviet casualties; and he had subscribed to the propaganda extolling the invincibility of the greatest army. Whether he really believed in Soviet superiority at arms is perhaps open to doubt for, according to Bagramian, who headed the operations directorate in the Kiev Military District, Zhukov said at that time 'that it was Stalin's opinion that the superiority of the *Wehrmacht* was such that at first the Red Army would be unable to hold the frontier areas, let alone contain the sector of the enemy main attack, for the Germans had both battle experience and greater technical ability'. Bagramian continued: 'I remember that this statement absolutely staggered us all (*chrezvychaino vsekh porazilo*) as if it were sedition'.[78]

In early June Maisky, the Soviet Ambassador in London, had been informed by the Foreign Office that an invasion of the Soviet Union was imminent.[79] In Moscow the diplomatic corps talked of little else.[80] Air and frontier violations were frequent, but Stalin had forbidden the firing on German aircraft in case Berlin should treat such incidents as a provocation.[81] On 14 June, Molotov is said to have rejected Kuznetsov's information showing the lack of German mercantile shipping in Soviet ports, with the remark that 'only a fool would attack Russia'.

On 13 June, Stalin had refused Timoshenko's request to bring the border districts to war readiness, but two days afterwards he agreed to the deployment, from 17 June, of the second echelon rifle divisions in the border areas. By 19 June the situation was sufficiently tense for Timoshenko, undoubtedly with Stalin's agreement, to order the move of the front headquarters in the border areas.[82] On Saturday 21 June a further telegram was received from Maisky and, at 2 p.m., Stalin himself telephoned Tiulenev, the Commander of Moscow Military District, ordering the anti-aircraft defences to be brought to combat readiness.[83] Timoshenko, Zhukov and Vatutin were summoned that evening to see Stalin, who was, according to Zhukov, clearly worried, for a German deserter was said to have brought news of the imminence of war. Stalin's reaction, which had already been telegraphed to Kiev Military District, was that the line-crosser 'has perhaps been sent by the German generals to provoke a conflict'. He declined to authorize the draft directive, brought by the Commissar for Defence, ordering the districts to war readiness, and would agree only that the districts be warned of the possibility of provocations; they were specifically ordered 'not to be incited'. Fortified border posts were to be occupied during the night and aircraft dispersed and camouflaged. The salient points of the order were dictated by Stalin to Zhukov who, together with Vatutin, then drafted the directive in the antechamber; it was taken back to Stalin, who first had it read aloud, before reading it himself; he made some alterations in his own hand, and then gave the signal to Timoshenko to sign. Because the message went out as a text and not a code word it was not received by the field units until 0230 hours.[84] Timoshenko, the general staff and the headquarters of districts and lower formations remained at their posts all night.

The Soviet armies from the Baltic to the Black Sea had been clustered hard against the frontier since April, with the new and incomplete mechanized corps shared out between them. In the view of Halder, the German Chief of General Staff, the Red Army deployment made little military sense, and by May the OKH department of *Fremde Heere Ost* judged it to be merely a political demonstration of force.[85] The German High Command reasoned, quite rightly, that, if attacked, the Soviet formations would defend ground and so be unlikely to escape from the great seething cauldrons in which they would finally meet their end.

# 5

# *From Brest to Vyazma*

The Commissar for the Navy had not been consulted on the developments immediately before the outbreak of war and it was not until 11 p.m. that Kuznetsov was sent for by the Commissar for Defence and told to bring the fleets to combat readiness. Meanwhile Zhukov continued to receive messages from the military districts reporting unusual activity on the other side of the border. At 30 minutes after midnight the situation report was telephoned to Stalin who asked whether the warning order had already been transmitted to the districts; the dictator then went to bed.

At 3.27 a.m. Oktiabr'sky, the Commander of the Black Sea Fleet, telephoned Zhukov from Sevastopol reporting the approach of unidentified aircraft from the sea, and he sought confirmation of the telephonic orders just received from Kuznetsov. Timoshenko agreed that the naval anti-aircraft defences should open fire and he continued the check and double check by telling Oktiabr'sky to report the latest situation to Kuznetsov. By the time Kuznetsov was called, Sevastopol was already under attack. When Kuznetsov tried to reach Stalin, Malenkov came on the line, irritable and disbelieving, then rang off quickly since he wanted confirmation direct from Sevastopol.[1] By 3.40 a.m. Zhukov received further reports of air raids from Klimovskikh and Purkaev, the chiefs of staff of the Belorussian and Kiev Military Districts, and was told by Timoshenko to telephone Stalin. When Zhukov made his report to the dictator, there followed a long silence and the only sound to be heard at the other end was that of breathing. Zhukov asked whether he had been understood. Still there was no answer.

Finally, Stalin instructed Zhukov to go to the Kremlin and tell his secretary Poskrebyshev to summon the Politburo.[2]

When, shortly after 4.30 a.m., Timoshenko and Zhukov were called in to the Politburo meeting, Stalin sat pale and silent, cradling an unlit pipe in his hands. Molotov returned from a meeting with the German Ambassador with the news of the Berlin declaration of war. According to Zhukov, Stalin sank in his chair, lost in thought.

Even after the formal declaration of war Stalin still appeared to believe that the attacks were a provocation on the part of the German generals. Directive No. 2, issued at 7.15 a.m., ordered the Red Army to destroy the enemy penetration, but to keep out of Germany and restrict air activity to a limit of 90 miles within enemy territory. Meanwhile the Politburo kept open the radio link with the German Foreign Ministry and asked Japan to mediate.[3]

When Tiulenev met Voroshilov early on 22 June he was taken aback by the former Commissar of Defence's first question, as to where the High Command was accommodated.[4] No plan had in fact been made for a joint command of the Commissariats of Defence and the Navy until Timoshenko sent a draft to Stalin that morning proposing the setting up of a High Command, with Stalin as the Commander-in-Chief. When Stalin signed the decree, twenty-four hours later, it had been redrafted. Stalin named Timoshenko as the Commander-in-Chief and established a General Headquarters of the High Command which consisted of a council of war with Timoshenko as chairman, and Stalin, Molotov, Voroshilov, Budenny, Zhukov and Kuznetsov as members.[5] Although this body took the somewhat grandiose title of *Stavka*, with its imperial echoes, it was, in fact, merely a committee, without a separate secretariat or staff, and had nothing in common with the organization of the last tsarist *Stavka* at Mogilev which, in February 1917, consisted of three chancelleries and 16 directorates (*upravleniia*) employing 250 officers and officials. Stalin's first *Stavka* had merely an institute of permanent advisers which included Vatutin, Voznesensky, Voronov, Zhdanov, Zhigarev, Kulik, Meretskov and Mikoian.[6]

Although Timoshenko had been nominated as chairman, he was not, according to Zhukov, empowered to take any decisions of importance, and Stalin continued to write his ministers' directives. On the evening of 22 June 1941 Stalin had drafted the Commissar of Defence Directive No. 3 and ordered that Zhukov's name be affixed to it, although the Chief of General Staff was at that time 600 miles away at Tarnopol and unaware of its contents.[7] At a later date Zhukov took the blame for the order.

On the first day of war the border military districts had been converted to fronts. Stalin followed the example of Lenin at the beginning of the Civil War, sending his own personal representatives from the Politburo and the Central Committee to the fronts and armies, Zhdanov to the North, Khrushchev to the South-West and Voroshilov to the West Fronts; in due course nearly all the professional military commissars filling the appointments of political members of front military councils were replaced by Stalin's close associates. Personal military representatives followed, for Zhukov was already in the Ukraine and Shaposhnikov and Kulik were sent to Belorussia. Budenny took over the command of the Reserve Front, and Tiulenev the new South Front based on the former Odessa Military District. The South-West and South Fronts outnumbered the invaders to the south of the Pripet, and, because they escaped the full weight of the German air attack, Kirponos and Tiulenev managed to retain a tenuous and intermittent control over their troops. Elsewhere between the Pripet and the Baltic the Soviet communication system was largely destroyed by enemy air attack and saboteurs.

In 1941 the Soviet government and military communications system was based almost in its entirety on the use of line. In the capital the state telephone served both the civil and the military, this being additional to a separate Kremlin telephone for party and government leaders. The main Union system, controlled by the Commissariat of Communications (NKS), was based on a line network which ran out radially from Moscow to the republic and region capitals, each of which in turn had a separate spider based on the *oblast'* centre. The connections relied on one circuit, or more usually, on one wire, and there were few alternative or bypass systems. Trunk cable was not in use in the Soviet Union at that time. Most of the lines were suspended aerially on poles running alongside the railway tracks and main roads, where they were particularly vulnerable to air and saboteur attack. The reliability and capacity of the line was not high and a break in a single connection might cause a communications black-out over a considerable area.

Telegraph was widely used over this line system, and although the Wheatstone morse-typing automatic instrument and the Hughes letter-typing machine were still in service, reliance was placed on the Baudôt telegraph printer, which could work duplex on four or six channels over a single circuit. Accord or isochronism had to be maintained between the dispatching and receiving machines, but the training of telegraphists was a simple matter as the keyboard had only five keys. The Baudôt was the mainstay of the Soviet governmental, civil and military communications, and Stalin had such faith in it, being convinced that it was secure from interception, that he marked his own signals 'for transmission only by Baudôt' and required that the general staff did the same. Shaposhnikov would wait patiently for hours for a Baudôt link to transmit urgent and important telegrams, refusing to use morse facilities which were available. In fact Baudôt could be intercepted if the receiving equipment had access to the line; although Baudôt had great capacity it was only as reliable as the line system it used.[8]

Shortly before the war a separate communication network had been introduced throughout the Soviet Union for a limited number of subscribers, this being known as high frequency (*vysokochastotnyi*) line, popularly called *V Ch* or *V Ch NKVD*. This system, which had been used commercially in the USA since 1917 and in the United Kingdom since 1934, was based on line using a carrier frequency from 6.3 to 28.5 kilohertz, and was used for both voice and telegraph. It had important technical advantages over the normal state telephone system, one being that the transmissions above the 15–20 kilohertz frequencies were beyond audio range and therefore secure against aural interception unless equipment was available to translate the carrier wave. Frequencies were changed from time to time and lines were duplicated to provide alternatives in case of failure. The system was manned by the NKVD. Although *V Ch* terminals were allocated to the Red Army shortly after the war started, eventually being taken into use by all front and army headquarters, there were so few available in 1941 that military commanders had to travel great distances to the nearest *V Ch* telephone when required to talk to Stalin. Stalin had his own signal centre, equipped with *V Ch* and Baudôt, in the Kremlin room adjoining his secretary Poskrebyshev's office.

The Commissariat of Defence had accepted that the line system operated by the NKS would provide the basis of the military signal service at both strategic and operative level. Only in wartime would the Red Army take over line operation, construction and maintenance, and the troops for this would be found by the conscription of NKS personnel. Peresypkin, the Commissar for Communications, became overnight a deputy commissar for defence and head of a new military signals main directorate, in addition to his other posts. In June he was made a colonel and in December a lieutenant-general. Other NKS administrators and engineers were similarly inducted and given appropriate army ranks.

The scale of provision of command radio was meagre and its range so limited that it was regarded of little significance. The general staff had a number of RAF, RAT, 11 AK and 12 AK stations, and the RSB(40) was the basic set between divisions and armies; the divisions used the 6 PK, 5 AK and 71 TK radio. The Red Army started the war with only two radio codes. At divisional level and below a two digit system was used, known in Russian as the PT 39A; behind the divisions, messages were transmitted in five digit code taken from block list tables. But the system became complicated and, in the forward areas, largely unworkable when further codes were superimposed for formation and unit designations, names and co-ordinates, with the result that commanders avoided using it.[9] According to the German intercept service, Russian call signs and frequencies were changed every three hours.

The breakdown of the signal communications to the north of the Pripet left Kuznetsov's and Pavlov's formations paralysed. Kuznetsov, like Kirponos in the south, was lucky, however, in that he was assailed by only one panzer group which attempted, in vain, to pin him against the coast. Yet his armies fell back in such disorder that it was 18 days before the general staff in Moscow could get a situation report from them.[10] Pavlov was less fortunate, for his three armies were deployed forward close to the frontier in the great Bialystok salient, inside what was in effect a gaping German mouth. On 27 June Hoth's and Guderian's panzer groups met near Minsk encircling the main element of the West Front. It may have been at this time that Stalin, hearing of these defeats, thought that the end had come and gave way to hysteria, saying that 'all Lenin has created is lost for ever'; he then ceased to do anything 'for a long time'; Khrushchev's version, strangely reminiscent of Ivan IV, said that Stalin returned to the helm of state only after a deputation had pleaded with him to do so.[11] Zhukov has denied that this happened; but, whether it did or not, Stalin's inactivity could have hardly lasted more than a day or two for, according to other accounts, he was in control of the Soviet war machine on 26, 29 and 30 June.

According to Voronov, Stalin was unable to assess the scope of the war or estimate the effect of time, space and the relation of forces.[12] Stalin's Directive No. 3 issued on the night of 22 June ordering the South-West Front to take Lublin, 50 miles inside the *General Gouvernement* of Poland, by 24 June, was greeted with incredulity by both Purkaev and Bagramian.[13] The North-West and West Fronts were similarly directed to make a concentric attack on the Suwalki salient of East Prussia. At the West Front, Boldin, Pavlov's deputy, remonstrated that it was impossible to carry out the order.[14] The South-West Front, instead of attacking, was already retreating when Malandin, in a direct wire conversation on 26 June, forbade – in Stalin's name – any further withdrawal.[15]

That day Stalin had telephoned Zhukov at Tarnopol telling him that the enemy was nearing Minsk, that Pavlov was in a state of confusion, Shaposhnikov was ill and Kulik had disappeared. Zhukov was to return to Moscow immediately. Late that evening Zhukov was ushered into Stalin's office, where Timoshenko and Vatutin were stiffly at attention, their faces pale and drawn and their eyes red from lack of sleep. The generals could do little except suggest that a rearward defence line be occupied by two armies behind the line Polotsk-Mozyr, which was about to be prepared and occupied by the four armies of Budenny's Reserve Front. On 27 June Zhukov sent a Baudôt order to Minsk, rambling in its content and full of generalities and promises of glory.[16] If Stalin did seek seclusion, this was probably the day on which he did so.

On 29 June, after Minsk had fallen, Stalin appeared twice in Timoshenko's office and, in Zhukov's words, 'on both occasions reacted extremely harshly (*kraine rezko*)'. The next day, on 30 June, Stalin instructed Zhukov to summon Pavlov to Moscow.

It would appear that the decision to remove Pavlov had been taken on or before 28 June, for on that night Timoshenko had interviewed Eremenko in Moscow and appointed him as the Commander of the West Front. It may be indicative of Stalin's absence that Eremenko was not seen by the dictator. Malandin was to take over the duties of front chief of staff. Together Eremenko and Malandin arrived at the West Front command post the next morning and presented Pavlov with the written order removing him from his command, establishing a precedent frequently used by Stalin for the dismissal or arrest of high ranking officers.[17] Starinov, who was present, has described how the exhausted Pavlov at first showed relief at his release from responsibility, supposing that Stalin's punishment would not go beyond dismissal.[18] Pavlov was, however, arrested together with Klimovskikh, the chief of staff, Klich and Grigor'ev, the heads of artillery and signals, and Korobkov, the Commander of 4 Army. These luckless generals 'were brought to trial on the proposal of the military council of West Front [Eremenko and Malandin]', and although Zhukov does not say so, they were shot.

During Stalin's lifetime Pavlov was held responsible not only for the destruction of the West Front but also for the decision taken in November 1939 to break up the large tank formations. In Khrushchev's time the fault was said to be Stalin's, in that the West Front was deployed close to the border, against Shaposhnikov's advice, Zhukov being censured 'for his unwillingness to withstand Stalin's pressures'.[19] Zhukov excused himself by blaming Voroshilov.[20] At the time, according to one senior officer, the generals did not believe the sensational announcement of the treachery within the West Front, although they did fear that this might herald a new purge. What Shtemenko has since called 'the inexplicable change round of commanders' unnerved the general staff. The commissars there were not slow in making their suspicious presence felt, accusing a general staff colonel, engaged on a routine marking up of enemy dispositions on a battle map, of exaggeration and panic-spreading.[21] The Pavlov *affaire* did much to shake the confidence of the troops and the people in its commanders. It was a pattern which was not to be repeated, for thereafter during the war the disappearance and subsequent fate of unlucky or incompetent commanders remained a state secret.

The commissars now came in for preferment. In a decree of the Presidium of the Supreme Soviet of 16 July, signed by Kalinin, the former powers of the military commissars, no longer to be known as political deputies, were restored, these powers being defined as 'similar to those which they had during the Civil War against the foreign interventionists'. The need for the change was explained by 'the transition from peace to war'.[22] By a directive of 29 June, grave measures, that is to say shooting, had been announced against rumour-mongers, panic-spreaders and cowards.

On 30 June Kuznetsov and his political member Dibrova were replaced by Sobennikov and Bogatkin in command of the North-West Front, Vatutin being sent from the general staff as the chief of staff. Eremenko's West Front no longer existed, for all fighting ceased in the Bialystok pocket on 3 July and five days later 290,000 Soviet prisoners, including several corps and divisional commanders, were in German hands together with 2,500 captured or knocked out tanks and 1,500 guns.[23]

A State Committee of Defence (GKO) had been brought into being on 30 June, this being responsible for all the wider aspects of the war, political, economic and military, its functions being similar to those of Lenin's Council of Defence of the Civil War. It originally consisted of Stalin, Molotov, Malenkov, Voroshilov and Beria, and its orders, in the form of numbered GOKO resolutions, were supreme, being enacted by the Council of People's Commissars through the machinery of the commissariats.[24] The *Stavka* continued as the main directing organ for military matters but, on 10 July, it was reformed with Stalin as its chairman, and Molotov, Timoshenko, Budenny, Voroshilov, Shaposhnikov and Zhukov as members, and was renamed the *Stavka* of the Supreme Command. On 19 July Stalin nominated himself as People's Commissar for Defence and, on 8 August, he became the Supreme Commander of the Armed Forces of the USSR, his military committee taking the name of *Stavka* of the Supreme High Command (VGK). The fact that Stalin was the Commander-in-Chief was concealed, however, from the Soviet Union and the outside world, and orders of the day and public announcements signed by the dictator described him as the Commissar for Defence. Only after Stalingrad did he admit to being the Supreme Commander.[25]

On 1 July Timoshenko had been given the command of a new West Front, reconstituted from the recently arrived armies of Budenny's Reserve Front and the remnants of Eremenko's force, Eremenko and Budenny being appointed as Timoshenko's deputies. Bulganin became the political member of the military council, Malandin remaining as chief of staff until 21 July when he was replaced by Shaposhnikov. Reserves in depth were collected for a Reserve Front under Bogdanov of six armies, and a Moscow Front under Artem'ev of three armies covering the outskirts of the capital.[26] On 4 July, by GOKO decree No. 10, 270,000 citizens of Moscow city and *oblast'* were mobilized to form 25 divisions of the people's military reserve (*narodnogo opolcheniia*), another description borrowed from the tsarist empire.

On 10 July Stalin had decided to establish three theatres (*napravleniia*) each controlling two or more fronts. Timoshenko's West Front became the West Theatre, controlling the West, Reserve and Moscow Fronts and F. I. Kuznetsov's Central Front consisting of two armies detached from the left wing of the West Front. Budenny, together with Khrushchev, took command of the South-West Theatre, commanding Kirponos's South-West and Tiulenev's (later Riabyshev's) South Fronts and Oktiabr'sky's Black Sea Fleet. Voroshilov and Zhdanov formed the North-West Theatre comprising Popov's North and Sobennikov's North-West Fronts and Tributs's Baltic and Golovko's North Fleets.[27] By a decree of 15 July, corps headquarters were temporarily abolished in order to economize in staffs. The great tank losses could not be readily replaced and the mechanized corps were disbanded, the remaining tank divisions, soon to become tank brigades, being allocated to rifle armies. For some time to come there could be no question of combating the panzer thrusts with massed armour.

On the German side there was only a short delay in launching the second stage of the offensive along the main Moscow highway, another great pincer movement starting from the area of Minsk and closing over 150 miles to the east. Timoshenko's West Front was soon broken open, and by 17 July Hoth and Guderian met east of Smolensk having entrapped a vast number of troops. By 5

August, the Germans recorded the taking there of 309,000 prisoners, 3,000 guns and 3,205 captured or knocked out tanks.[28] The total number of German tanks in action was barely over a 1,000.

Stalin was, as Zhukov put it, beside himself with rage at the Smolensk defeat. 'We generals', he said, 'felt the full weight of his anger'. Towards the end of July Poskrebyshev telephoned Zhukov and Timoshenko to go to a Politburo meeting in Stalin's *dacha*. No reason was given. Stalin wasted no time in preliminaries and told Timoshenko that the Politburo had decided to appoint Zhukov in his place. Timoshenko was silent. Zhukov has said that he spoke out in Timoshenko's defence, emphasizing the confidence which Timoshenko enjoyed among the troops and the unsettling effect of the frequent change of commanders. 'For Stalin', Zhukov tells his latter-day readers, 'was not always objective in his judgement of military leaders'.[29] Stalin put the question to the Politburo members and eventually Timoshenko was allowed to return to his post.

---

Hitler had always intended that Leningrad should be taken before Moscow, and very early on he had come to regard the seizure of the whole of the Ukraine, the Donets Basin and even Caucasia as having priority over an eastwards advance from Smolensk. His attention was fixed on the Crimea, the occupation of which would, he thought, enable German troops to invade the Caucasus by way of Kerch. On 30 July Hitler ordered von Bock's Army Group Centre to go over to the defensive and this was followed by the order of 12 August turning Hoth's panzer troops northwards towards Leningrad and Guderian's armour south into the Ukraine.[30] The great Smolensk battle of 1941 in which, according to Soviet accounts, the Red Army defenders are said to have defeated von Bock in his eastward march on Moscow, inflicting on the Hitlerite forces 250,000 casualties, did not take place.

Zhukov subsequently said that he himself became convinced, towards the end of July 1941, that the enemy's intention was to move southwards and strike at the flank and rear of the South-West Front in the Ukraine.[31] If this was indeed Zhukov's belief, it could have been based on nothing but surmise, for the German Army Commander-in-Chief, the Chief of General Staff and the three army group commanders were all agreed that the immediate objective should be Moscow; only Hitler was determined that the advance should be deflected south into the Ukraine. The arguments in favour of the Moscow offensive were still being presented in Rastenburg as late as 23 August.[32]

On 29 July Zhukov asked Stalin to receive him, so he said, to hear his appraisal of the situation. Stalin saw Zhukov in the presence of a hostile Mekhlis. Zhukov wanted to move a number of divisions from the Far East and evacuate the whole of the right bank Ukraine. When Zhukov recommended that Kiev should be given up Stalin became angry. Forty minutes later Zhukov had been relieved of his appointment and transferred to the command of the Reserve Front, and Shaposhnikov was on his way from the West Theatre to take over once more his old post as Chief of General Staff; this is Zhukov's version of how he came to be removed from his appointment, although the reasons given by him are unlikely to be the real ones. Vasilevsky and Shtemenko are silent on the matter. The naval staffs had found Zhukov difficult to work with and Khrulev intimates that he had already lost a measure of Stalin's confidence, at least in so far as staff and organizational matters were concerned.[33] Yet there is no doubt that Stalin still had great confidence in Zhukov's command ability.

On the evening of 30 July Hopkins, Roosevelt's personal representative, arrived in Moscow. It was arranged that, as a preliminary, Hopkins should talk to Iakovlev, of the main artillery directorate. But Hopkins found that no one dared give any information or offer an opinion on any subject, Iakovlev saying that he was not empowered to disclose 'whether the Soviet Union does or does not need equipment'. Any question as to the holdings of Soviet armament or its capabilities met with an evasive answer. Only Stalin could give any information; and Hopkins noted the awful fear with which any subordinate regarded his superior.[34] At the second meeting Stalin assured Hopkins that the Leningrad-Smolensk-Kiev line then held was 'more easy to defend than the original frontier'; he did not say that the Soviet withdrawal had been deliberate and part of Soviet strategy.

On 8 August, only three days after the Smolensk cauldron had been cleared, Guderian's panzer group had attacked Kuznetsov's Central Front between Mogilev and Gomel; two weeks later the front had been destroyed with the loss of a further 78,000 prisoners. This new German thrust was interpreted by Stalin and Shaposhnikov as an enveloping movement to outflank the West and the Reserve Fronts from the south, as part of a general advance on Moscow through Bryansk.[35] This was indeed what von Bock wanted to do, but the arguments with the Führer continued and meanwhile Guderian's troops marked time on the Desna awaiting the decision to march to the east or south.[36]

The destruction of the Central Front caused Zhukov, who was still a member of the *Stavka*, to send a signal to Stalin on 19 August warning him of the likelihood of a German thrust southwards to the rear of the South-West Front.[37] Zhukov advocated the concentrating of a force of ten infantry and four cavalry divisions with 1,000 tanks and 500 aircraft on the Desna athwart Guderian's route to the south, and suggested that the necessary forces could be found 'from the Far East, Moscow and the military districts of the interior'. This optimistic proposal, which disarmingly overcame all difficulties of time and space, evoked a polite but cool acknowledgement from Stalin and Shaposhnikov.

On 8 August Stalin had talked to Kirponos on the direct line, accusing him of 'light-heartedly being about to give up Kiev'.[38] On 14 August, while the Central Front was under attack, Stalin had created a new Bryansk Front under Eremenko, originally consisting of two hastily formed armies, concentrated, not south of the Desna, but to the flank covering Bryansk and the route to Moscow. Stalin and Shaposhnikov had produced their own plan, whereby Eremenko, together with the left wing of Zhukov's Reserve Front, was to attack due westwards. The offensive was to start at the end of August.[39]

Vasilevsky, by then head of the operations directorate and deputy chief of general staff, had not met Eremenko before he saw him in Stalin's presence at the time of his appointment to the Bryansk Front. Eremenko was known, however, to Stalin and members of the GKO. Stalin was friendly and solicitous, asking him about the battle on the West Front. Eremenko, who had once been a noncommissioned officer in the tsarist cavalry, conducted himself, said Vasilevsky, with great dignity, answering questions quickwittedly and skilfully; he appeared confident and resourceful and told Stalin that the enemy was already losing his arrogance (*spes'*).

Eremenko said that he had no doubt that he would destroy Guderian in the next few days. According to Vasilevsky, Stalin was visibly impressed and, as Eremenko took his departure, he looked admiringly after him with the remark 'that is the sort of fellow we want in a tight corner'.[40]

When on 16 August Shaposhnikov hinted that it might be necessary to retire behind the Dnieper, Stalin was still full of Eremenko's praises. Zhukov, however, was uneasy about the fighting value of his left-hand neighbour, and when, on 23 August, he communicated his fears to Shaposhnikov, the Chief of General Staff told him that he, too, doubted whether Eremenko would be able to block the path of the German armour. On 25 August Stalin again cross-examined Eremenko by Baudôt and asked for an assurance of success, Eremenko replying 'I will smash this scoundrel Guderian without any doubt'.[41] Eremenko's offensive was to come to nothing, his armies, despite Stalin's messages of severe displeasure, retreating eastwards in disorder. Yet, a fortnight later, Stalin still appeared to be unaware of the extent of the Bryansk Front's defeat.

Guderian, having received final orders to move south, crossed the Desna on 2 September and began his rapid advance deep in the rear of the South-West Front. In the far south, the German Army Group South was to secure a bridgehead over the Dnieper at Kremenchug on 9 September, from which, three days later, von Kleist's panzer group was to strike northwards and join Guderian in the area of Romny and Lokhvitsa, these panzer thrusts cutting off about six Soviet armies to their west in the great bend of the river.

On 7 September the South-West Front reported the threatening situation to Budenny and Shaposhnikov. Shaposhnikov and Vasilevsky, so Vasilevsky has said, went to see Stalin, who reproached them for wanting to run away. Two days later, however, the dictator issued an order permitting the South-West Front to make a limited withdrawal to the Desna except that Kirponos was to continue to hold Kiev.[42]

Bagramian, a former tsarist *praporshchik* with the Armenian cavalry who was Kirponos's deputy chief of staff, has said that the front had been aware since 7 September of the threat from Guderian, and that this was foremost in their thoughts during the

military council meeting held on the night of 10 September. The
political members Burmistenko and Rykov were cautious. Tupikov,
the chief of staff, recently the military attaché in Berlin, considered
the threat to be so serious that he advised an immediate withdrawal
to the River Psel, 180 miles to the east. Kirponos, too, was outspoken, and he regretted that Budenny was not allowed to decide
any matter of importance without first seeking Stalin's permission.[43] Nor could Kirponos realign his own armies without
prior *Stavka* approval. He had little faith in the academician
Shaposhnikov, who would weigh up all the courses and present his
evaluation without making a single concrete proposal, merely
asking Stalin for orders. For Kirponos did not believe 'that this
very competent officer of the old general staff could not see the
mortal danger . . . he simply could not muster the courage to tell
Comrade Stalin the whole truth'. Finally, the military council
decided to send a telegram to Moscow asking for permission to
withdraw troops from the Kiev area and prepare a general withdrawal to the line of the Psel. At 0200 hours that morning Shaposhnikov came on the direct line, speaking in the name of the *Stavka*,
describing any withdrawal as premature, and not permitting any
troops to be removed from the area of Kiev.[44]

Following an appeal from Kirponos, Budenny spoke to Shaposhnikov on the telephone but failed to move him. That same day, on
11 September, Budenny addressed a signal to Stalin protesting
against Shaposhnikov's reply. Budenny thought that the enemy's
intention was clear, a double envelopment from north and south,
and that delay in withdrawing the South-West Front might result
in the loss of troops and an enormous quantity of armament.[45]
Budenny was thereupon relieved of his appointment, Khrushchev
being permitted to remain, an indicator that the political member
may not have been so loud or insistent in his requests for a withdrawal as he subsequently claimed. Budenny's successor was to be
Timoshenko.

Zhukov, by tampering with the calendar, has given a somewhat
different account. He was, he said, called from the Reserve Front
to the Kremlin on 8 September and ordered to assume command
of the Leningrad Front the next day, for the city had already been
surrounded by the enemy. Stalin told him that 'we have also
decided to replace the command of the South-West Theatre'.

Discussion took place as to whether the Kiev group should be withdrawn east of the Dnieper, and, Zhukov adds, Stalin consulted not only himself but also Shaposhnikov and Timoshenko.[46] This account is presumably intended to disarm censure of Stalin for arbitrarily rejecting advice and removing a commander who was in fact right, for Zhukov's version conveys the impression of a collective and well-considered decision which had no connection with Kirponos's and Budenny's signals of 11 September. Yet Zhukov's new dates are not attributable to a slip of the pen because his story continues in chronological sequence starting with his air flight to Leningrad, which he said he made on 9 September. If this meeting described by Zhukov took place at all, it would appear to have done so on Thursday 11 September shortly after Budenny's signal had been received in Moscow, for Zhukov was appointed to the Leningrad Front on that day. Fediuninsky, who accompanied Zhukov to Leningrad, has described taking off together from Vnukovo airport on the morning of 13 September, the same day that Timoshenko arrived in Poltava.[47] Kuznetsov was sent for by Stalin on 12 September and was told that Zhukov had been appointed to the Leningrad Front, the decision having been taken 'only yesterday'.[48]

Meanwhile, on 11 September, Stalin held a Baudôt teleprint conversation with the South-West Front military council. Stalin began by telling Kirponos that the South-West Front proposal to withdraw to the Psel seemed dangerous, and he would want a guarantee from the South-West Front that previous failures would not be repeated. The proposed withdrawal, said Stalin, would lead to encirclement, since the enemy was advancing, not only from the north in the area of Konotop, but also from Kremenchug in the south and from the west; these attacks would be stepped up as soon as the Red Army troops started to fall back again. The proposal to withdraw the South-West Front before the positions on the Psel were in fact prepared, was hazardous; a bold offensive against the north grouping in co-operation with the Bryansk Front was a prerequisite, without which a withdrawal could lead to catastrophe.

According to Bagramian, who was himself retelling Tupikov's account, Kirponos sat motionless studying the lengthening Baudôt ticker tape as Stalin talked on. The dictator appeared to be reasoning with himself. 'There might', said Stalin, 'be a way out'.

*First.* Regroup the forces. . . . Make attacks against the Konotop grouping together with Eremenko. . . .

*Second.* Prepare a defensive line on the Psel by withdrawing five or six divisions and a powerful artillery group facing north and west.

*Third.* After the forces have been concentrated against Konotop . . . and after the Psel defensive line has been prepared . . . the evacuation of Kiev can begin . . . when Kiev is evacuated the east bank must be held secure.

*Finally.* You must cease looking for rearward defensive lines . . . and must seek only ways of stopping, I repeat, stopping the enemy.

This *Stavka* order shows that the earlier disasters of Minsk, Smolensk and Uman had apparently left Stalin ignorant of the speed with which the German panzer leaders developed their encirclement operations. He was still pinning his hopes on Eremenko. Yet, even though this is taken into account, the directive is illogical and contradictory.

When the Baudôt tape stopped ticking, the military council of the South-West Front sat silent. Tupikov, who appeared dumb-founded, later confided to Bagramian that, when the second paragraph appeared, his hopes began to rise that the South-West Front could withdraw, but Stalin's closing words were shattering. Kirponos, pale and silent, turned to the other members for their views. Burmistenko said that they had no alternative but to remain; Rykov merely ran his hands through his hair. Stalin was waiting for an answer. Kirponos turned to the telegraphist and began to dictate the reply straight on to the machine. He was much unnerved by Stalin's Baudôt presence, for he denied that the proposal to withdraw had originated from him, but had, said Kirponos, 'been in response to requests from above'.

The Baudôt began to tick away once more as Stalin's reply was received. The request to withdraw *did* come from the South-West Front *and* Budenny, and to illustrate his point Stalin read out extracts from Budenny's signal of the same day. Shaposhnikov, said Stalin, was against a withdrawal, but Budenny and Kirponos were for it. Kiev was not to be given up nor were the bridges to be blown without *Stavka* approval. The substance of Bagramian's account is supported by Zhukov and by Vasilevsky.[49]

On 14 September Tupikov drafted and sent to Shaposhnikov his own signal, since Kirponos refused to sign it, placing the responsibility for the impending catastrophe on the Supreme Command and ending by forecasting disaster at the end of two days.[50] Stalin himself penned the reply branding Tupikov as a panic-monger, and handed the draft back to Shaposhnikov to sign.[51] On 15 September, the day that Guderian and von Kleist made contact, Stalin sent a signal to London asking for twenty-five to thirty British divisions to be transported to Archangel or to the southern regions of the USSR.[52]

On 16 September the encirclement of the South-West Front was complete, and two days later, as if to distract public and world attention from the area, a special NKO order announced the award of a newly introduced guards status to formations heroically defending the area of Smolensk.

Bagramian, who was on a visit to the theatre headquarters on 16 September, was told by Timoshenko that the theatre military council had decided to order the South-West Front to organize a break-out 'in anticipation that the Supreme Commander will allow the withdrawal to the Psel'. Bagramian was instructed to give Timoshenko's verbal orders to Kirponos. Bagramian subsequently said that he felt vaguely uncomfortable about not having a written directive, but he associated this with the security risk of being flown back into the pocket. That same afternoon he rejoined the South-West Front headquarters.

At first the front military council was in high spirits at the news of Timoshenko's order. But then Kirponos refused to act unless he received an order from Stalin or a written authority from Timoshenko, and no urging by the other members of the council could move him. On the evening of 16 September Kirponos sent a radio message to the Supreme Commander asking for instructions, adding that he, Kirponos, thought that withdrawal to the Psel River was the correct course.[53] Twenty-four hours later, at midnight on 17 September, a radio reply was sent by Shaposhnikov in the name of the *Stavka* authorizing the pulling back of troops from the Kiev area.[54] But no word was said about a front withdrawal out of the encirclement back to the Psel. Stalin appears to have washed his hands of the affair and left his subordinates to their own devices. In desperation, Kirponos ordered a general retirement; by then many of his forward formations were already outflanked and being broken up.

By 26 September the South-West Front had ceased to exist; the German count of prisoners and booty taken by both Army Groups Centre and South from the beginning of September amounted to 665,000 prisoners, 3,400 guns but only 800 tanks.[55] The four members of the military council of the South-West Front perished. The Soviet accounts of the circumstances of their fate have been contradictory.

---

Meanwhile Leningrad and the Soviet north-west had been under heavy attack and the Red Army troops had given ground. In consequence, on 23 August, Voroshilov's North-West Theatre was broken up. Kurochkin's North-West Front reverted to the direct control of Moscow and was joined by a *Stavka* commission, consisting of Bulganin, Mekhlis and Meretskov, to investigate its lack of success. Popov's North Front had been redesignated as the Leningrad Front and it gave up its responsibilities in the far north to a new Karelian Front under Frolov. When Zhukov arrived at the Smolny on 13 September, he gave a Moscow authority to a dejected Voroshilov, instructing him to hand over command. According to Bychevsky, Zhukov telegraphed to Vasilevsky in Moscow asking him to tell the Supreme Commander that he, Zhukov, proposed 'to conduct the defence more actively than his predecessor'.[56] It is not clear whether this referred to Popov or Voroshilov.

At about this time Stalin instructed Kuznetsov to send a telegraphed order to Tributs, the Commander of the Baltic Fleet, to carry out preparatory work for the scuttling of all warships, in case it should be necessary to abandon Leningrad. Kuznetsov, who apparently lived in fear that the NKVD was, at Stalin's direction, preparing a dossier of documents to incriminate him in charges of treason, blurted out almost involuntarily that he could not, as so important an order would have to come from the dictator himself. It was, thought Kuznetsov, apparent that Stalin did not want to sign this directive, for he then sent the admiral to Shaposhnikov with orders to dispatch the telegram over their joint signatures. Shaposhnikov was aghast and refused point-blank. Eventually Kuznetsov and the Chief of General Staff drafted an instruction for Stalin to sign. Nothing more was heard of it.[57]

On 5 September Hitler decided that his aim was already achieved, for the South-West Front was about to be destroyed and Leningrad could henceforth remain as a secondary theatre. The main strategic task now, he reasoned, was to go for Moscow before the onset of the bad weather.[58] Army Groups North and South were ordered to give up panzer and air formations to von Bock.

The West Front, commanded by Konev, was deployed due west of the capital astride the Smolensk-Vyazma road. Behind the West Front lay the Reserve Front, commanded by Budenny, only two of his six armies, those in the south linking the West to the Bryansk Front, being in contact with the enemy. Yet further to the south was Eremenko's Bryansk Front.

The German plan envisaged Hoth's panzer group attacking in a wide encircling sweep north of the Moscow road and joining up near Vyazma with the southern pincer formed by Hoepner's panzer group. Meanwhile Guderian was to outflank the Bryansk Front from the south and advance on Moscow by way of Orel and Tula. Guderian's offensive was to begin on 28 September and was to be taken up by the German troops further to the north on 2 October.

Konev, who had been a non-commissioned officer in the tsarist artillery and a military commissar until 1927, subsequently said that he informed Moscow of the imminence of an enemy offensive on 26 September. In reply he received a *Stavka* directive forbidding any form of mobile defence.[59] Konev in his turn was obliged to veto his subordinate Rokossovsky's plan for a fighting withdrawal.[60] The strength of the West, Reserve and Bryansk Fronts was said to have totalled eighty-three divisions, in all 1,252,000 men, but only 820 tanks and 360 aircraft.[61]

Meanwhile in Moscow, on 28 September, Harriman and Beaverbrook had the first of three evening meetings with Stalin. The dictator was cordial and gave a review of the military situation as he wished it to be known to western powers. Stalin felt that British divisions might be sent to the Ukraine, but he dismissed

Beaverbrook's suggestion that British troops in Persia could be moved into the Caucasus, with the retort that 'there is no war in the Caucasus, but there is in the Ukraine'. Beaverbrook's proposal that strategic discussions should take place between the British and Red Army general staffs was rebuffed.[62]

At the meeting the next day Stalin was surly and hostile, abrupt and rude, restlessly walking about and smoking, making three telephone calls unconnected with the discussion and each time dialling the number himself. Beaverbrook believed that the dictator was under some intense strain; this may have been the case, although Guderian's probing attacks of 28 and 29 September had as yet been unsuccessful. Stalin showed little interest in western help. Deliberately offensive, he inferred that the Soviet Union was bearing the whole burden of the war and that the proffered aid was of little consequence. The following day Stalin performed the Pavlovian *volte-face* which was to be the common feature of the meetings with foreign statesmen and their envoys. He was all smiles, geniality and co-operation, and agreement was speedily reached, even though this represented hardly more than a readiness by Stalin to accept material assistance.

The only intelligence concerning the state of the Soviet armed forces was that which could be deduced from Stalin's requirements. He wanted tanks, aircraft, anti-aircraft and anti-tank guns, and raw materials, and since the dictator showed no interest in field branch artillery or small-arms it was assumed that the Soviet Union, in spite of its losses, still had plentiful stocks. Harriman noted that Stalin was the only man to deal with in foreign affairs and 'that dealing with others was almost a waste of time'. Ismay used the same words in describing the military sub-committee discussions with Soviet generals. Ismay noted Stalin's shrewd eyes, full of cunning; his handshake was flabby and he never looked one in the face. But he had great dignity and his personality was dominating; as he entered the room every Russian froze into silence and the hunted look in the eyes of the generals showed all too plainly the constant fear in which they lived. It was nauseating, said Ismay, to see brave men reduced to such servility.[63]

On 1 October Guderian had broken into open country in the Soviet rear and was on the move towards Orel, having turned the southern flank of the defence line. That night Leliushenko, a commander awaiting an appointment, was interviewed by Stalin and ordered to organize the defence of Mtsensk and Orel, taking with him a motor-cycle regiment, the only troops readily available in Moscow. At Tula, according to Leliushenko's account, he picked up some guns from the artillery school together with municipal buses as towing vehicles. He was in constant telephonic communication with Shaposhnikov who began to route to him, by road and rail, units and part formations, offering him *Katiusha* multiple-rocket batteries, provided that there was no risk of losing them to the enemy. 'But', added Shaposhnikov, 'take care of them, my dear fellow, otherwise you will answer for it with your head; so says the Supreme Commander'.[64] Shortly afterwards Leliushenko was joined by part of a tank brigade, which happened to be on rail flats, and his command grew rapidly from a motor-cycle regiment to that of two guards rifle divisions, two tank brigades, part of an airborne corps and a tactical support air group.[65] On 2 October Stalin sent Artem'ev, the Commander of Moscow Military District, to Tula to organize the defences there.

The main enemy offensive on the axis of the old Moscow highway at first went unnoticed, for the breakthrough was unreported by the West and the Reserve Fronts. So it came about that Moscow Military District knew of the penetration before the general staff in Moscow. Telegin, the political member of the military district council, has said that on the morning of 5 October he heard that Hoepner's tanks were in Yukhnov, as close to Moscow as Tula, and it was some hours before he could convince Shaposhnikov and Stalin of the truth of the reports.[66]

According to Rokossovsky, the army commanders of the West Front were poorly informed and controlled. Rokossovsky stayed in his original position unaware of developments elsewhere until, on the evening of 5 October, he received a signal from the West Front telling him to transfer all his divisions to the command of his neighbour and withdraw his army headquarters to Vyazma where, on 6 October, he would form a new force to counter-attack on Yukhnov, about fifty miles to the south-east. He was suspicious of the order and asked for it to be confirmed in writing. When he entered Vyazma, German troops were already there. Having escaped from encirclement and arrived at the West Front headquarters, he was to find Stalin's investigators, Voroshilov and

Molotov, already with Konev and Bulganin. Voroshilov was reluctant to believe that Rokossovsky had been ordered to leave his
troops behind and the army commander was obliged to produce
his written order. Konev and Bulganin appear to have suffered
from a lapse of memory. Altogether it was, as Voroshilov said at the
time, 'a strange affair'.[67]

If Budenny was aware of the extent of the German success he
made no report to Stalin but dealt with the emergency in the only
way he knew, by going forward into the battle area. Konev, for his
part, remained unaware until 6 October that Hoth had broken his
right flank and was rapidly approaching Vyazma from the north.
The Vyazma encirclement of Konev's West and Budenny's
Reserve Fronts resulted in the destruction of forty-five divisions
and the loss of 673,000 prisoners.[68]

The primary cause of the defeat would appear to have been the
*Stavka* directive of 27 September committing the troops to a rigid
defence. Within the West Front the defence preparations and the
command exercised by Konev could not have been of a high order,
for an Army Group Centre war diary entry on 2 October said that
'all subordinate armies are agreed that the enemy has been surprised and has put up little resistance'.[69] Konev replied to criticism by pointing to his over-extended front and his lack of depth,
and emphasized the inadequacy of his reserves; for this he
subsequently blamed the *Stavka*. Yet a cogent reason why information and intelligence was not passed back to the *Stavka* would
appear to have been that commanders feared to report reverses;
for if they were in any way responsible they might be punished as
traitors, and if they were merely reporting the failure of others
they could be arrested as panic-spreaders. This happened to
Sbytov, the head of the Moscow Military District air force, who
was threatened by Abakumov with NKVD arrest for producing the
air reconnaissance reports confirming that Hoepner's tanks were in
Yuhknov.[70]

On 5 October Stalin held a leisurely Baudôt conversation with
Zhukov in Leningrad. The Supreme Commander wanted Zhukov
to come to Moscow the next day so that they might 'discuss action
to be taken on the Reserve Front's left wing in the area of Yukhnov'.[71] The following day Stalin, obviously not yet aware of the
encirclement at Vyazma, agreed to Zhukov's postponing his flight

for yet another twenty-four hours. But during the course of that day German troops entered the city of Bryansk cutting off all signal communication with Eremenko, whose forces had been partially encircled, and news came from Cherevichenko's South Front of the envelopment of two Soviet armies near Osipenko against the Black Sea, eventually leading to a further loss of 106,000 prisoners. Konev was still unable or unwilling to give a coherent account of the battle situation on the West Front. That night Stalin ordered Zhukov to hand over the command of the Leningrad Front to Khozin and return at once to Moscow.

# 6

# *The Winter Campaign*

The German winter offensive from October until December was launched along the whole of the eastern front from Leningrad to the Black Sea, having as its strategic objective the north south line of Vologda-Stalingrad-Maikop, extending up to 300 miles to the east of Moscow.[1] During the first few days the weather had been generally dry, with favourable ground and air conditions giving the firm going and the clear skies and visibility needed for reconnaissance and air and artillery support. From about 7 October, however, heavy and continuous rain began to fall over the whole of the front.

When Zhukov arrived in Moscow on the night of 7 October, Stalin ordered him to go out to the West Front headquarters to investigate and report from there. Zhukov found the West Front military council, Konev, Bulganin and Sokolovsky, in session; the extent of the encirclement was known to them, but they had not told Stalin and they left this unpleasant task to Zhukov. As Zhukov subsequently judged the situation, the West Front 'might have averted the Vyazma disaster by the display of more energy and determination'. Zhukov moved off once more in search of the headquarters of the Reserve Front; when he found it, Mekhlis, the *Stavka* representative, was already there, but little information was to be gleaned from him except that it was feared that Budenny was captured. In Maloyaroslavets, already a deserted town, Zhukov came across Budenny, but he knew little except that two of his armies had been cut off. Zhukov went on towards Yukhnov to ascertain personally if the enemy was there, despite the fact that the Moscow air reconnaissance sorties had definitely confirmed, three days before, that panzer troops were in the town. Like other senior army commanders he was without mobile radio, and he reported his movements by detailing local units to phone messages to the general staff in Moscow.[2]

The GKO investigating commission already with the West Front, consisting of Voroshilov, Molotov and Malenkov, and attended by Vasilevsky, was not idle, and, according to Konev, Molotov dictated 'with the greatest of persistence' the manner in which the withdrawing troops should be redeployed.[3] On 10 October the commission recommended to Stalin that Zhukov should replace Konev and that the West Front be amalgamated with the Reserve Front. Budenny had been removed from his command on 8 October. The commission's recommendation was accepted by Stalin. New forces were rapidly concentrated and grouped into four armies to defend the western approaches to the capital, and, on 17 October, the *Stavka* ordered the detachment of the four northern armies of the West Front's right wing to form a new Kalinin Front under Konev. Three weeks later, on 10 November, the Bryansk Front was broken up. All fronts were then directly subordinated to Stalin and the *Stavka,* except that Timoshenko still had a co-ordinating responsibility for Cherevichenko's South Front.

On the south-west approach to the capital Leliushenko's hastily assembled force, aided by the rain, snow and the *rasputitsa,* the breaking up of the roads, had brought Guderian's force to a temporary halt at Mtsensk. When Leliushenko was recalled to the Kremlin on the night of the 11 October, to be given the command of a newly raised army, he felt that he had accomplished his mission in holding the enemy on the Zusha, the *ne plus ultra* line which Stalin had marked on the map. Leliushenko entered the dictator's conference room to find Stalin walking up and down in silence, while Shaposhnikov bent over the maps. Molotov opened the interview by turning to Leliushenko, looking at him severely and demanding, most unexpectedly, why the enemy had not been pushed back out of Orel. The surprised Leliushenko replied that he had so few troops available that, even if he had done so, the enemy would have outflanked him from north and south. Stalin stopped his walking for a moment, then nodded silently, which, said Leliushenko, was Molotov's cue to break off the interrogation with a wintry smile. Leliushenko had the feeling that this little scene had been discussed and rehearsed before his arrival.[4]

On 7 October *Pravda* had reported the giving up of the city of Vyazma 'after a glorious and heroic struggle', but the fact that the West and the Reserve Fronts had suffered an overwhelming defeat could not be concealed. There was panic and looting in the capital, and the diplomatic corps and a number of government commissariats were moved to Kuybyshev. Werth has described what he called 'the great skedaddle' and Birse, of the British Military Mission, has said that there was everywhere among the Muscovites a sense of defeat and impending calamity. Leaflets could be found strewn in public places, blaming the Soviet Government for the misfortunes.[5] When, on the night of 19 October, Artem'ev and Telegin, the military council of Moscow Military District, were ordered to attend a meeting of the GKO in Stalin's office, the atmosphere there was tense, and Stalin was nervous and irritable. Artem'ev, a NKVD general, suggested the proclamation of a state of siege. Stalin instructed Malenkov to draft a GOKO decree to this effect, there and then; but it proved, on being read aloud, to be verbose and so little to the dictator's liking that, according to Telegin, he became angry, 'rushed to Malenkov and snatched the papers from him'. The decree was then dictated by Stalin to Shcherbakov, the Moscow party secretary, 'and approved by all present'. The decree provided for 'the strengthening of controls, the setting up of military tribunals and the shooting on the spot' of real or suspected offenders.[6]

In the second half of October, the enemy advance fell off rapidly due to the exhaustion of his troops, the over-extended fronts, the bad weather and the difficult going conditions. The air situation, too, was gradually changing in favour of the Red Army since much of the *Luftwaffe* was being withdrawn. The defenders were falling back on their Moscow base, and reinforcements began to arrive at the fronts, the West Front alone receiving 100,000 men, 2,000 guns and 300 tanks by the first fortnight in November.[7] In late October, three reserve armies had been brought into being, and in November a further six armies were deployed in depth on a line from Onega to Astrakhan.[8] In Vasilevsky's opinion, the forming of these nine armies was one of the most important factors in deciding the outcome of the winter war.[9] In order to ensure that these armies could be moved forward, the Moscow railway complex and the main east-west lines from the interior were put under military control from 24 October.[10]

All the reserve formations were not formed from the *opolchenie,* however, for the forty or more divisions in the Far East were being steadily reduced, an attempt being made to conceal from Tokyo the decrease in the real fighting strength by a proliferation of formation headquarters, so that, where before there had only been an army, Apanasenko's Far East Front deployed four armies. Kovalev's Transbaikal Military District became a front, though it commanded but one army. By a NKO directive of 16 April 1941, three days after the signing of the Soviet-Japanese Pact, two rifle corps, two rifle divisions and two air brigades were moved to the west, and by the end of November 1941, the total troops ordered to Europe had increased to 17 regular divisions.[11] More were to follow after the attack on Pearl Harbour.

---

The organization and responsibilities of the Soviet general staff were in some respects similar to those of the tsarist general staff, except that the description 'general staff' was applied in tsarist times to the corps of staff officer graduates who served either in the body of the general staff at the capital or were accredited to formation staff vacancies. The Soviet general staff, however, comprised only the command and staff centre in the capital and, in 1939, was in fact called the general staff of the NKO. The Soviet general staff in Frunze Street thus approximated to what was once *der grosse Generalstab* in the Berlin Königsplatz. With the departure of Timoshenko at the beginning of July 1941, the general staff became independent of the Commissariat of Defence and directly subordinate to the newly formed *Stavka*. It took its orders only from Stalin.

When Zhukov quitted the general staff at the end of July it was in confusion, for not only had it been inadequately prepared for war, but its organization had been drained of its principal experienced members. On Stalin's orders, officers were dispatched from the general staff, as well as from the directorates of the Commissariat of Defence, to field formations or as members of the many investigating commissions, which he used as eyes and ears; for

Stalin believed that any officer of ability ought to be at the front. Sokolovsky and Malandin had gone to the West Theatre. Vatutin went to the North-West Front; Golikov left for London; Sharokhin, Kurasov and Kokorev, the chiefs of the theatre and sector operations departments, were appointed as chiefs of staff to fronts or armies. Zlobin, the new chief of the operations directorate, was replaced almost immediately by Vasilevsky.[12]

In July, by order of the GKO, the responsibility for rear services, signals and army organization were removed from the general staff, in order that it might concentrate its attention on strategic and operative matters.[13] The lot of the general staff was not, however, enviable, for Stalin held the general staff in low regard in the first few months of war and he constantly vented his anger on it. It was rarely consulted, and military decisions were usually taken above its head, it being used merely to transmit Stalin's orders.[14]

Stalin covered the widest range of subjects and demanded exhaustive information on any matter under discussion, occasionally asking the Chief of General Staff for comment, but more often than not deciding himself and, said Vasilevsky, giving out his orders without using a single superfluous word. He spared neither himself nor others. According to Vasilevsky, he was an excellent organizer and this organizing ability was eventually to play an enormous role in bringing strategic and operative plans to fruition. He alone found and allocated reinforcements and *matériel*. Yet, in the first year of war, continued Vasilevsky, Stalin 'made miscalculations, some of them grievous', for he was unjustifiably self-confident and presumptuous (*samonadeian*) and overrated his knowledge and ability in the military field. He often changed commanders without good reason, and his interference brought unsatisfactory results. He demanded that others should not be enslaved by old ideas and should learn by modern methods, but in the beginning he could not do this himself. His leadership, said Vasilevsky, was personal and arbitrary.[15]

Zhukov bore witness to Stalin's work in organizing strategic material and technical resources, and he has said that Stalin's real achievement during the winter of 1941 was the creation of carefully husbanded *Stavka* reserves, details of which he guarded from his front commanders. Both Zhukov and Shtemenko have described the dictator's capacity for work and for detail, his retentive memory

– he was never at a loss for a name and he never forgot a face – his gift for sifting essentials and factual data and his ability to uncover the weakness of others; they have told how he demanded clarity and exactitude and of his intolerance of verbosity, of his sternness, formality and reserve, broken by spiteful anger.[16] He was also fervent, impetuous and headstrong and, as Zhukov put it, 'if Stalin was already decided there would be no further argument – discussion ceased anyway as soon as Stalin supported one of the parties'.[17]

In Rotmistrov's judgement the main reason for the 1941 losses was Stalin's personality cult, 'for he concentrated in his own hands great powers, believing himself to be infallible in his ability to decide all questions, including military ones'. At this time he also appears to have had firm faith in his Old Guard supporters, and Rotmistrov has criticized the former Commissars of Defence and the tyranny and incompetence of those who enjoyed Stalin's confidence.[18] Although Rotmistrov names only Mekhlis, the censure would also appear to include Shchadenko, Beria, Voroshilov, Budenny and Kulik. In the autumn of 1941 Mekhlis and Shchadenko still worked hand in glove, and, as Gorbatov has recounted, could effect the arrest and imprisonment of senior army commanders.[19]

Stalin at first sought to improve the high command and general staff by innovation and experiment. In the winter of 1941, he came to believe that the senior officers of the general staff lacked combat experience and therefore authority in their relationship with the staffs of the fronts and armies; so he had commanders and chiefs of staff of armies posted to the general staff to head the theatre and sector departments. This was a failure because, as Shtemenko said, many of these warriors lacked staff training, and the others had lost the habit.[20] The morale of the general staff suffered, and its efficiency was criticized by the fronts and by the directorates of the Commissariat of Defence.[21]

The heads of the operations directorate, and the theatre and sector departments within the directorate, came into daily contact with the Supreme Commander since he preferred to deal directly on points of detail. It proved difficult to find officers of quality and stamina suitable for these onerous duties and, more particularly, satisfactory to Stalin, for if they met with his approval they were soon posted to the fronts. Vasilevsky, a former tsarist *Shtabs-kapitan* in 409 Novokhopersky Regiment, a man of ability and great lucidity in thought and expression, narrowly escaped being sent to Leningrad to help out Voroshilov. He remained heading the operations directorate from August 1941 until June 1942, being appointed deputy chief of general staff in March of that year. But because Stalin believed that a good staff officer was also a competent commander, Vasilevsky, when still head of the operations directorate, began, on Stalin's instructions, to spend most of his time in visits or attachments to the fronts, the day to day direction of the general staff being left in 1942 not to a general staff officer, but to Bokov, its political commissar, merely because Stalin had got used to his face. As Shtemenko said, the Supreme Commander asked no one's advice on this subject and apparently considered such a situation normal.[22]

In the first year of the war Shaposhnikov, inclining towards von Moltke's precedent and perhaps hoping to protect the operations directorate against Stalin's misuse of its staff, introduced the 'corps of officers of the general staff', the first time that the word *ofitser* had been used since the revolution. Their function was to keep the general staff informed of the actions of the commanders to whom they were attached.[23] Many commanders resented their presence as 'spies and overseers'.

The accommodation for the Soviet High Command was unsatisfactory since the work was shuffled backwards and forwards daily between the Kremlin, the Kuntsevo *dacha*, the 'far house' on the Dmitrov road, Frunze Street and later Kirov Street and other addresses in the capital. But, for lack of better, this peacetime accommodation continued to be used throughout the war. The German air raids on Moscow, which started at the end of July, made it necessary to move part of the general staff each night to the Kirovskaia underground station, no trains being allowed to stop there. The platform which served as a general office was screened from the rails by plywood partitions, a communications centre being installed in one corner and an office for Stalin in the other. Later the general staff was given a building in Kirov Street with an annexe set apart for the dictator.[24] After December 1941 the underground shelters were no longer used, but the general staff remained in Kirov Street; Stalin was usually to be found in the

**12** Stalin, c. 1941 aged 63 years, on becoming Chairman of the Council of Commissars, Commissar for Defence and the Supreme Commander.

**13** *Above left.* Shaposhnikov, a tsarist colonel, who was Chief of General Staff from 1937–40 and again from 1941–42 (died 1945).

**14** *Above right.* Zhukov, a tsarist cavalry NCO, who was Chief of General Staff from February to June 1941 and Deputy Supreme Commander from 1942–46.

**15** *Below left.* Bagramian, an Armenian, a tsarist junior cavalry officer, later a Sovient front commander.

**16** *Below right.* Tiulenev, a Red Army cavalry brigade leader who later commanded Soviet fronts.

Kremlin. The rump of the old signal centre continued a separate existence in providing a telegraph service for the Commissariat of Defence, while the main element served Stalin's Kremlin office and the general staff in Kirov Street.

Stalin took a close interest in military communications and many of his instructions bore the influence of his experience during the Civil War. In one directive he said he was averse to 'excessive reliance by commanders on the telephone, for they should do as the military did at the time of the imperialistic war', that is to say make fuller use of the teleprint telegraph. On 23 July the dictator signed a general signals directive to his field commanders, having, said Peresypkin, 'characteristically' altered the draft to emphasize once more the value of teleprint; he pointed out that all fronts and armies had been re-equipped with Baudôt taken from government and industry in the rear areas.[25] That September the Supreme Commander required that Baudôt terminals with an alternative line layout should be established between the general staff and the armies, bypassing the front headquarters, so that, in the event of signals failure, armies could be controlled from Moscow.

Stalin's working day began an hour or so before noon when he would himself dial the operations directorate for a briefing on what had happened during the night. According to Shtemenko, the answering officer would verbally describe the situation, using a ten yard long telephone lead as he walked from one battle map to the next, Stalin having a corresponding set of maps in his own office which were brought up to date every five days by Platonov. The most important fronts were dealt with first, fronts, armies and armoured formations being referred to by the names of their commanders, the lesser formations by their number and designation. Even though there were twenty or thirty armies in contact with the enemy, Stalin never allowed a single one to be passed over without mention. Occasionally, he would interrupt and dictate an order to be sent to a particular front and this was taken down verbally, read back to the dictator, and dispatched. The second briefing would be at about 1600 hours, sometimes by telephone but usually in the form of a written summary collated by Shaposhnikov; this also went to members of the Politburo and the government. Shortly before midnight the Chief of General Staff or his deputy, the head of the operations directorate, and the theatre or sector chiefs if required, would drive either to the Kremlin or to Kuntsevo with their maps and folders for the nightly report to Stalin and the Politburo or GKO. The heads of main arms and services, usually Voronov, Fedorenko, Novikov, Vorob'ev, Iakovlev and Khrulev, might be in attendance.

Stalin's study and conference room, which was entered through Poskrebyshev's office and the cubby-hole occupied by the chief of the dictator's NKVD bodyguard, has been frequently described by its many visitors; the vaulted ceiling and light oak panelling, the portraits of Suvorov and Kutuzov, Marx and Engels; the long table with the Politburo members sitting against the wall facing the military; Stalin's desk near the death-mask of Lenin under a glass case, and the globe. Stalin would walk up and down, his hands behind his back, smoking his pipe and listening to the reports of operations over the last twenty-four hours. After the reports came the draft directives, which were signed by Stalin and counter-signed by the Chief of General Staff or his deputy or by one other member of the *Stavka*. Less important orders were agreed by Stalin and signed by Shaposhnikov or Vasilevsky after the conclud-ing words 'by order of the *Stavka*'; a distribution copy was sent to Stalin. Directives and orders were often formulated on the spot at Stalin's dictation, many of them being handed untyped to Poskrebyshev's signal centre for immediate transmission to the fronts. Stalin dealt personally with proposals for the promotion, decoration and appointment of senior officers. These nightly meetings often lasted until three or four in the morning.[26]

In the first few months of the war the claims of the field com-manders had been optimistic; their failures they had tried to conceal. As the true situation emerged, Shaposhnikov had borne the weight of Stalin's rage, usually in silence. Some angry scenes were caused by nothing more serious than the late rendition of a front situation report, and, when he could, Shaposhnikov apparently attempted to protect his subordinates.[27] According to Voronov, Stalin wanted to know everything, but his commanders and staff feared to tell him the truth; Iakovlev, the aircraft designer, on the other hand, considered that Stalin was more angry at failure to report than with the lack of success reported.[28]

On 17 October Shaposhnikov and the general staff were evacuated from Moscow, Vasilevsky and Shtemenko remaining as Stalin's immediate assistants.[29] Shaposhnikov, however, soon returned to Moscow until he became ill at the end of November, when he handed his duties over to Vasilevsky. Vasilevsky, like Shaposhnikov, was a man of education, culture and tact, and of charm and modesty; he was also circumspect in his relationship with Stalin and the party. He was of a different stamp from Zhukov, who, like Timoshenko, had much of the cavalry non-commissioned officer about him, being particularly blunt and outspoken, offensively so to his subordinates, according to his colleagues. Belov and Rokossovsky would have their readers believe that Zhukov was capable of speaking sharply even to Stalin; but this is scarcely to be credited, for western observers noted how subdued Zhukov was in the presence of his political masters.[30]

Stalin's mentality was devious, for in October 1941 Voronov proposed to him that a reserve of 160 guns should be formed into ten artillery batteries to thicken up Moscow's anti-tank defences. Stalin pondered aloud, and wished that he had twice as many. Finally he agreed to the ten new units but, to Voronov's surprise, suggested that they should be called regiments. For, said Stalin, this would ensure that 'proper attention would be paid to the units'; and, as for the commanders, 'commander of an artillery regiment – that had a proper ring to it – not only a divisional commander but even a corps commander would have to take notice of him!'. Stalin pointed out to the doubting Voronov, that many infantry divisions had been reduced by casualties to shells, with a fighting strength of less than a regiment, but they still remained on the order of battle as divisions, these numerous cadres swelling the totals of the formations said to be in action on the Russo-German front. When, ten days later, the new artillery regiments had been formed, Voronov suggested to Stalin that the general staff should allocate them. The Supreme Commander, he said, looked at him in surprise, asking, 'Who there could do it?'. Stalin thereupon himself deployed the regiments from his reading of the map.[31]

---

Zhukov has said that no master plan existed for the winter counter-offensive, and Vasilevsky has confirmed that there was no thought in Moscow of a military initiative until the beginning of November when the German attacks had died down. Events made this impossible, however, for it soon became apparent that the Germans intended to resume the offensive.[32]

On 13 November Stalin telephoned Zhukov, instructing him to mount pre-emptive attacks on the German flanks according to a plan which he and Shaposhnikov had thought out, and so disorganize the enemy's preparations. When Zhukov objected that he could not spare a man for the purpose, Stalin became angry and ordered him to 'consider the matter as settled'. Stalin then spoke to Bulganin to tell him that both he and Zhukov had got too big for their boots (*zaznalis'*). The attacks were mounted as ordered, with little time for preparation, and both Zhukov and Rokossovsky confirm that they failed.[33]

The new enemy offensive, which had as its primary aim the taking of Moscow, began on 15 November, when the wet weather had given way to cold. The German troops on the Nara were to pin the Soviet West Front, while Hoepner's and Reinhardt's panzer groups outflanked the capital from the north and Guderian came up from the south. When Reinhardt struck his main blow north of Moscow, Khomenko's 30 Army on Konev's left wing was routed. That the blame lay with the *Stavka* did not save Khomenko, for at Stalin's order he was immediately relieved by Leliushenko, who had been briefed personally by the dictator. Leliushenko's arrival was Khomenko's first intimation that he had been dismissed.[34] In the next ten days Reinhardt and Hoepner moved forward fifty miles almost to the northern outskirts of the capital; then, like Guderian in the area of Tula, they could do no more, and they waited impatiently for von Kluge to begin his offensive from the Nara, due west of the city.

During the last ten days in November Stalin became increasingly agitated, and, on or about 30 November, occurred the Dedovo-Dedovsk incident when Stalin, under the mistaken impression that the town of Dedovsk, only twenty miles west from the Kremlin, had fallen, 'lost no time in expressing his anger' and ordered Zhukov, together with Rokossovsky and Govorov, both army commanders, to go to Dedovo and supervise an attack by a rifle company and two tanks to retake the locality. Stalin was deaf to entreaties that it would be ill-advised to leave the front headquarters at such a time, and became furious when told there had been confusion in place names. The three generals had to go to Dedovo.[35]

Rokossovsky, a former tsarist non-commissioned officer of 5 Kargopolsky Dragoons, at one time, prior to his three years imprisonment during the purges, a cavalry corps leader and Zhukov's senior commander, has said that Zhukov, too, was very nervous during this period. If Rokossovsky is to be believed, Zhukov forfeited much of the respect of his army commanders because of his impetuosity and lack of self-control and his distrust of his subordinates.[36] The Istra incident which occurred at this time, while of no great consequence in itself, has subsequently attracted much attention in the Soviet military press. Rokossovsky wanted to fall back a few miles and use the Istra as an obstacle, and, as Zhukov disagreed, Rokossovsky appealed to Shaposhnikov, who gave his assent. Rokossovsky reasoned that since the Chief of General Staff rarely assumed any direct responsibility, then Shaposhnikov would have told Stalin of the change. He was surprised, therefore, when Zhukov shortly afterwards countermanded Shaposhnikov's agreement.[37] Although some western commentators have assumed that Zhukov dared to oppose Stalin's will, it is more probable that Zhukov had first taken his complaint to Stalin; and it is in character that Stalin would, with the intention of reaffirming his confidence in the front commander, have told Zhukov to issue his own order.[38] A day or two afterwards Stalin, who, as Anders said, on occasion liked to play the role of *bon papa,* had a telephone conversation with Rokossovsky 'in a kindly and fatherly voice'. Rokossovsky judged that the Supreme Commander merely wanted to express his trust in the army as well as the front commander.[39]

On 29 November, Zhukov had telephoned Stalin asking for two further armies from the *Stavka* reserve in order to destroy the enemy panzer penetrations to the north and south of the capital before they should be reinforced. Stalin, according to Zhukov, listened attentively but was doubtful whether von Bock might still hold a reserve. But when Zhukov assured him that the enemy was exhausted, Stalin said that he would first talk to the general staff.[40] Later that day Zhukov was informed that three armies would be released to him, but that plans as to their use would be required in Moscow on the morrow. This, said Zhukov, was the seed of the winter counter-offensive which was to throw the enemy back 200 miles. A few hours later, at dawn on 30 November, Stalin telephoned asking whether the whole of the West Front could not go over to the offensive. Zhukov pleaded lack of resources, but, as an alternative, suggested that the offensive might be extended beyond the flanks of the West Front. This, however, had been done the day before, for a newly confident Timoshenko had already driven the enemy out of Rostov, and his proposal to use his right wing against von Bock's flank was readily accepted by Stalin. Zhukov gave his own plan to Vasilevsky on 30 November, requesting that he should lay it before the Supreme Commander quickly. It was agreed without amendment that day.[41]

At 0330 hours on 1 December, Stalin and Vasilevsky signed the directive to the Kalinin Front, the Supreme Commander telling Konev that he was dissatisfied with his conduct of the battle; Konev was to concentrate his forces and strike along new axes. Later that day Konev told Vasilevsky that such an offensive was impossible in view of his depleted strength and lack of tanks. Vasilevsky countered by quoting back the strength returns furnished by the Kalinin Front. Was not Konev aware of the successes at Rostov. It was necessary to strike now, said Vasilevsky, for any delay might be fatal.[42] The earlier West Front defeats had presumably undermined Konev's confidence, and Stalin became concerned at his lack of determination. On 4 December Vasilevsky arrived at the Kalinin Front, personally to ensure that Konev gave out his orders in the spirit of the directive. Eight days later Shaposhnikov was well again and both he and Vasilevsky were present when Stalin spoke on the direct line to Konev, demanding that he cease his hairsplitting tactics (*krokhoborskuiu taktiku*).[43]

Zhukov's plan concerned itself only with the West Front and the three recently allocated armies. Cherevichenko, the hero of Rostov, took command of Timoshenko's right flank, forming a new Bryansk Front on 18 December, and began to envelop the German Army Group Centre from the south. Konev's Kalinin Front moved forward, cautiously at first, supported by Kurochkin's North-West Front, Purkaev's and Eremenko's armies outflanking the enemy from the north and penetrating westwards almost as far as Smolensk and Vitebsk.

The success of the Moscow battle, which involved four fronts, was at one time popularly attributed to Zhukov. Rotmistrov's 1963 study has said that the offensive originated from the plan forwarded by the military council of the West Front. Neither Stalin nor

Zhukov is mentioned by name.[44] Sokolovsky, who was a member of that council, writing in the following year does not make that claim, but he blames Stalin for interfering in the conduct of the front battle.[45] Zhukov's 1968 account, that the overall plan was drawn up by the general staff and Stalin in consultation with the front commanders, is substantially the same as that written by Vasilevsky in 1974. Whatever the truth of the matter, there can be little doubt that Stalin remained in overall military control, and that neither he nor Timoshenko ever needed prompting to undertake offensive operations.

---

On 2 December 1941 Anders, a former Polish officer of the tsarist army only recently released from the NKVD Lubianka prison, was, together with Sikorski, received in audience by Stalin. Anders's description of Stalin differs little from that recorded by other western observers, his eyes black, cold and dull, wrinkled into a smile which seemed only skin-deep, the salesman's joviality, the quiet deliberate tones and the pronounced Caucasian accent, and 'the unmistakable atmosphere of power about him'. Anders noted the subservience shown to Stalin, particularly by the obsequious Molotov 'with his quick offer of a light every time Stalin drew out a cigarette, more like a lackey than a colleague'. At this meeting, Stalin, when asked concerning the fate of 4,000 missing Polish officers, replied, imperturbably according to Anders, that 'they must have escaped to Manchuria'.[46]

A fortnight later when Eden visited Moscow, Japan had attacked the American and British dependencies in the Pacific, and Hitler had declared war on the United States. Stalin showed none of the nervousness and strain apparent during the previous September, and Eden found him 'a quiet dictator in his manner'. He sympathized with Eden on Britain's defeats in the Pacific, saying that 'we, too, have had our difficult periods'. Stalin was particularly interested in Japanese air power and told a sceptical Eden that his military advisers believed 'but were not absolutely certain' that Germany had given Japan 1,500 aircraft together with pilots. If the German aircraft had not been transferred to Japan, said Stalin, where had they gone. For the last six weeks he had noticed a considerable decrease in German air power on the Russian front and he did not believe the aircraft had gone to Libya.

Stalin gave Eden a *resumé* of the military situation as it appeared to him on 16 December. Putting the best gloss that he could on the earlier Russian defeats, the extent of which had never been admitted either at home or abroad, the dictator said, quite falsely, that the war policy of the Soviet Union had hitherto been that of a fighting retreat so as to wear down the German forces. By now, the enemy was tired and ill-clad, having made no preparation for a winter campaign, whereas on the Soviet side the new formations arriving at the front had enabled the Red Army to counter-attack. Counter-attacks, said Stalin, had gradually developed into counter-offensives, and he would 'try and carry this on all through the winter'. He had, he thought, two months in hand before the Germans could organize a counter blow; it was difficult to say how far the Red Army would be able to move forward, but that would be its aim until the spring. The Red Army had air superiority continued Stalin, but not a great one, and needed tanks, 'especially Valentines which have been found to be much better for winter use'. In the south the position was quite satisfactory. The secret of the recent successes was the opportune arrival of fresh reinforcements; 'the German Army was not so strong after all, in spite of its enormous reputation'.[47]

On 17 December Stalin asked that the talks either be postponed for a day or else held after midnight as 'he had a conference of generals'. Timoshenko and his staff were in Moscow and this meeting probably centred around the formation of the new Volkhov and Bryansk Fronts, and the directive issued on 18 December concerning a fresh offensive in the north-west. On 19 December Eden was driven out to Klin, which had been reoccupied only four days before, and sat down to lunch next to 'the Russian general who had described to us the battle'. Eden believed him to be a major-general 'on the staff of an army'. It was in fact Leliushenko. At the banquet on the final day of the meeting Stalin was clearly embarrassed at the spectacle of a somewhat drunk Timoshenko. Yet, when the Ribbentrop-Molotov pact was discussed, he showed no shame, said Eden, in brazenly giving Molotov the discredit for it.[48]

---

In the south the situation was, as Stalin had told Eden, satisfactory, for the enemy Army Group South, ordered to secure the line Stalingrad-Maikop, had overreached itself in trying to enter the

Caucasus and had been forced back from Rostov to the line of the Mius.

In the north, near Leningrad, von Leeb's Army Group North had moved north-eastwards preparatory to joining up with the Finns on the Svir. Tikhvin fell on 8 November and the defending Red Army troops began to disintegrate. The rear of 7 Independent Soviet Army, facing north against the Finns, was threatened, and its commander Meretskov telephoned the Stavka, presumably Poskrebyshev, for Meretskov said that 'there and then Stalin came on the phone'; having heard Meretskov's report, the dictator ordered him to hand his army over to his deputy and take over the command of the routed troops facing von Leeb.[49] Stalin told Meretskov he could give him no reinforcements, but authorized him to use the three armies in the area as the situation demanded. By 11 November the energetic and jovial Meretskov had already organized the first counter-attack and this steadily built up into an offensive. On 9 December, Meretskov's troops entered Tikhvin.

Two days later Meretskov was summoned to the general staff in Moscow and told by Vasilevsky that he was to form a new front headquarters, the Volkhov Front, interposed between the Leningrad and North-West Fronts. The following day Meretskov was called to the Kremlin where he found Stalin and Shaposhnikov, together with Khozin and Zhdanov from the Leningrad Front, grouped round a map of the Leningrad-Volkhov area. The task was to plan an offensive which was intended to link up by land with Leningrad.[50]

In addition to the four armies already allocated to him, Meretskov wanted to take over yet another from the Leningrad Front; Khozin and Zhdanov objected. Stalin listened to the argument and finally sided with Khozin; 'if that is best for Leningrad, let it be that way'.

The main difficulty that was to bedevil the new offensive was that of timing, because Meretskov still awaited the arrival of his troops. Meretskov has said that he was given no time to prepare his offensive, but was goaded into the attack as soon as he had arrived back on the Volkhov; he has cited the Stavka directive of 17 December and 'one in the clearest terms' on 24 December. 'On top of that' continued Meretskov, 'Mekhlis arrived as the Stavka

representative to speed up operations'. Consequently Meretskov
had been obliged from 20 December onwards to make fruitless
and costly tactical attacks before the main offensive was launched.
Voronov, one of the few to earn Meretskov's thanks, came to assist
in artillery matters, but, by the first week in January, the attacks by
the two armies already in place were dying out and the other two
reserve armies were not yet assembled. On 10 January Meretskov
was still not ready, and he subsequently said that he needed,
in fact, another fifteen to twenty days to complete his
concentration.

On 11 January Stalin and Vasilevsky had a direct wire conversation with Meretskov in which they stated that 'according to the
information available to them' the Volkhov Front was not ready,
and they suggested that the offensive be postponed to ensure success.
Meretskov has admitted that he grasped 'at the additional two
days offered', still knowing that he could never be prepared in
time. Then, on the eve of the offensive, the divisional commanders
of a shock army, the main striking force, complained to Meretskov
that their army commander did not know what he was about.
Meretskov reported the facts to the *Stavka,* and Stalin had the
commander replaced immediately. The offensive, born of these
inauspicious beginnings, failed. The *Stavka* accused the front
military council of turpitude and indecision and Voroshilov, as
Stalin's representative, arrived for a tour of inspection of the armies,
returning once more with Malenkov and Novikov as part of a GKO
investigating committee.

According to a Soviet reviewer of Meretskov's memoirs 'the
Volkhov Front did not have the courage to tell Stalin the true
state of affairs before or after the offensive was launched'. This may
indeed have been the case, but this criticism must also have applied
to Mekhlis, Voroshilov, Voronov, Vasilevsky, Khrulev and Novikov who went there in turn. However this may be, Stalin afterwards put the blame on Meretskov, saying 'the offensive has been
hurried without preparation and has set people laughing; if you
remember, I proposed that you delay the attack, but you refused and
now you reap the fruits of your rashness'.[51]

Stalin may indeed have used these admonitory words to Meretskov; whether he would have agreed to a delay of three weeks is
another matter. For, on 5 January, Zhukov had been called to a

GKO meeting where Shaposhnikov had outlined the plan for a massive counter-offensive from Leningrad to the Black Sea, and this included the lifting of the Leningrad blockade and the re-occupying of the Donets Basin and the Crimea, all to be done in the shortest time possible. Stalin summarized the presentation by saying that the enemy was in confusion and unprepared for winter warfare; the need for offensive action was immediate. He asked if anyone had anything to say.

Zhukov has said that he spoke against a general offensive on the grounds that this might starve his own West Front of troops and material and put its advance at risk; his address, he said, was obviously unwelcome to Stalin who interjected a number of critical remarks. Voznesensky, Chairman of the Economic Council of the Defence Industry, supported Zhukov on the grounds of the general shortage of equipment. Stalin retorted by saying that he had talked to Timoshenko, who was all for the offensive. 'We must', said Stalin, 'finish the Germans off quickly so that they will not be able to come back in the spring'. This was the cue for Malenkov and Beria to take the floor and attack Voznesensky. In Zhukov's opinion, which was reinforced by what he afterwards heard from Shaposhnikov, the immediate and general offensive was Stalin's brain-child and was not initiated by the general staff.[52] Zhukov could see no reason why he had been told to attend since discussion was superfluous, and he came to the conclusion that it had been Stalin's intention merely 'to put pressure on the military'; in this case himself. Vasilevsky has said that on 10 January, on Stalin's initiative, a directive was sent to all fronts concerning the coming offensive 'which was going to drive the aggressor out of the country'.[53]

Stalin continued to act as the co-ordinator of the fronts immediately to the west of Moscow. On 16 December he had, against Zhukov's wishes, transferred Leliushenko's army back to Konev. On 19 January Zhukov was told to transfer a shock army to the *Stavka* reserve from whence it was to go to Kurochkin. When Zhukov and Sokolovsky appealed to the general staff against the order, they were informed that the decision was that of the Supreme Commander. Zhukov telephoned Stalin, only to be told that he was to send the army back 'without any more argument'; when Zhukov attempted to continue the conversation Stalin replaced the receiver. By the end of February the West Front had already outrun its logistic support and resources; the enemy had regrouped and was counter-attacking strongly, enveloping Soviet armies one after the other. But, said Zhukov, the appeals of the front for a respite so that the position might be consolidated were ignored by Stalin, who constantly repeated his self-formulated principle of offensive action: 'Attack! If you have no results today, you will tomorrow; even if you achieve nothing except the pinning of the enemy, the result will be felt elsewhere'. Yet by his harsh measures, continued Zhukov, Stalin achieved the well-nigh impossible; he was attentive to advice but he made his own decisions, decisions which, in Zhukov's opinion, did not always correspond to the demands of the situation.[54]

Stalin's simple philosophy has been criticized in the six volume history, published under Khrushchev, for over-optimism and dispersal of effort. The troops, it said, were thrown into battle piecemeal without proper preparation and with inadequate tank or artillery support. But the main charge levelled against Stalin concerned the allocation of the nine reserve armies; of these, three went to the West and two to the Volkhov Fronts, and one each to the Kalinin, Bryansk, North-West and South-West Fronts; if most had gone to the West Front, Army Group Centre might have been destroyed.[55]

The gains made by the Red Army in the north and south, measured in territory, were admittedly small and, in the south at least, transitory. Kozlov's Transcaucasus Front in the Kuban crossed the Kerch straits on 26 December and established a bridgehead in the Crimea, so enabling the besieged Sevastopol garrison to hold out for a further few months. In the Ukraine Timoshenko, once more a theatre commander, used the left wing of Kostenko's South-West Front and the right wing of Malinovsky's South Front in an offensive which, starting on 18 January, achieved an eighty mile wide breakthrough in the area of Izyum, penetrating sixty miles into the enemy rear in eighty days and threatening the supply artery to Stalino. In the north von Leeb had fallen back, his left flank still being under pressure from Meretskov's Volkhov Front, when his right flank was unexpectedly assailed on 7 January by Kurochkin's North-West Front. By 8 February Kurochkin had encircled a German force of 90,000 men at Demyansk. Over the whole of the eastern front there was a nervousness and tension never experienced before by the German command.

Hitler's intention had been to occupy the line Vologda-Stalingrad-Maikop that winter. Yet, throughout the course of the further three and a half years' fighting, the Germans did not succeed in advancing beyond the line on which they had halted in the spring of 1942, roughly in the area Leningrad-Velikiye Luki-Spas Demensk. Only in the Ukraine were Axis troops to resume the advance in the great summer offensive.

---

Khozin, the Commander of the Leningrad Front, had complained, during a teleprint conversation with Moscow, that the efforts of the Leningrad and Volkhov Fronts so lacked co-ordination that the enemy could easily parry their blows in turn. He urged, so he has since said, that the *Stavka* should exercise a more centralized control over both fronts, so directing their efforts and reserves in the decisive sectors. Meretskov has imputed to Khozin less disinterested motives. Khozin was called to Moscow on 21 April to report to Stalin and the GKO, Shaposhnikov and Vasilevsky being present. Having heard Khozin's address, Stalin proposed that the Leningrad and Volkhov Fronts be merged into a single front, this proposal, according to Khozin, surprising not only himself but all the others present. The decision, as Khozin admitted, subsequently proved to be a bad one, 'but at that moment no one could think of any objections, and indeed, in view of the colossal authority which Stalin wielded, hardly anyone could in fact object'.[56]

The directive covering the reorganization and the disbandment of the Volkhov Front was signed that night and the front was downgraded to the status of a group under Khozin's Leningrad Front. Meretskov learned on 23 April, he said to his 'utter surprise', that he was to be transferred to the West Front firstly as a deputy commander and then to command an army. The Leningrad Front, however, could provide no remedies and, in Khozin's words, 'the situation instead of improving steadily worsened'. The armies, he said, were worn out, with formations sixty or seventy per cent short of establishment; tank brigades had no tanks and the artillery no ammunition. On 8 June Meretskov received a telephone call from Moscow informing him that the Volkhov Front was to be reconstituted with himself as the front commander.

Meretskov has recounted, with satisfaction, his version of the GKO meeting which took place in the second week in June. Stalin summed up the situation by saying that '*we* committed a grave error in joining the two fronts' and that Khozin had seriously mismanaged things. Meretskov, together with Vasilevsky, was to go to the Volkhov and bring out Vlasov's encircled shock army no matter what the cost, even if it had to abandon heavy weapons and equipment.[57] As for Khozin, he lost the advancement and subsequent fame which went to Govorov, the former artillery officer of the White Guards, who, on 3 June, relieved him as the Commander of the Leningrad Front.

# 7
# *Further Defeats*

The German Führer had abandoned his intention of resuming the offensive on Moscow and had decided to occupy Caucasia in the summer of 1942; he intended to get to the Volga, but the taking of Stalingrad was unimportant, except that every effort was to be made to reach the city 'or at least control the area by the fire of heavy weapons' so that the Soviet Union could no longer use it as an industrial or communications centre.[1] The campaign was to open by a thrust in the north from the area of Kursk, striking due east towards Voronezh. The German motorized forces were then to change direction south-eastwards, moving rapidly along the right bank of the Don and enveloping the South-West Front from the rear. In order to conceal the direction of the offensive, Keitel, the head of the OKW, had issued a directive, on 12 February, for an intelligence cover plan to disseminate false information that the next German offensive was to be directed on Moscow.

In the spring of 1942 Stalin and the Red Army general staff believed that the seizure of Moscow would be the main enemy strategic object, and, according to Vasilevsky, 'the majority of the front commanders thought so too'. It was considered that any enemy offensive in the Ukraine was likely to have as its aim not the occupation of Caucasia, but the envelopment from the south of both the West Front and Moscow. Shaposhnikov urged Stalin to go over to the strategic defensive in order to accumulate reserves, so that the expected enemy offensive could be met with a counter blow.[2] Stalin accepted Shaposhnikov's proposals in principle, but it transpired that the dictator's interpretation of 'active defence'

143

was a series of major offensives at Demyansk, the Crimea, Kharkov, Kursk, Smolensk and Leningrad. Meanwhile the strategic reserves were held in the areas of Tula, Voronezh, Stalingrad and Saratov, so that, as Vasilevsky said, 'looking at the plan critically, one must say that we intended both to attack and defend'.

That March Shaposhnikov received from Timoshenko a request for additional forces for a grand offensive to be made by the Bryansk, South-West and South Fronts with the aim of clearing the enemy from the Ukraine as far west as Kiev. Although the general staff begged the Supreme Commander not to agree, Stalin sanctioned as much of Timoshenko's offensive plan as could be undertaken with his own resources.[3] At the end of the month, at a GKO planning conference, Shaposhnikov attempted to decry the merits of Timoshenko's proposal, but he was silenced by Stalin, who asked whether they should idle and allow the enemy to attack first. It was necessary, said Stalin, to strike a number of blows over a wide front.[4] Timoshenko spoke in favour of his plan and Voroshilov agreed with him. Zhukov supported Shaposhnikov in general terms but adhered to his own view that there should be one offensive, that by his own West Front. Shaposhnikov took no further part in the discussion. Vasilevsky shared Shaposhnikov's opinion and he subsequently condemned Stalin's strategy as a frittering of strength and effort. He later commented: 'Many might rightly censure the general staff for failing to tell Stalin the negative consequences of his plans, but would only do so if they did not know the difficult conditions under which the general staff had to work'. The only comfort which Vasilevsky could draw was that these errors were fully taken into account a year later at Kursk.[5]

Timoshenko intended to use the larger part of two fronts to attack out of the Izyum bulge, a salient surrounded on three sides by the enemy. Notwithstanding Shaposhnikov's opinion that 'an offensive mounted from an operative bag (*iz operativnogo meshka*) was attended by great risks', Timoshenko assured Stalin that it would be successful. The dictator thereupon ruled that the South-West Theatre offensive was 'an internal matter in which the general staff should not interfere'.[6]

Zhukov agreed both with Stalin and with the general staff that the main German thrust would be from Orel and Kursk, the enemy then wheeling in a north-easterly direction behind Moscow, and that the Bryansk Front, newly under Golikov's command, was holding a key sector. Increased tank production had made possible once more the raising of large armoured formations, and Golikov had been heavily reinforced; in addition, a new 5 Tank Army under Liziukov, part of the *Stavka* reserve, was concentrated behind the Bryansk Front. Stalin had refused to allow Golikov to support Timoshenko's offensive, and, on 24 April, he ordered Golikov to move his main forces further north to the Orel area where they would be closer to the capital.[7]

Timoshenko's offensive began on 12 May, Kostenko's South-West Front attacking out of the salient northwards on Kharkov.[8] Hitler had already ordered operation *Fridericus I* to be mounted on 18 May, having as its aim the destruction of the Izyum bulge.

At first Timoshenko's operation was most successful and this caused Stalin to make some bitter comment on the worthlessness of the general staff.[9] Hitler countered the Soviet offensive by bringing *Fridericus I* forward and, on 17 May, von Kleist's panzer army began its attack on the south face of the salient, cutting through Malinovsky's South Front and making rapid progress into Kostenko's rear, so that the Izyum bulge, held by part of two fronts, was in immediate danger of encirclement. What Shaposhnikov had forecast was about to come to pass.

On the evening of 17 May Vasilevsky suggested to Stalin that part of Kostenko's attacking force be turned round to assist Malinovsky in its rear. Timoshenko, however, told Stalin that the situation was under control. Although Khrushchev has said that he warned Stalin on 17 May of the danger, it would appear that this really occurred late on 18 May. Stalin would not agree to break off the attacks on Kharkov; Khrushchev then spoke to Vasilevsky, at about 1800 hours that day, and pleaded with him to intercede with Stalin; but Vasilevsky declined, telling Khrushchev that he had more than once attempted, in the face of Timoshenko's and Khrushchev's opposition, to dissuade Stalin from the operation and from maintaining the Kharkov attacks; Khrushchev must now deal directly with the Supreme Commander himself.[10] When Khrushchev telephoned the Kuntsevo *dacha* Stalin refused to speak to him but suffered the conversation to be conducted through Malenkov, at the end of which he directed that everything should remain as it was.[11] Khrushchev criticized Stalin only after his death.[12] Timoshenko subsequently tried to place the responsibility for the Kharkov defeat on Kharitonov.[13]

Against a German loss of 20,000 men, the Red Army casualties in prisoners alone totalled 214,000, in addition to 1,200 tanks and 2,000 guns. Kostenko and a number of army commanders were said to have been among the killed and the South-West Front had ceased to exist. The South-West Theatre was downgraded to a front. With this defeat the Soviet Union had lost all strategic initiative.

Kharkov was not the only defeat suffered by the Red Army during the Stalin offensives. In March the dictator had sent Mekhlis to Kerch as the *Stavka* representative to Kozlov's Crimea Front. Stalin had confidence in Mekhlis, trusting him, according to Meretskov, 'because he reported everything and concealed nothing'; Meretskov, himself not distinguished for urbanity or tact, described Mekhlis as 'suspicious, rude, curt, obstinate and rigid'. Shortly after arriving in the Crimea, Mekhlis had replaced Tolbukhin, the front chief of staff, by Vechny; and, according to Shtemenko, 'true to his usual practice, instead of helping he began capriciously to shuffle around (*peretasovyvat'*) other senior commanders and staff'.[14] The Crimea Front neither began its own offensive nor deployed defensively to meet that of the enemy. Finally, on 8 May, the German blow fell and Kozlov's troops began to disintegrate.

On that day Mekhlis sent a telegram to Stalin commencing with the words, 'this is not the time to complain, but I must report, so that the *Stavka* will know the front commander for what he is'; Mekhlis placed the responsibility for the unreadiness for battle on Kozlov's shoulders. Stalin, however, dispatched what Shtemenko called 'a no less remarkable reply'. Stalin thought Mekhlis's position, 'as a mere observer without responsibility, strange . . . and very comfortable', reminding him that as a *Stavka* representative he was answerable for failures, and was in duty bound to rectify mistakes on the spot. If, continued Stalin, Mekhlis had confined himself to passive criticism, so much the worse for him. 'You demand that we replace Kozlov by somebody like Hindenburg, but you must know that we have no Hindenburgs in reserve'.[15]

Two days later, at 0300 hours on 10 May, Stalin is said to have ordered Kozlov to withdraw immediately, and, at 2350 hours the next day, he instructed Budenny to go to the Crimea and compel Kozlov to disengage.[16] By then, however, the Crimea Front had been routed and, against German casualties totalling 7,500 men, Kozlov lost 170,000 in prisoners alone, 1,100 guns, 250 tanks and 300 aircraft. A month later Sevastopol fell with a loss of a further 90,000 prisoners. For this failure Mekhlis was recalled, degraded in rank and replaced as head of the main political directorate by Shcherbakov. Kozlov, two army commanders and other more junior commanders were removed, losing rank or being otherwise punished. Budenny's North Caucasus Theatre was redesignated as a front.

Elsewhere the Leningrad, North-West and West Front offensives gained no real advantage; the enemy Demyansk salient still held and Army Group Centre began to make limited attacks to pinch out the salients near Vyazma and Byelyi defended by Zhukov's West Front. These resulted in the loss of a further 70,000 Red Army men as prisoners.

---

On 19 June a German light plane, carrying the luckless Major Reichel bearing plans for von Bock's summer offensive into the Ukraine, lost its way in bad weather and was brought down on Soviet territory. Details of the plans were hurriedly transmitted to Moscow. When, the next day, Stalin and Vasilevsky asked on the direct line for the South-West Front's evaluation of the documents, Timoshenko replied that he had no reason to doubt their authenticity. Stalin, however, was not convinced, and in a short telegraphed instruction he told Timoshenko to keep the incident secret, for he himself believed that the captured order covered only part of the German plan.[17]

On the morning of 28 June the left wing of von Bock's Army Group South drove a great gap between the Bryansk and the South-West Fronts and moved rapidly towards Voronezh, which von Bock was to take if he should so please, provided that it did not delay the departure of the motorized force south-eastwards to the lower Don bend.[18] Von Bock, however, became nervous about Golikov's tank strength and allowed himself to be drawn into the heavy fighting. Hitler subsequently blamed von Bock's delay at Voronezh for the failure of the whole Stalingrad campaign.

Stalin and the general staff had predicted that the enemy

thrusts would be made on the Orel-Tula and Kursk-Voronezh axes.[19] Von Bock's tank attacks into Voronezh reinforced the Moscow interpretation of the enemy's strategy, and, so that Timoshenko should keep this foremost in his mind, Stalin sent a message at 1605 hours on 2 July, through Vatutin, warning him that the penetration threatened the rear of the Bryansk Front as well as that of the South-West Front.[20] Since Golikov's front reserves had already been committed, Stalin put at his disposal two further armies together with Liziukov's tank army, with orders that it should attack, in conjunction with the tank corps already forming part of the front, on a north-south axis and envelop von Bock's left wing. Although Rotmistrov has said that Liziukov had only 400 tanks, Golikov, according to Vasilevsky, had a further 600, and, of the total, 800 were of modern T34 or KV type; this force was sufficient, Vasilevsky reckoned, 'to change the whole situation'.[21]

Golikov had been sent to Voronezh, probably on 2 July, leaving his deputy Chibisov at the Bryansk Front headquarters at Elets in control of the northern wing; Vasilevsky, appointed Chief of General Staff only a week before, arrived there on 3 July. According to Vasilevsky, 5 Tank Army was still without orders on 4 July. Vasilevsky took command himself and issued verbal instructions to Liziukov, Vasilevsky subsequently justifying his action by quoting Kazakov, the Bryansk Front chief of staff: 'the front commander was in Voronezh, the deputy commander Chibisov had only just arrived; in this situation the general staff representative took over control'.[22] The tank army offensive failed, according to Vasilevsky, 'because of lack of leadership and poor front support'. The tank army commander's account remained unwritten, for Liziukov was said to have died in the battle.

Rotmistrov, the commander of one of Liziukov's tank corps, has a different story. Rotmistrov's 7 Tank Corps had just arrived from Kalinin, and the other two tank corps were still sixty miles to the north. Vasilevsky decided to send 7 Tank Corps forward, presumably to establish contact, and he personally gave Rotmistrov preliminary orders. On 4 July Liziukov, 'after spending two hours with Vasilevsky', issued his own orders, but Rotmistrov had difficulty in understanding them because they had been framed by someone 'accustomed to command infantry and not tanks', that is to say by Vasilevsky, for Liziukov was an armoured leader. The other two tank corps did not go into action until 7 and 10 July. The offensive failed, Rotmistrov said, because the force was committed piecemeal without proper artillery and air support, and his 1963 account held Stalin and Vasilevsky responsible.[23]

Meanwhile, however, there was a further lack of harmony in the Soviet High Command. On 7 July, when Liziukov's tank battle was at its height, Stalin had recalled Vasilevsky to Moscow in order to split the armies of the Bryansk Front by interposing a new head-quarters to the south, Golikov and his staff becoming the nucleus of a new Voronezh Front headquarters. The old Bryansk Front headquarters remained in being, still under Chibisov.[24] Vasilevsky escaped censure for Liziukov's defeat, but Golikov and Chibisov suffered an immediate, if temporary, eclipse. According to Kazakov, Stalin had heard from the NKVD that 40 Army under Popov, who was frequently in Stalin's disfavour, was allowing the two NKVD regiments in Voronezh to bear the brunt of the fighting. Since Golikov was reluctant to give Stalin an assurance that Voronezh would be held, he was replaced on 14 July as the Commander of the Voronezh Front.[25] On the other hand, others, including Vasilev-sky, say that Golikov was directly relieved of his command *of the Bryansk Front* by Rokossovsky.

This point is relevant to Rokossovsky's description of his interview and appointment by Stalin, in the presence of the out-going front commander, whom Rokossovsky does not name. Stalin's views were contrary to those expressed two months before, when he censured Mekhlis for failing to interfere with the actions of the Crimea Front commander. The former Bryansk Front commander complained to Stalin that he thought that he was being removed from his post unjustly, because Vasilevsky had 'got in the way by interfering, holding conferences when it was necessary to act, and in general overriding the front commander'. Stalin retorted that 'the party and the government had entrusted the front to *you*, not to the *Stavka* representative'. Soviet military organization and functions were often what Stalin happened to say they were at the time. Stalin may have been talking to Golikov. Yet the quick-witted Golikov, who had been a military commissar for many years, had not scrupled formerly to complain directly to Stalin; and in any case Golikov had been at Voronezh. On the other hand the slow tempo of command activity, about which Vasilevsky complained, is more suggestive of Chibisov's Olympian calm; for Rokossovsky has described how Chibisov was wont to go his own unhurried way, cheerfully dispensing tea from his *samovar* in the most difficult and threatening situations. The lesson which Rokossovsky learned was to refer all disagreements, difficulties and reverses, however unpalatable, directly to Stalin by telephone.[26]

When the replacements for Golikov and Chibisov were being nominated, Vasilevsky, together with his deputy Vatutin, were attending Stalin in his Kremlin office. The first suggestion, Rokossovsky for the Bryansk Front, was immediately agreed; but Stalin rejected the list of candidates for the Voronezh Front. The long and thoughtful silence was broken by Vatutin who rose to his feet with the words, 'Comrade Stalin, nominate me to command the Voronezh Front'. Vatutin, a friend of Zhukov's, was not highly regarded by the dictator. The interruption surprised both Vasilevsky and Stalin who, in open amazement, said 'What, you!' (*Vas*), and sat frowning, lost in thought. 'What does Vasilevsky think?'. Vasilevsky supported Vatutin. After further reflection Stalin gave a grudging acquiescence. 'If Comrade Vasilevsky is satisfied with you, I will not oppose it'.[27] Vatutin, a lieutenant-general of infantry, who had entered the Red Army as a recruit in 1920, had held no commands other than a temporary group at the time of the Moscow battle; he had been Vasilevsky's immediate senior, both in appointment and rank, in 1940 and 1941.

Timoshenko's South-West and Malinovsky's South Fronts fell back rapidly to escape envelopment. The 1961 account says that the Soviet command, presumably the South-West Front of which Khrushchev formed part, 'skilfully combined the defence of natural features with a timely withdrawal'.[28] This description hardly accords with the panic felt at the time and Stalin's standstill order No. 227 of 28 July.

On 12 July a new Stalingrad Front had been raised from three reserve armies, together with two tank armies in the process of formation, absorbing also the remnants of the South-West Front. Timoshenko was given the new command, but, eleven days later, he was replaced by Gordov, Khrushchev remaining with the front military council. A large part of the Stalingrad Front was deployed on a narrow bridgehead on the right bank of the Don covering the approaches to Stalingrad, the area once defended by Voroshilov against Krasnov's Don Cossacks. On 23 July, the day that Gordov assumed his new post, the enemy began his offensive to destroy the bridgehead, preparatory to an advance to the Volga.

On 23 July Vasilevsky arrived in the bridgehead, having been told by Stalin to take control of operations, and there he ordered two separate counter-attacks, by one tank army on 25 July and by the second, two days afterwards; for this piecemeal employment of armour, though it totalled only 240 tanks, he was, two decades later, criticized in the Soviet military press. Stalin, or so Vasilevsky said in 1965, was reluctant to use tanks in this fashion, but on this occasion he did not interfere.[29] The counter-attacks failed and Gordov was driven over the Don, leaving behind him about 48,000 dead and prisoners, 270 tanks and 600 guns.

Further to the south the approach of Hoth's panzer army along the Kotelnikovo railway, over which Budenny had skirmished in 1918, posed a second threat to Stalingrad, for Hoth was already east of the Don. Gordov's Stalingrad Front stretched from its junction with Vatutin's Voronezh Front down to the Sarpa Lakes, a distance of over 450 miles. Stalin met the problem of the extended front and the exposed southern flank by interposing yet another headquarters there, and conjuring up new forces, in the first instance by cutting the Stalingrad Front in two.

In the early hours of 2 August the wounded and still lame Eremenko was brought from a Moscow hospital to the Kremlin, where a GKO meeting was in session, and Stalin appointed him as the commander of 'a front in the Stalingrad area'. At a second GKO meeting the following night, Eremenko, still decisive and confident in his manner, objected that he did not like the proposed inter-front boundary which was to run from Kalach-on-Don to the Tsaritsyn stream; since enemy attacks were usually directed along Soviet boundaries, the whole of Stalingrad, Eremenko felt, ought to be the responsibility of a single front. Stalin's irritable outburst, unexpected by Eremenko, surprised, so he believed, even the GKO members; the dictator said, with some emphasis, that the boundary would remain exactly as he had laid it down. The formations and resources were then divided between the two fronts, and Eremenko was appointed to the more southerly, the new South-East Front. The necessary directives were drafted in the light of the decisions taken and, said Eremenko, the changes were confirmed there and then by Stalin.[30]

On 4 August Eremenko took off from Moscow without a head-quarters or staff, and the next day the South-East Front came into being, temporarily sharing the Stalingrad Front headquarters in the Tsaritsyn river gorge. Eremenko's account, published at the time of Khrushchev's ascendancy, recounts without inhibition the events which led to his establishing a close relationship with Khrushchev at Gordov's expense. Gordov appears to have been an excitable and difficult character. Konev considered him experienced but wilful and unbalanced; Rokossovsky called him an abusive (*maternyi*) commander. Zhukov was more tolerant of such a failing but told Stalin that Gordov did not get on well with people.[31] He was certainly on unsatisfactory terms with Khrushchev. Vasilevsky was sent to Stalingrad to suggest a solution.

Vasilevsky had come to disagree with Stalin's recent action in splitting the former Stalingrad Front and in siting the inter-front boundary in the city, and he apparently succeeded in passing on his doubts to Stalin; and, because Khrushchev had no confidence in Gordov, a compromise was arrived at whereby the front boundary remained temporarily where it was, but Eremenko was placed in the overall command of the two fronts, with Khrushchev acting as the political member for both military councils.

Eremenko has stressed his closeness to Khrushchev and, like some of his fellows during Khrushchev's ascendancy, was critical of both Stalin and Vasilevsky. Vasilevsky in his turn has recounted *verbatim* the Baudôt teleprint conversation of 9 August, in which Moscow asked Eremenko to comment on Stalin's proposal that Eremenko should command the two fronts, with Gordov and Golikov acting as his deputies. For Eremenko is said to have replied 'my answer is that no one is wiser than Stalin'.[32] The coupling of the two fronts under one commander was not to prove a success, for Eremenko lacked confidence in his subordinates. Instead of directing the battle through Gordov and Golikov he began to act as the field commander for both forces, passing orders direct to armies and holding consultations with the military councils and arms commanders of both fronts.[33]

As in the summer of 1918, the civil population of Stalingrad were digging field works to the west of the city, except that this time it was the proletariat not the *bourgeousie* who had been con-scribed. By 5 August Hoth had reached the outer defence ring, not thirty miles south-west of the city, and ten days later Paulus's 6 Army was preparing to cross the Don and come to Hoth's support. In the Caucasus, List's Army Group A had, on 5 August, taken Voroshilovsk (Stavropol), and Maikop fell immediately after-wards; by mid August German troops were in the old Kuban Cossack capital of Krasnodar (Ekaterinodar) and moving up the foothills of the Caucasus, hardly fifty miles from Novorossisk and the other Black Sea ports.

It was at this time that Churchill and his military staff arrived in Moscow to bring news to the dictator that there would be no second front in Western Europe that year.

# 8
# *Stalingrad and the Caucasus*

On the evening of 12 August Churchill and Harriman, Roosevelt's representative, attended the meeting with Stalin, Molotov and Voroshilov, during which Stalin took issue at every point with a degree of bluntness amounting to insult, telling his allies that they could not win wars if they were afraid of the Germans and were unwilling to take risks. He did, nevertheless, show some interest in the proposed allied landings in French North Africa, and accurately predicted their political and strategic merit in that they would provoke French and Germans to fight each other, put Italy out of action and ensure Spain's neutrality.[1]

At the next meeting, on the night of 13 August, Churchill and Harriman were handed a long *aide-mémoire*, signed by Stalin, accusing his allies of failing to fulfil their undertaking of a second front in Europe in 1942. Stalin wanted an immediate landing of six to eight allied divisions on the Cherbourg peninsula.[2] When Harriman asked about plans for ferrying American aircraft across Siberia, Stalin curtly dismissed the question with 'wars are not won with plans'. Brooke recorded in his diary that night:

Stalin is a realist . . . facts only count . . . plans, hypotheses, future possibilities mean nothing to him, but he is ready to face facts, even when unpleasant.[3]

On the afternoon of 15 August Brooke, Wavell, Tedder and Jacob attended the Spiridinovka Street military conference with Voroshilov and Shaposhnikov, whom the British delegates believed to be the Chief of General Staff. Brooke considered Voroshilov to be 'an attractive personality, a typically political general who owed his life to his wits', and believed that 'in the early days when Voroshilov commanded a battalion, Stalin was attached to his unit as the political commissar'. Voroshilov's military knowledge, thought Brooke, was painfully limited, and only the charming Shaposhnikov had a well-trained military brain. Shaposhnikov said little, most of the talking being left to Voroshilov, who, 'with his squat figure, round head, bluff manner and uncultured speech, seemed the typical Russian peasant'. Behind the friendly, pleasant, rather disarming and mischievous smile there lurked, Birse felt, the ruthless obedient-to-existing authority spirit to be found in the USSR, a view shared by Deane, who has described how the chummy and cherubic Voroshilov could drop the hard *peretsovka* drinking guise of the previous night's bacchanalia and, with the dawn, assume to order the cold or offensive demeanour so common to Soviet officials.[4] Voroshilov could not reveal the Soviet strength in Caucasia without first obtaining Stalin's permission, and the meeting, which Birse considered to be futile, appears to have been a political exercise, for Voroshilov had been instructed merely to press for a second front. Shaposhnikov and the twenty other Soviet generals attending the conference raised no points and answered no questions.

Over the whole visit Jacob had been impressed only with Stalin, with his complete self-possession and detachment and his cold and calculating mastery of the situation.[5]

On the final night, Birse met Stalin for the first time when he accompanied Churchill to the Kremlin. Much of Birse's description confirmed what was already widely known, Stalin's uncomfortable office, the limp handshake, the shifty glance usually directed to the ground, the unfamiliar Georgian accent and the foreign sounding Russian. When the time came to depart, Stalin invited the British Prime Minister to supper at his Kremlin apartment – Birse thought 'on the spur of the moment'; according to Stalin's daughter, however, she had been brought to the capital earlier in the day 'to be shown off to Churchill that night'.[6] Inside Stalin's flat Birse noted the same sparseness of furnishing, described many years before by Bazhanov. Later, Stalin surprised and impressed his visitors by his knowledge of Wellington's campaigns. Stalin

might, as Birse imagined, have made a special study of the Napoleonic Wars; on the other hand, to judge by his daughter's account
of the preparation, with 'the Commissariat for Foreign Affairs
explaining the etiquette for dealing with foreigners', it is possible
that the dictator's knowledge was based more on the reading of
notes hurriedly prepared that day to provide him with table talk.

---

Meanwhile the real Chief of General Staff was on the Don when,
on 23 August, Paulus's panzer troops crossed the river, reaching
the west bank of the Volga by nightfall. On 23 and 24 August
Stalingrad, which had up till then been turning out tanks, guns
and other armament, was heavily bombed from the air and left a
sea of flame. It was not until the night of 24 August, when the *V Ch*
telephonic link had been re-established, that Vasilevsky spoke
again to Stalin, and the unpleasant conversation remained forever
in his memory for he was subjected to a torrent of what he has
called 'painful, insulting and mostly undeserved abuse, directed
not only at the Chief of General Staff but at all Red Army military
commanders'. It was all that Vasilevsky could do, he said, to convince the Supreme Commander that the city was still in Soviet
hands.[7]

At midday on 23 August, Eremenko received a radio message of
exhortation from Stalin, telling him that 'the enemy forces involved
are not large and you have sufficient resources to annihilate them;
concentrate the air forces of both fronts; mobilize the armoured
trains and bring them forward on the city loop line; lay smoke to
confuse the enemy and strike home by night and by day, using
every gun and rocket launcher that you have. Above all do not
give way to panic. Have no fear of this impudent (*nakhal'nogo*) foe
and do not lose faith in victory'. When this message was received,
Stalingrad was alight from end to end, the asphalt roads were
aflame, the telegraph poles were crackling like matchsticks, and
the burning oil and petrol spreading across the surface of the Volga
had set the river craft on fire; from the tractor works, German tanks
could be seen immediately to the north, fighting it out with anti-
aircraft gun detachments.[8]

By 24 August the city itself had already lost its strategic and
economic significance, except that Hitler by degrees became determined to take possession of it. Yet Stalin's instruction that day

forbidding the evacuation or demolition of industrial equipment in Stalingrad, showed that the dictator was sensitive to giving up a locality which bore his name and which had contributed to his fame, and to the effect which he imagined this would have on the morale of the Soviet people.[9] Stalin sent a further directive to Vasilevsky, Eremenko and Malenkov in which he ordered that the German penetration should be destroyed without fail.[10]

Because of the serious situation at Stalingrad Zhukov had been withdrawn from the West Front on 27 August and appointed as Deputy Supreme Commander. From the time of Zhukov's arrival at Kamyshin at midday on 29 August, it would appear, contrary to what Eremenko has said, that Gordov's front was taken out of Eremenko's and Khrushchev's hands, henceforth being controlled directly from Moscow.[11]

Stalin had told Zhukov to begin a Stalingrad Front offensive using Moskalenko's army, with two more reinforcing *Stavka* armies being committed as they arrived; in addition Stalin held out a promise of further formations, although he would not allot 'the newly formed strategic reserves intended for later tasks'. When it became clear that Moskalenko could not be ready by 2 September, Zhukov postponed the attack for twenty-four hours, at the same time reporting the reasons to the Supreme Commander. Yet the attack, when launched, failed for lack of preparation and support. That same day, on 3 September, Zhukov received a teleprint, signed by Stalin, reminiscent of a Lenin missive in the Civil War, saying that Stalingrad might be lost that day or the next, and ordering all commanders 'to attack immediately – no delay permissible – any delay would be criminal'.[12]

When Zhukov telephoned Stalin to say that an offensive could be ordered the following morning, but only if it was to be made without artillery support, Stalin asked whether he (Zhukov) thought that the enemy would wait for the Deputy Supreme Commander to bestir himself. A compromise was eventually arrived at whereby Gordov would put off his attack until 5 September but would come to Eremenko's support earlier if Stalingrad should be directly threatened. The attack on 5 September was a failure, the Red Army men being driven back to their start line by fresh enemy forces being moved up from Gumrak. Stalin, however, was pleased with these meagre results and he told Zhukov 'to keep attacking and so divert the enemy from Stalingrad'. The fighting continued, Zhukov remaining with Gordov while Vasilevsky paid flying visits to Eremenko. 'Only once and with Stalin's permission', said Zhukov, did Eremenko and Khrushchev visit the Stalingrad Front to familiarize themselves, in Zhukov's presence, with the situation there.[13]

In the latter part of August Stalin called Rokossovsky and Vatutin to Moscow to discuss an offensive against Voronezh. Both wanted to play the main role. Stalin listened to their arguments and finally sided with Vatutin. 'But since Rokossovsky was finding life a little dull he had better come to Moscow'. Rokossovsky was named commander-designate of a new front which was to attack the Stalingrad enemy from Serafimovich in the northern Don flank, and the Bryansk Front was given to Reiter, at one time a tsarist regular officer. In the event, this plan came to nothing, because the troops earmarked for the operation were drawn into the Stalingrad fighting.[14] Towards the end of September, Rokossovsky was appointed by Stalin to take over the Stalingrad Front from Gordov. On 28 September, the Stalingrad Front was re-designated as the Don Front while Eremenko's South-East Front became the new Stalingrad Front. Both were directly subordinate to the *Stavka*.

The concept of a massive counter-offensive was born, according to Zhukov, in Stalin's office on 12 September. He and Vasilevsky had given their estimate of the additional formations needed for Stalingrad, and while Stalin began to study what Zhukov called 'his own map showing the detail and location of the *Stavka* reserves', the two generals moved away from his desk and began a whispered discussion saying that they would have to seek 'some other solution'. Zhukov was surprised that Stalin had such a keen ear, for the dictator looked up and asked, 'What other solution?'. He sent both back to the general staff to prepare outline proposals for other forms of a counter-offensive.[15]

Zhukov's and Vasilevsky's preliminary planning on 13 September was influenced by the long exposed Rumanian held flanks to the north and south of the German salient which stretched eastwards to the Volga, and by the absence of German mobile reserves. The decisive blows should be made, they thought, against the Rumanians, but these could not be mounted until Stalin's strategic reserves were ready, and this in its turn depended on the production of the tanks and vehicles needed to equip the reserve formations; November appeared to be the governing date.[16] That same night Vasilevsky and Zhukov explained their ideas to Stalin, who was alone. Stalin wondered whether a deep double envelopment was not too ambitious; would it not be better, he suggested, to keep it on the land-bridge between the Don and Volga. His advisers thought not, since this would be too close to Stalingrad, allowing the German armour to turn about and quickly engage the new Soviet thrusts; the envelopment should be made well inside the Don bend before the river froze over. Stalin ordered the planning to continue, but meanwhile no one else should know what had been discussed.

Neither Zhukov nor Vasilevsky have outlined any proposals they might have made concerning the battle still being fought in the far south by Tiulenev's Transcaucasus Front, which had absorbed both Malinovsky's South Front and Budenny's North Caucasus Front. The key to the Caucasus lay of course in the area between Stalingrad and Rostov. Yet it is doubtful whether such strategic factors received much consideration within the Soviet High Command that September. Zhukov has said that Stalin 'emphasized that the main task was to hold Stalingrad and prevent an enemy advance along the west bank of the Volga to Kamyshin'.[17] But this is only a half truth. In reality Stalin was obsessed by the conviction that Hitler's strategy was based on an advance northwards up the Volga. Five years after the war had ended and before the captured German archives had been investigated, the dictator was still stating that this was so, for the 1950 *Kratkaia Biografiia* contained the following paragraph:

Comrade Stalin promptly divined the plan of the German command. He saw that the idea was to create the impression that the seizure of the oil regions of Grozny and Baku was the major and not the subsidiary objective of the German summer offensive. He pointed out that in reality the main offensive was to envelop Moscow from the east, to cut it off from the areas of the Volga and the Urals, then to strike at Moscow, and in this way end the war in 1942.[18]

This misappreciation is no longer mentioned in Soviet war histories.

In the years immediately following the Second World War, Stalin was credited with personally planning the Stalingrad counter-offensive. In 1963 Rotmistrov rejected this, but dwelt on the part played by Khrushchev and Eremenko.[19] Khrushchev had his own story.[20] Eremenko, writing in the comforting warmth of Khrushchev's patronage, has said repeatedly that it was he who suggested to Stalin a double envelopment, meeting at Kalach-on-Don.[21] Vasilevsky has supported Zhukov.[22] The unravelling of Russian contemporary history is complicated not only by Soviet pretensions of infallibility, by prejudices and politics, but also by writers with revisionist tendencies, some of whom have seen Vatutin as the architect of victory. Zhukov, in denying this, has stressed that a number of fronts were involved together with 'concrete calculations of the availability of *matériel*'. This could be done only by Stalin and the general staff.[23]

On the enemy side, Hitler was not unaware of the course open to the Soviet High Command, for even as early as 16 August he had been concerned in case the Red Army should mount a counter-offensive against Germany's weak allies in the area of Serafimovich. His own bold style of planning and the Civil War map, which was said to have been brought to his notice, led him to believe that Stalin might repeat '*den russischen "Standard-Angriff" von 1920*', with Rostov as its strategic objective.[24] But Hitler had no idea of the strength in which such an offensive could be launched, nor did he take into account an envelopment from the area to the south of Stalingrad.[25]

The main Soviet blow was to be struck from the north by a newly formed South-West Front under Vatutin, interposed between the Don and the Voronezh Fronts, Vatutin handing over his former command of the Voronezh Front to Golikov.[26] Vatutin's force, concentrated in the Serafimovich and Kletskaya bridgeheads, was to begin the offensive against Dumitrescu's Rumanians, while, one day later, the left flank of Eremenko's Stalingrad Front, about thirty miles to the south of the city, was to attack a Rumanian corps holding the Axis southern flank; Eremenko would thrust northwards to meet Vatutin's armour in the area of Kalach-on-Don. A subsidiary offensive was to be made by the flanks of Rokossovsky's Don Front, aimed at pinning Paulus

**17** *Above left.* Vatutin, who had entered the Red Army infantry in 1920, became deputy chief of general staff in 1941. From 1942 he was a front commander (killed 1944).

**18** *Above right.* Golikov, who joined the Red Army in 1918, was for many years a commissar before becoming an infantry commander. In 1941 he headed military intelligence.

**19** *Below left.* Eremenko, a tsarist cavalry NCO and Red Army cavalry corps commander, was an army and front commander from 1941–45.

**20** *Below right.* Popov entered the Red Army infantry in 1920, eventually to become a mechanized corps leader. From 1941 he commanded successively fronts and armies.

**21** The military council of the South-West Front, destroyed at Kiev in September 1941; from the left, the commander Kirponos, the commissar Burmistenko and the chief of staff Tupikov.

**22** Stalin's aircraft designers *(from the left)*, Lavochkin, Tupolev, A. S. Iakovlev and A. I. Mikoian.

and putting a barrier between him and Dumitrescu. The operation was to be named *Uranus*.

During the second week in October the front military councils began work on their own plans, these being co-ordinated by Zhukov at the South-West Front and by Vasilevsky with the Stalingrad Front. On 7 November Zhukov gave a presentation to the GKO.[27] Four days later he was back at Serafimovich, where he came to the conclusion that the offensive would have to be delayed because of logistic problems and he signalled to Stalin the reasons. Stalin agreed, but raised a new factor in reminding Zhukov that the outcome of the battle must depend on a favourable air situation; if Novikov had any doubts then the offensive should be further postponed.[28]

Stalin apparently took a close and controlling interest in air force organization and reserves. In the early summer of 1942 all tactical air forces had been removed from the command of ground armies and had been concentrated under the fronts.[29] During that year the air forces of several fronts began to be used, together with the long range air force (ADD), in single co-ordinated blows, the commander of the VVS often being on the spot as the air representative of the *Stavka*; his duties were never defined in writing but were given to him on each occasion by Stalin. At the end of each day the *Stavka* air representative sent a personal report to Stalin outlining the results of the air operations, with a copy to the chief of staff of the VVS.[30]

Nikitin, a deputy commander of the VVS, has said that Stalin's air reserves were at first quite meagre. By June 1942, however, two fighter and one bomber air armies were in existence, each having from three to five air divisions and numbering from 200 to 300 aircraft. According to Nikitin, Stalin was carefully accumulating and equipping air corps of the *Stavka* reserve during 1942, 'daily noting in his own notebook' the deliveries from aircraft production; Stalin personally made the allocation of equipment to the air forces in the field and to those in reserve, and even during the difficult Stalingrad days the process of building up the air reserve continued. On 1 October 1942 Stalin was interesting himself in 'live-firing two-sided tactical air exercises' for the reserve air corps, prior to committing them to battle, requiring that Nikitin should personally brief him on the results.[31]

On the morning of 14 November Zhukov and Vasilevsky saw
Stalin again and made their reports; the dictator was satisfied, 'for
he listened attentively and did not interrupt even once'. They
then suggested to Stalin, so Zhukov has said, that a new offensive
should be mounted by Konev's West and Purkaev's Kalinin
Fronts in the area of the Rzhev salient, in order to prevent the
movement of enemy troops to the south, it being proposed that
Zhukov should prepare the offensive to the west of Moscow while
Vasilevsky should co-ordinate the Stalingrad operation.[32]

Zhukov's account of the events which led to the successful
counter-offensive conveys an impression of mutual respect between
superior and subordinate, and of close co-operation and goodwill
between the civil, military and political organizations. Yet it is
questionable whether this description corresponded with reality.

Lugansky has told how, in September 1942, Khriukin, the
Commander of 8 Air Army, was hurriedly summoned, together
with a number of his officers, to the South-East Front headquarters
at Stalingrad; they imagined that they were about to receive
decorations. Malenkov, Zhukov, Vasilevsky and Eremenko were
there, but the talking was done by Malenkov and not by the
generals. Malenkov wanted to know the names of the commanders
of air regiments or units which, 'according to the notes which he
held in his hand', had been insufficiently effective in the air fighting
over Stalingrad. The majority of those named were present.
Malenkov, the Politburo member, according to Lugansky, 'without raising his voice gave brief orders for their court-martial or
reduction in rank'; he abused and insulted Khriukin in front of his
junior officers.[33]

Nor did the Red Army in the Caucasus fare better at the hands
of Beria, the GKO representative. He told Tiulenev that 'he would
break his back' and he threatened Malinovsky with arrest. According to Tiulenev, Beria deliberately discredited the generals of the
Red Army.[34]

---

On 17 November, hardly more than twenty-four hours before the
counter-offensive was due to begin, Vasilevsky was recalled to a
GKO meeting in Moscow to discuss a private letter sent to Stalin
by Vol'sky, the commander of a mechanized corps of the Stalingrad Front, stating 'that the plan was unreal and doomed to failure'.

Vasilevsky re-affirmed that the counter-offensive should not be delayed or altered. Stalin instructed Vasilevsky to get Vol'sky on the telephone and, said Vasilevsky, 'to the amazement of everybody present' Stalin had a short comradely and 'not at all brusque' conversation with him. Stalin then told Vasilevsky to take no further notice of the incident, for 'the final decision regarding Vol'sky would be made in accordance with his performance during the next few days'.[35]

The Stalingrad Front offensive on 20 November was delayed by a few hours because of heavy fog, and the general staff in Moscow plagued Eremenko with messages demanding an immediate start. Stalin himself does not appear to have intervened. Later Eremenko reported the course of the battle direct to the Supreme Commander three times during that day, for, like other Soviet generals, he was quick to notify success.[36] On 23 November, Eremenko joined with Vatutin near Kalach-on-Don, so encircling 6 Army and part of 4 Panzer Army. Twenty German and two Rumanian divisions had been enveloped in an operation which had lasted only four days.

Vasilevsky proceeded with method and circumspection. On the evening of 23 November he telephoned Stalin from the South-West Front to suggest that a westward looking cordon, strong in mobile troops, should be established to prevent the enemy forcing a new corridor into Stalingrad. This was agreed by Stalin.[37] But since some of the intelligence communicated by Vasilevsky was not to the dictator's liking, Stalin sent a signal to Rokossovsky, saying that Galanin was slack, that Zhadov should attack and pin the enemy, and that Rokossovsky should give Batov 'a bit of a push' (*podtolknite*), since he could have re-acted more energetically. This was, presumably, an arbitrary exerting of pressure on the army commanders.

Stalin had instructed Vasilevsky that same evening to explore the possibility of launching *Saturn,* a second strategic blow which had already been discussed in Moscow, this being close to what Hitler had earlier termed the 'standard Stalin offensive of 1920'. *Saturn* was to take the form of a thrust by the left flank of Golikov's Voronezh Front, and the right wing of Vatutin's South-West Front, from the area of Pavlovsk and Kalach-in-Voronezh southwards to Rostov, along much of the same route travelled by Budenny's 1 Cavalry Army a quarter of a century before.

On 25 November Vasilevsky was at the Voronezh Front with Golikov, Voronov and Novikov, and the next day he was in the forward area with Vatutin on the right flank of the South-West Front. From there Vasilevsky had a direct line conversation with the Supreme Commander, telling him that both the Voronezh and South-West Fronts would need to be heavily reinforced before they could carry out *Saturn*. Vasilevsky's estimates were, however, acceptable to Stalin. The dictator directed that Vasilevsky should henceforth apply himself 'only to the business in hand', that is to say the liquidation of the Stalingrad pocket, leaving the co-ordination of *Saturn* to Voronov. Stalin intended, he said, to transfer the left-flanking formations of the South-West to the Don Front, so that Vatutin could concentrate on *Saturn*. Vatutin would remain responsible for the defence of the outer perimeter as far south as the Chir. The area beyond that would be covered by Eremenko.[38]

Vasilevsky, who had meanwhile based himself on the Don Front, asked for his orders in writing, and these were teleprinted to him by Stalin in five short paragraphs. Vasilevsky was to control the Don and Stalingrad Fronts, his mission being to destroy the encircled enemy, to the exclusion of any other activity; he was to receive a further tank corps which he could use at his discretion, and an air corps of Pe2 bombers. Stalin followed up this conversation by dictating new orders to Vatutin, and Rokossovsky and Eremenko were informed of the change of plan.[39]

The earlier attempts to destroy Paulus's 6 Army had been unsuccessful, so Vasilevsky believed, because both he and the Soviet High Command had estimated that there were only 90,000 troops in the pocket, whereas in fact the strength stood at a quarter of a million. The first hastily mounted offensive on the shrinking pocket had been undertaken by three fronts. Rokossovsky has said that he telephoned Stalin urging that all the besieging troops be put under a single command, and it is in fact possible that this conversation prompted Stalin to order Vasilevsky's return to the Volga. But when Vasilevsky did arrive from the South-West Front on 29 November, he brought with him what Rokossovsky called 'Stalin's insistent order' that the Don Front renew the offensive at the beginning of December. Thereupon Rokossovsky drove the enemy back another twenty miles, where, in the Rossoshka valley, in a temperature of minus 32 degrees centigrade, the offensive came once more to a standstill.[40] On 4 December Vasilevsky reported this check to Stalin, who agreed, with reluctance, to divert Malinovsky's 2 Guards Army from Vatutin to Rokossovsky, 'for Stalin had set great store on the use of that newly formed and well equipped formation for *Saturn*'. Stalin demanded that the Stalingrad offensive be resumed by 18 December. On 9 December Vasilevsky signalled to Moscow his new plan known as *Kol'tso*, to destroy 6 German Army, but in the event it came to nothing due to the intervention of von Manstein's relief thrust from the south-west.[41]

Meanwhile, Zhukov, who was still with the West and Kalinin Fronts, told Stalin on 29 November, in response to a request for his views, that he considered that the enemy relief attempt would be made either from the south-west along the Kotelnikovo railway, or by the more direct approach from the west from the enemy bridgehead near the junction of the Don and the Chir. Zhukov suggested that 'a reserve of about 100 tanks' should be concentrated in each of these areas.[42] In consequence, that same day, Rotmistrov, still commanding 7 Tank Corps, was ordered to the Stalingrad area, arriving at the Nizhne-Chirskaya *stanitsa* on 7 December. According to Rotmistrov, Vasilevsky told him, 'with a look at the telephone', that the Supreme Commander 'demanded the immediate destruction of the enemy strong point', that is to say the Chir bridgehead and the Rychkovsky *khutor*, preparatory to an offensive beyond the Chir against what was believed to be an enemy relief force near Tormosin. When Rotmistrov asked for two days in which to prepare his attack, Vasilevsky, so said Rotmistrov, 'still very much under the influence of his recent conversation with Stalin', declined to agree without first telephoning Moscow. When Rotmistrov presented his final plan on 11 December, his intention to make a surprise attack without artillery preparation was greeted by Vasilevsky with amazement; the Chief of General Staff insisted on quizzing Rotmistrov's tank brigade commanders to confirm that they were in agreement with their chief, and even then, said Rotmistrov, reported the details back to Stalin.[43] Rotmistrov, however, tends to overelaborate his criticism, for this degree of centralization was common everywhere. On the other flank of the South-West Front, Krasovsky had no fighter formations to cover the concentration of ground troops for *Saturn*, so he suggested using a division of *Shturmoviki* II-2 single-engined ground attack aircraft for that purpose. He put the proposal to Voronov, and did not consider it unusual that Voronov, in his turn, should obtain the necessary permission from Stalin.[44]

Eremenko's Stalingrad Front covered both of the likely approaches to Stalingrad. Eremenko was convinced, or so he has subsequently said, that the main German offensive would come from Kotelnikovo on his left flank; Stalin and Vasilevsky believed that the main danger lay on his right flank at Tormosin.[45] When the Stalingrad Front military council pleaded with Stalin for more armour for the Kotelnikovo sector, he promised them only 'an insignificant reinforcement of sixty tanks'. For Eremenko had no power to use his front resources as he thought fit.

Between 28 November and 3 December cavalry probes into Kotelnikovo revealed the presence there of a strong panzer division, off-loading from the rail flats. Eremenko, believing that the arrival of these enemy troops presaged von Manstein's main offensive, reported this intelligence to Stalin. The Supreme Commander, however, was not convinced by Eremenko's deductions and replied that he would reinforce Kotelnikovo 'as far as the situation would allow'. Nine days later, at dawn on 12 December, von Manstein's main offensive in the area of Kotelnikovo began in earnest; when the news was reported to Stalin, the dictator became agitated, telling Eremenko that the Stalingrad Front should not give ground for it would be sent reserves immediately.[46]

On the evening of 12 December Vasilevsky was unable for many hours to get a signal connection to Moscow; while waiting he spoke, presumably by telephone, to both Rokossovsky and Malinovsky warning them that he intended to ask the *Stavka* for permission to transfer 2 Guards Army from the Don to the Stalingrad Front.[47]

Later that night Vasilevsky explained the situation to Stalin. The suggestion, that 2 Guards Army should be moved south and that the destruction of the encircled 6 German Army should be delayed, met with an angry refusal from the dictator, 'coupled with some plain and unpleasant speaking'. He who had so often presented crude ultimata to Lenin accused Vasilevsky of trying to blackmail the *Stavka* into handing over reserves to the sectors for which he was responsible.[48] Vasilevsky was indeed unfortunate in that 2 Guards Army had already been re-routed twice, following in the wake of the Chief of General Staff, but he said that he felt Stalin's anger to be unjustified since he, Vasilevsky, had been charged with the destruction of the encircled pocket, and the removal of Malinovsky from the Don Front was against his (Vasilevsky's) interests since he had 'no responsibility for the outward defence against a relieving enemy force'. Stalin's directive of 27 November certainly said so; yet if Vasilevsky was not responsible for the outer perimeter, it is not clear why he had, only the day previously, presided over Rotmistrov's preparations for the westward attack towards Tormosin.[49]

Stalin declined to give Vasilevsky a decision, saying that he would first discuss the matter with the GKO. Vasilevsky waited the whole of that night in a state of anxiety and tension, and not until 0500 hours did he hear that Malinovsky would be released to the Stalingrad Front, 'the sole responsibility for the defeat of von Manstein being placed on the shoulders of the Chief of General Staff'. Voronov was to be responsible for Stalingrad.

Rokossovsky, in an account which is probably based on recollection, has said that a *V Ch* telephone conversation took place at this time between Stalin and Vasilevsky. Vasilevsky handed him the instrument, saying that Stalin wanted to hear what Rokossovsky thought about the transfer of 2 Guards Army. The Commander of the Don Front was emphatically against it, preferring, he said, to finish off Paulus quickly and then turn on von Manstein. Stalin then took up his conversation again with Vasilevsky, at the end of which Stalin told Rokossovsky that 'his plan was a bold one and certainly merited attention, but in the circumstances was too risky'. Stalin agreed that the Stalingrad operation should be postponed.[50] But the *Stavka* directive, issued at 2230 hours on the night of 14 December, ordered Eremenko and Rokossovsky 'to continue the systematic destruction of the encircled enemy, allowing him no respite, by night or by day'.

On the night of 13 December the *Stavka* took the decision to alter Vatutin's axis from due south to Rostov, to another running south-eastwards on Tatsinskaya and Morozovsk, in the immediate rear of von Manstein's Army Group Don. The altered plan was known as *Malyi Saturn*. The reasons for the change were set out in a clear and concise five paragraph directive sent to Voronov, Vatutin and Golikov over Stalin's 'Vasil'ev' signature. Von

Manstein, Stalin said, posed a serious threat, and Tatsinskaya and Morozovsk were *Luftwaffe* air supply bases; secondly, the removal of 2 Guards Army from the South-West Front had weakened Vatutin's striking power; and, finally, Vatutin's outer cordon armies could not be counted on to assist the main thrust.[51]

On 18 December Vasilevsky sent to the *Stavka* a draft proposal for the counter-attack to be made on 22 December against von Manstein's relief thrust, Vasilevsky subsequently publishing his draft in full, in order to disprove Eremenko's claim that the plan was his own.[52] The draft proposal timed at 1520 hours on 18 December was approved by Stalin in a signal timed at 0050 hours on 19 December.

Von Manstein reached a point about twenty-five miles from Paulus's perimeter where he was brought to a halt by that part of Malinovsky's 2 Guards Army which had arrived in the forward area. Paulus, contrary to the Soviet expectation, made no attempt to break out to the south-west. The Stalingrad Front counter-offensive towards the south, beginning on 24 December, was immediately successful, but in any case the outcome of the Stalingrad Front's battle had already been decided by the success of *Malyi Saturn* being fought nearly 200 miles away to the north-west.[53]

The military and geographical conditions which made *Malyi Saturn* possible were the same as those which contributed to the success of *Uranus* – a long over-extended enemy salient, with the exposed northern flank held by German allies inferior in fighting quality to the Red Army. Vatutin repeated his south-eastward thrust deep in the Axis rear, and in five days his armour had advanced nearly 150 miles, scattering and largely destroying 8 Italian Army. Von Manstein was forced firstly to move his armour westwards, to meet the new threat, and then finally to give up the Stalingrad relief attempt. This led to the loss both of the encircled 6 German Army and of Caucasia.

Since Voronov had departed for the Stalingrad area on 20 December, the control of Vatutin's South-West Front was undertaken directly by Stalin and Zhukov.[54] Meanwhile, on 1 January, Vasilevsky had been instructed to quit the Stalingrad Front and join the Voronezh Front to organize and co-ordinate the last of the succession of offensives, this to be made by Golikov and Reiter against 2 Hungarian Army to the west of the defeated 8 Italian Army. The Hungarian force was speedily destroyed and 2 German Army, north-west of Voronezh, had to withdraw rapidly westwards to escape encirclement. Much of its heavier equipment was abandoned. Von Weichs's Army Group B had ceased to exist as a fighting force and Army Groups A and Don were already with-drawing rapidly westwards so that they should not be pinned against the Sea of Azov. The German Army in Russia had lost the strategic initiative.

———

Towards the end of December 1942, during a GKO meeting, Stalin proposed, probably at Voronov's or Rokossovsky's prompt-ing, to make the Don Front alone responsible for the destruction of 6 German Army. The committee agreed. Zhukov, when asked for his opinion, said that Eremenko would be offended; Stalin im-mediately silenced him. That night, when Zhukov informed Eremenko of the GKO decision, Eremenko 'gave way to his emotions'. Zhukov was sufficiently hardy to raise the matter once more with Stalin, and for this the dictator abused (*vyrugal*) him. Only the susceptibilities of the two generals might occasion some surprise.[55]

The *Stavka* directive was issued on 30 December, and, on 1 January 1943, Eremenko's Stalingrad Front became the new South Front responsible only for operations against von Manstein's withdrawing troops. Eremenko's three armies on the southern perimeter of Stalingrad were transferred to Rokossovsky's command.

At the beginning of January Zhukov was sent to Leningrad with Voroshilov as the *Stavka* representatives responsible for co-ordinating the offensive of Govorov's and Meretskov's fronts. Meretskov described an incident when Mekhlis, the political member of the Volkhov Front, addressed 'some curt and insulting remarks to Voroshilov'. Normally, if Mekhlis and Meretskov only had been present, Voroshilov would, thought Meretskov, have put Mekhlis in his place and no more would have been heard of the matter. 'But we were not alone', said Meretskov, 'and that meant that Stalin would hear of this unpleasant incident'. From whom, Meretskov does not say, but Zhukov was undoubtedly there. On Meretskov's advice Mekhlis sent an immediate written report to

Stalin before the dictator should hear of the incident from other sources.[56] Meretskov, like Rokossovsky and Kuznetsov, preferred to deal directly with Stalin.[57]

The *Stavka* directive of 30 December instructed that the offensive against Paulus should be mounted by 6 January and be completed in the course of five or six days. The chief of the front intelligence department still put the encircled enemy at 86,000 men, and it was only when a German transport plane was brought down carrying soldiers' mail destined for the Reich that it became apparent that he had much underestimated the German strength. On 3 January Rokossovsky called on Voronov to tell him that he must have a further six or seven days to prepare for the offensive. Voronov, who was certain that the *Stavka* would not allow so long a delay, sent an immediate report to Moscow, using the same tactic he later criticized in Eremenko, in that he compromised by making an arbitrary cut in the postponement suggested by Rokossovsky. Stalin telephoned 'some harsh reproaches' about both Voronov and Rokossovsky, but finally agreed the new date of 10 January.[58]

The first phase of the Don Front offensive began on 10 January, followed by the second twelve days later. All enemy resistance ceased by 2 February. With the surrender of Paulus the Red Army claimed to have counted 147,000 enemy dead and 94,000 prisoners. According to German documentary sources the loss at Stalingrad, not including the two Rumanian divisions, was 209,000 men. German losses outside the encirclement probably amounted to a further 100,000 men and two Rumanian armies, an Italian and a Hungarian army had been virtually destroyed.

Voronov and Rokossovsky were brought to Moscow on 4 February. At the Kremlin Stalin was 'obviously very pleased', coming forward to meet them, shaking them warmly by the hand and congratulating them. 'For', said Rokossovsky, 'when he felt it to be necessary, Stalin could literally charm a person by his warmth and attention'.[59]

---

On 28 July 1942 Budenny's North Caucasus Front had absorbed the remnants of Malinovsky's South Front after its retreat from the Ukraine. Malinovsky lost his command. Tiulenev, whose Transcaucasus Front had hitherto been responsible for the defence of the Turkish-Iran frontier, then assumed the overall command of the theatre and Budenny returned to Moscow. From September onwards the Transcaucasus Front was reinforced by levies from the local peoples, and by formations sent from the Russian interior over the railway track hastily constructed along the west shore of the Caspian. Once more a proliferation of GKO commissions and representatives of the GKO and *Stavka* appeared in the area, some coming from the Politburo or NKVD and others from the general staff, their activities and rivalries, according to Shtemenko, causing duplication and confusion.[60]

Officers of the general staff sent back their findings to Moscow, and Tiulenev began to receive a volume of directives and critical reports, issued over Stalin's signature or in his name, with the shortcomings set out in detail, illustrating the lack of supervision by front and army commanders.[61] Control, including close tactical control, was not lacking from Moscow, however. A *Stavka* directive of 2 October 1942 outlined the general mission of the Black Sea Group as 'the defence of Tuapse and the Black Sea ports', and then detailed the tasks of each of its formations.[62] Yet this tight control from the centre did not appear to have lessened Tiulenev's responsibility in the event of failure.[63]

At the end of that month Stalin became interested in a proposal originating from Tiulenev, at one time a cavalry brigade commander under Budenny, that a new cavalry army should be formed in the North Caucasus, where horsemen were particularly plentiful. Stalin had asked the opinion of Kirichenko, a cavalry corps commander, but, in the end, he agreed with the general staff that cavalry was too vulnerable for modern war except in support of other mobile troops.[64]

On 29 December Zhukov, speaking on behalf of the Supreme Commander, instructed Tiulenev that Petrov's Black Sea Group should strike north to Rostov and the rail junction of Tikhoryetsk, joining up with Eremenko's Stalingrad Front. A successful double envelopment of this kind would have closed the two exits from Caucasia and trapped von Kleist's Army Group A. Tiulenev could see no means by which he could carry out his orders, for the lowlands were flooded and deep snow lay on the mountains, the few roads and tracks were unusable and he lacked engineer resources. On the other hand some road and track preparation had already been carried out in the Maikop direction. But when

Tiulenev spoke to Stalin on the telephone urging that a thrust on Maikop further to the east would be more practical than the Krasnodar axis, Stalin would hear none of it.[65] Tiulenev's and Petrov's plans, sent to Moscow on 31 December, were rejected that same day since the forces were, in the opinion of the *Stavka*, too widely dispersed. With the rejection Moscow sent back its own proposals for the offensive which was to start not later than 12 January.[66]

On the afternoon of 4 January Stalin telephoned the general staff and dictated to Shtemenko the outline of a directive formulating his strategy. The centre of gravity of the whole of the Transcaucasus Front rested with the Black Sea Group 'and neither Maslennikov nor Petrov as yet understood that fact'. It was not to the Soviet advantage to push the enemy out of the Caucasus and for this reason Maslennikov would henceforth have only a secondary role; so he could give up a rifle corps to Petrov immediately. Petrov was to start his offensive on time without awaiting the arrival of his reserves, and 'because he has had little experience of offensive action he must get himself into an offensive frame of mind'. In conclusion, said Stalin, Tiulenev should be in attendance all the time with the Black Sea Group.[67] On 7 January the general staff prepared a memorandum for the Supreme Commander complaining about Maslennikov and this resulted in an angry signal being sent by Stalin to Maslennikov and Tiulenev on 8 January, reminding them that he held them both personally responsible; henceforth he wanted, he said, reports twice a day.[68]

Stalin had told Petrov to submit two separate plans, one for the Novorossisk area which the dictator called *More* and another, *Gory*, covering the thrust over the Caucasus range. For Stalin alone selected nicknames and code names.[69] On 8 January these plans were received by the general staff; no exception was taken to *More*, but it was noted that the *Gory* plan took the Black Sea Group only as far as Tikhoryetsk, no provision being made for exploitation northwards to Bataisk-Rostov. Although Shtemenko considered that Petrov would indeed be fortunate to get as far as Tikhoryetsk, he could, he said, foresee trouble with Stalin, for 'the Supreme Commander never forgot what he had ordered or suffered others to do so'. So it transpired, for, on 8 January, Stalin dictated another signal requiring the Transcaucasus Front to repair this omission.[70]

Stalin had hoped to entrap another 20 divisions, but Army Group A had already begun to withdraw and Eremenko and Petrov could make little headway. On 24 January Maslennikov's North Group became the new North Caucasus Front, independent of Tiulenev, and on 16 March Petrov's Black Sea Group was amalgamated with Maslennikov's command. Tiulenev's Transcaucasus Front then returned to its earlier responsibilities of guarding the southern frontiers.

The German 17 Army continued to hold a bridgehead in the Taman peninsula, covering the Crimea and the Sea of Azov and forming, as Hitler intended that it should, a springboard for a renewed campaign into the Caucasus in the following summer. Stalin wanted the bridgehead eliminated and in March Beria was sent to the area once more. Zhukov followed on 17 April, taking Novikov, N. G. Kuznetsov and Shtemenko with him. Zhukov's activity took its usual whirlwind pattern.[71] But throughout the next three weeks fighting he was unable to drive in the bridgehead and the party were obliged to return to Moscow on 13 May, Shtemenko says 'in low spirits for they knew Stalin would be displeased and they prepared themselves for his rebukes'.[72] Maslennikov, however, was the only casualty, for he was replaced as front commander by Petrov.

---

Kuznetsov's descriptions, published in 1966 and 1968, have said that Stalin was completely immersed in the affairs of the fronts, that he knew their needs and talked regularly to the military leaders, with whom he had developed close ties. Several times Kuznetsov observed how front commanders were unable to agree with Stalin's opinion, 'and Stalin would then re-examine the question', Kuznetsov believing that the dictator even admired people who were not afraid to stand up for their own point of view.[73] Kuznetsov confirmed that the dictator's immediate reaction to failure was to remove or punish the commander.[74]

Samsonov, describing in 1968 Stalin's role during the Stalingrad battle, has said that Stalin had the particular ability to evaluate the recommendations of the military men about him, since his great experience of state and political matters enabled him quickly to master the specialist knowledge necessary for the day to day conduct of operations. Stalin 'had other competent advisers [*sic*] in addition to Vasilevsky and Zhukov' and during the course of the Stalingrad battle the level of generalship within the *Stavka* continued to improve. The concentration of power in Stalin's hands and 'his undisputed authority' endowed all his orders and demands with a special arbitrariness (*kategorichnost'*), which, on the whole, thought Samsonov, played a decisive role. However, the dictator's confidence in the infallibility of his own judgements and opinions and his intolerance of any objections, gave rise to occasions when his interpretation of the situation was incorrect. 'While punishing severely [this could mean shooting] those who were answerable for failure at the front, Stalin did not always judge the causes of lack of success with objectivity'. These facts, said Samsonov, 'are known, but one should not evaluate the *Stavka* on the basis of the characteristics of one personality or underestimate the contribution of the military figures forming the *Stavka* or its executive'. Although Stalin and the *Stavka* were far from the theatre of operations, continued Samsonov, they directed the day by day struggle in the greatest of detail, and this applied to the direction of the political and government bodies remaining in Stalingrad. Admittedly, the *Stavka* decisions of an operative-tactical nature were, in some cases, a hindrance, restricting or stultifying initiative and action on the spot. 'However, in analysing the events of the battle, if one examines not any one part in isolation but the whole, then the firm and positive aspect of the function of the High Command during the Stalingrad battle is apparent for all to see.'[75]

Vasilevsky considered that political acumen and political strategy endowed Stalin with a fine sense of military strategy; moreover, Stalin soon became expert in the operative field, especially after Kursk in 1943. Stalin's strategic and operative ability was far superior to his knowledge of tactics, but, concluded Vasilevsky, a detailed understanding of tactics was not necessary anyway.[76] The dictator's attitude to the general staff gradually changed during 1942, particularly after September when it showed its worth in the planning of the Stalingrad counter-offensive, and he began to take into account views, recommendations and plans, not only of the general staff, but also of the commanders of fronts and the deputy heads of the NKO. From this period onwards the general staff was sufficiently hardy to present its prognoses of future war developments, and Stalin was content at least to read them, although, as Shtemenko said, mindful of his own November 1941 forecasts when the dictator had declared that Germany was already worn out by its endeavours – he had given the Reich six months or 'a little year' (*godik*) at the most – the dictator now regarded any forecasts with some scepticism.[77] Stalin the bureaucrat, with his love of order and method, began to insist that responsible or interested commanders or staffs be consulted before he would commit himself to a new proposal, and he would ask, 'What is the view of the general staff?' or, 'Has this matter been cleared with Voronov?'. Shtemenko linked this new trend with Stalin's wish to uphold the authority and prestige of his immediate subordinates, for he was very conscious of the dignity of office. Voronov, on the other hand, stressed Stalin's demand for the highest degree of centralization; for not only did he require that he himself should know everything, but he expected his subordinates to be fully informed of what went on in their commands or departments. Yet there were many occasions, described by Shtemenko, when Stalin the autocrat asked the general staff if it had any comment, but it did not reply because it knew that he had decided the question 'and was only asking us for form's sake'.

Politburo, GKO or *Stavka* meetings, which were never held in Stalin's absence, usually took place either in the Kremlin office or at Kuntsevo. It was sometimes not clear whether a Politburo or GKO meeting was in session except in the recording of the protocol or issue of decrees, and the *Stavka* was frequently attended by Politburo and GKO members. Vasilevsky has related, with amusement, how some of his colleagues have since asked him for a photograph of the *Stavka* in session. Stalin was the *Stavka* and he frequently gave orders, personally or by signal, no other members of the Politburo, GKO or High Command being present, usually as a result of telephone consultations with the fronts or the general staff.

Stalin's confidence in the military had been partially restored and, on 9 October 1942, one man command was revived, the military commissars losing their right of veto and reverting to the status of deputies for political matters (*zampolit*). In December 1942, 140 political workers, mainly political members of front and army military councils and senior commissars, for the first time in the history of the Red Army, received general rank. At Stalin's order, Khrulev produced for his inspection tsarist officer shoulder boards (*pogony*), and the tsarist patterns were introduced, with only minor variations, into the Red Army.[78] So it came about that, according to the painting reproduced in the *Ukrains'ka Radians'ka Entsiklopediia*, Khrushchev was pleased to wear the uniform of a lieutenant-general, with the gold braided *pogony* and the traditional grey tsarist greatcoat edged with crimson.

Stalin expected Vasilevsky, Zhukov and his other *Stavka* representatives to make routine reports to him by *V Ch* telephone or Baudôt twice a day, at noon and again at 2200 hours; unusual or important events had to be notified straightaway. The routine reports were given in the form of a diary time-table showing how they had filled in their day and what they had seen or heard. The dictator had to be kept informed of their whereabouts and they were not allowed, without Stalin's prior permission, to leave the fronts to which they had been allocated.[79]

Vasilevsky's burden was particularly onerous since, at Stalin's order, he was constantly at the fronts; yet he was still responsible for the general staff in Moscow. Vasilevsky tried to overcome the problem by selecting an officer of experience and outstanding ability to remain in the capital as his deputy. In May 1942 when he had asked Stalin that Vatutin, then chief of staff of the North-West Front, be transferred back to the general staff, Stalin, 'in all seriousness', said Vasilevsky, had asked, 'Why? Isn't he any good at the front?'. A few months later, after Vatutin had succeeded in having himself posted away from the general staff to command the Voronezh Front, Vasilevsky had to find a replacement to be his first deputy, and his choice fell on Antonov, the chief of staff of the North Caucasus Front. Stalin agreed, but apparently without enthusiasm. Antonov, the son of a tsarist artillery officer, had started his military service as a *praporshchik* and junior officer in a tsarist *eger* regiment of chasseurs, which regiment is not clear, for the only *eger* unit remaining in the 1914 Army List was the Egersky Regiment of Foot Guards. Stalin, however, did not want Antonov, and he ordered that Bokov, the political deputy to the general staff, should continue to make the daily reports to him when Vasilevsky was away. Antonov notified Vasilevsky of this arrangement and asked to be relieved of the post, whereupon Vasilevsky telephoned Stalin from the Voronezh Front and again warmly recommended Antonov. Stalin listened without comment and then told the Chief of General Staff that he, Vasilevsky, could have Antonov as the deputy *Stavka* representative with the Voronezh Front. For, said Vasilevsky, 'Stalin was a careful and mistrustful person, particularly of new faces'. Antonov stayed with the Voronezh Front for three months, where he was to earn much distinction, before resuming his duties as deputy chief of general staff and chief of the operations department.[80]

# 9
## *From Kursk to Kiev*

The Voronezh Front offensive had caused the precipitate withdrawal of 2 German Army, so encouraging the *Stavka* to instruct Golikov to draw up hurried proposals for the occupation of Kharkov, nearly 200 miles away. Golikov's plan was confirmed by Stalin on the night of 23 January when he dictated to Bokov a directive for the new operation to be known as *Zvezda*.[1] Zhukov had been with the Voronezh Front, and when he returned to Moscow he was, according to Shtemenko, so optimistic that the general staff took the view that the Voronezh Front was strong enough to move west and south-west on divergent axes, taking Kursk as well as Kharkov. This variation to the original *Zvezda* directive was issued on 26 January. Contrary to established practice the offensive was not to be made in operative depth, that is to say with armies in echelon, but in line.

Meanwhile Vatutin had submitted to Moscow a plan, known as *Skachok,* for a southerly thrust aimed at cutting von Manstein's communications in the Ukraine. On 19 January Stalin agreed Vatutin's proposal in principle and ordered him to reach the Sea of Azov within seven days of starting the offensive; the launching was to be delayed, however, until after the taking of Kharkov. Meanwhile Stalin began to extend the scope of *Skachok* to include the cutting of the Crimean escape route from the Caucasus, and, on 8 February, he ordered Vatutin to widen his assault frontage to take in Dnepropetrovsk and Zaporozhe.[2] Golikov and Vatutin were sure that the enemy was in full retreat, and this confidence spread to the general staff.[3]

Stalin had formulated even more ambitious plans, for he had come to believe that, by turning Golikov's troops south-westwards towards Poltava, he could encompass a secondary envelopment of von Manstein, to the west of that to be mounted by Vatutin. In addition he intended to interpose another front between the Bryansk and the Voronezh Fronts, which, striking north-westwards, would outflank von Kluge's Army Group Centre from the south. Rokossovsky was given this assignment on 4 February, Stalin telling him that part of his front was to move from Stalingrad to Elets, there to be joined by two more armies from the *Stavka* reserve; then, as the newly designated Central Front, it was to launch an offensive in the direction of Gomel and Smolensk, this being co-ordinated with other offensives to be made by Konev's West and Reiter's Bryansk Fronts; the operation was due to start on 15 February. Rokossovsky considered this early date to be unrealistic, but his views failed to influence Stalin and he was given his written directive on 5 February.[4]

According to Shtemenko, Stalin personally took charge of the preparations for this operation and gave Reiter a severe dressing down for suggesting that the Bryansk Front attack might be delayed by only one day.[5] When Rokossovsky complained that the railway capacity was inadequate to ferry forward the troops of the new Central Front, Stalin's remedy was to hand over the railway personnel to the NKVD, who so terrorized the officials that the result, according to Rokossovsky, was near chaos. Eventually Rokossovsky's request for a nine days' postponement was granted, but, by 25 February, when Rokossovsky was obliged to begin the offensive, only half of his troops had arrived in the battle area.[6]

On 17 February, when Hitler was actually visiting Zaporozhe, Kursk and Kharkov had already fallen to Golikov's Voronezh Front, and Vatutin's South-West Front was nearing Dnepropetrovsk. Hitler had intended to dismiss the Commander of Army Group Don, redesignated that February as Army Group South, and he was mollified only when von Manstein produced a plan for a counter-offensive to envelop Vatutin's and Golikov's rapidly advancing troops and to retake Kharkov.

On 17 February Stalin telephoned Vatutin to implement *Skachok* and told him to take Zaporozhe. The Red Army troops had, however, outrun their supplies and tactical air support, and the reversal of the air situation in the German favour was to prove the key to the subsequent battle. Von Manstein's counter-offensive, beginning on 19 February, destroyed the advanced elements of Vatutin's South-West Front and then began to move rapidly north-eastwards through a great gap in Golikov's Voronezh Front, reaching Kharkov by 12 March. Six days later the Germans were in Belgorod and appeared to be threatening the southern flank of Rokossovsky's newly arrived Central Front. Meanwhile Rokossovsky's own offensive had petered out, in spite of Stalin's agreement that its axis should be changed to the nearer and less ambitious objective of Orel; Reiter had advanced only a few miles. Stalin was subsequently blamed for the reverse.[7]

Stalin's reaction was characteristic; he considered that the Voronezh Front needed strengthening from a political as well as a military point of view and Khrushchev and Vasilevsky were ordered to report there; but not until he had heard Vasilevsky's report from near Belgorod did the dictator realize the danger to the Central and the Voronezh Fronts. After Vasilevsky spoke again to Stalin on 10 March the Supreme Commander decided to allot Golikov two more armies and a tank army.[8]

On or about 13 March Stalin telephoned Zhukov, who was with Timoshenko at the headquarters of the North-West Front. At Zhukov's recommendation Stalin agreed that Konev should take over the North-West Front after handing over the West Front to Sokolovsky, so that Timoshenko could be attached to the South and the South-West Fronts as the *Stavka* representative. Zhukov himself was to return to Moscow and then go on to the Voronezh Front. Zhukov used the formations allocated by Stalin, the two armies detached from Rokossovsky and the tank army from the *Stavka* reserve, as the nucleus of a force for counter-attacks in the area of Belgorod to restore Golikov's broken front.[9] By the end of March the situation was stabilized and the great Kursk bulge came into being, its northern face being held by the Central and its southern by the Voronezh Fronts. To the north and south of the Kursk bulge the cities of Orel and Kharkov remained in German hands. Golikov was removed from the command of the Voronezh Front which was taken over by Vatutin, the vacancy at the South-West Front being filled by Malinovsky who gave up the South Front to Tolbukhin. The Central Front did not escape investigation, for a commission headed by Malenkov and including Antonov, Khrulev and Ponomarenko, of the Belorussian Central Committee, was sent to Rokossovsky to look into the causes of his failure.[10]

---

Hitler was of the opinion that the best means of defence in Russia would be a limited offensive, to be made immediately after the thaw had dried out and before the Americans and British could mount their second front in Western Europe, and in this belief he had been encouraged by the success of von Manstein's recent Kharkov battle. He wanted to attack the Soviet enemy before the Germans were themselves attacked, in order to reduce, if only temporarily, the offensive capability of the Red Army. Hitler chose the Kursk bulge as the area for his new *Zitadelle* operation, for what was to have been a repetition of the destruction of the Izyum salient, the great Kharkov victory of May 1942; he did not intend, however, to continue the offensive into the Russian interior. The planning for *Zitadelle* began in early March in preparation for an attack in mid April, but the date was repeatedly postponed because of delays in the assembly of the troops.

Zhukov took the view that the enemy preparations were a preliminary to a thrust between Elets and Voronezh, striking northeast towards Ryazan and enveloping Moscow from the rear; such a suggestion was in harmony with Stalin's obsession that all German strategy had as its aim the taking of the Soviet capital. In his written report of 8 April to Stalin, the Deputy Supreme Commander said that he was against a pre-emptive Soviet attack; although he was 'unfamiliar with the disposition of the Red Army operational reserves', he believed that they should be used in depth to cover the southern and south-eastern approaches of the capital.[11] When Stalin read this report Vasilevsky was present. The dictator already knew that the general staff supported Zhukov's paper, but he said that he must first have the front commanders' opinions; he himself spoke on the telephone to Rokossovsky and Vatutin. Meanwhile Vasilevsky was to go to Zhukov to discuss the situation on the ground.[12]

The appreciation from the Central Front dated 10 April was in the form of a personal signal to Antonov from Malinin, the front chief of staff. Malinin thought the enemy aim to be the reoccupation of the Ukraine and he urged that a pre-emptive attack should be made against the enemy's Orel grouping.[13] The appreciation of the Voronezh Front, sent on 12 April under the signatures of Vatutin, Khrushchev and Korzhenevich, considered that the enemy might have abandoned his aim to occupy the south-east in favour of the envelopment of Moscow; nothing was said about a pre-emptive attack.[14] On the evening of 12 April, Zhukov, Vasilevsky and Antonov attended a Kremlin meeting to consider these reports. Stalin was agitated and worried in case mass German attacks should result in a repetition of Izyum.[15] He showed anxiety about Moscow. But since the enemy offensive was not believed to be imminent, Zhukov, together with Shtemenko, was sent on 18 April to the North Caucasus Front, while Vasilevsky and Antonov began to marshal the necessary reserves for the Kursk battle.

The newly concentrated reserves to the south of Moscow were under a Reserve Front commanded by Reiter, who had given up his Bryansk Front to Popov. But Stalin appears to have been unwilling to entrust what was to become a key formation to this Latvian former colonel of the tsarist army, and he was replaced by Konev, Stalin personally impressing on Konev the importance of his role in the coming Kursk battle.[16] But whereas the general staff had proposed that the Reserve Front should be given no defensive tasks, in order that it might be committed fresh and intact to the counter-offensive, Stalin ruled, on 23 April, that Konev's force should be used for secondary defence in strategic depth, covering a great belt of rearward defences behind the Bryansk, Central, Voronezh and South-West Fronts.[17] From 10 April the Reserve Front was redesignated as the Steppe Military District.

Stalin was usually unwilling to hear out lengthy opinion as to the enemy's intentions. On this occasion, however, the situation, as Shtemenko said, forced him to give weighty consideration to the courses open to the enemy. Zhukov affirms that Stalin's natural inclination was to go over to the offensive before the German blow should fall, but he lacked confidence in the ability of his own troops, for hitherto the successful Red Army offensives had been in mid winter.[18] Zhukov, Vasilevsky and the general staff were opposed to mounting an offensive until after the enemy had dissipated his strength against the formidable Kursk defences. In the Central and Voronezh Fronts opinions were divided, but, on 21 April, Vatutin reported to Moscow that a pre-emptive Red Army offensive might be necessary if the enemy continued to delay his attack, this view, as Zhukov and Shtemenko have since stressed, being supported by Khrushchev. Rokossovsky had written a paper for forwarding to Stalin, favouring the defence.[19]

In May and June Vatutin began to press, firstly Vasilevsky and then Stalin, that the Red Army should begin the offensive, urging the dictator not to lose the benefit of the summer weather. Stalin told Vatutin to forward his proposals in writing. Vatutin's frequent urging began to have its effect, so that, Vasilevsky said, it took all his efforts and those of Zhukov and Antonov, to dissuade the dictator. From his daily conversations Vasilevsky noted, with concern, how nervous Stalin was becoming. On 22 June Stalin ordered that Vasilevsky should bring Malinovsky to the Kremlin as he wanted to hear the latter's views, and Vasilevsky afterwards learned, to his surprise, that Stalin had kept Zhukov in ignorance of his fact and opinion finding activities.[20]

Stalin would not commit himself as to which he believed to be the correct course and it became obvious to the general staff that he was unable to come to a decision. On 10 and 20 May, and again on 2 June, the German offensive appeared to be imminent and the fronts stood to, only to be stood down again some days later. Vacillation and the prolonged waiting affected Stalin's temper, and this, according to Shtemenko, was the underlying cause of the fearful Kremlin scene when the dictator was informed, in a personal letter written by fighter pilots, of the defective fabric paint on the wings of the Iak 9 interceptors, which was causing them to break up in flight.[21] Vasilevsky, Voronov and Iakovlev were sent for, and Iakovlev, who had had long and close dealings with the dictator, said he had never seen him in such a rage. He abused his silent staff, calling them 'Hitlerites'; Iakovlev, according to his own account, began to shiver with fear. They escaped further wrath only by promising that all planes would be repaired within two weeks, a promise impossible of fulfilment. Meanwhile Stalin ordered that the military prosecutor's office should begin its immediate investigations to seek out traitors.[22] So the long wait continued until the first week in July.

The Soviet counter-offensive, timed to begin after the enemy offensive had been contained, was to consist of two main thrusts, one in the south against von Manstein and the other westwards against von Kluge. The offensive to the south by the Voronezh, the South-West, and later the Steppe Fronts, had as its primary aim the destruction of von Manstein's grouping at Belgorod-Kharkov, this operation being known as *Rumiantsev*. Opinions were divided as to the strategy to be subsequently adopted. Vatutin and Khrushchev are said to have urged that the Voronezh, South-West and South Fronts, together with the left wing of the Central Front, should be deflected south-westwards and occupy the southern Ukraine as far as the 32nd meridian, securing not only the rich industrial and agricultural areas of the south but also a springboard for mounting a campaign into Rumania and Hungary. Stalin decided against this plan, since it bypassed Kiev to the south and left von Kluge's Army Group Centre intact and still within 200 miles of Moscow; he himself favoured a thrust from Poltava west-north-west on Kiev; and, added Shtemenko, it was believed that an extension of this Soviet axis from Kiev towards the Carpathians would drive a deep wedge between Army Groups Centre and South, threatening both with envelopment.[23] This is what happened and it proved to be the corner-stone of the 1943 and 1944 Soviet victories in Central and South-East Europe.

The Soviet counter-offensive to the north of the Kursk bulge, known as *Kutuzov*, was to be made by the West and the Bryansk Fronts against the flank and rear of the Army Group Centre's Orel grouping, as soon as this had become bogged down in its attack against Kursk. These two fronts, together with the Central Front, would then move westwards into Belorussia forming the north flank of the Kiev thrust.

The detail for *Kutuzov* had been worked out by Sokolovsky and Popov and forwarded to the general staff for approval. Stalin presided at the co-ordinating Moscow conference which was attended by the front and army commanders. Antonov's presentation was so exhaustive and clear, said Bagramian, that little remained to be said. Stalin asked a few questions and expressed himself in agreement with the general substance of the plan. Bagramian, then the Commander of 11 Guards Army, had some reservations as to his own role on the left wing, but judged that it was not the moment for him to express an opinion. So he kept silent. Those present began rolling up their maps, when suddenly Stalin asked whether anyone had any different views. Bagramian said that he had. Stalin looked up at him 'quite surprised', but told him to continue. Everyone unrolled their maps again. Determined not to panic, Bagramian outlined how he thought his army should be used. At the conclusion he waited to be crushed by what he called the great trinity, Stalin, the general staff and the front commanders. This did not happen, however; at first nothing was said while the maps were being studied; then Bagramian's proposals were accepted without serious amendment.[24]

However nervous and unreasonable Stalin might have been at this time, the military were not subordinated to purely factional party interests. He refused a party request that the civilian population should be evacuated from the Kursk bulge, not only because this might be construed as an indication of an intention to withdraw, but also because the construction of the military defences depended on civilian labour. Again, when Rokossovsky asked Stalin that Zaporozhets, a tried and trusted old Bolshevik of the Civil War, should be removed from his appointment as the political member of 60 Army since the youthful Cherniakhovsky found it impossible to work with him, the dictator immediately ordered Zaporozhets's recall.[25]

In mid April Peresypkin had been sent by Stalin to the Reserve, Voronezh and Central Fronts to organize the signal communications. The existing radial state line network was developed into a grid system (USON), based on connecting up a chequer board of signal centres with duplicated and triplicated telephone and telegraph links, so that severed connections could be bypassed by alternative routes.[26] Although each army headquarters operated thirteen separate radio networks, wireless was sparingly used, even in the forward areas, except by the air and tank forces.

On 30 June Vasilevsky was attached to the Voronezh Front while Zhukov was ordered to remain with Rokossovsky; in the first week in July Konev's district was converted to a front and ordered forward, Stalin recommending that Konev should report personally to Vatutin in order to familiarize himself with conditions in the area.[27] On 1 July 1943 the Central and Voronezh Fronts are said to have included over 1,300,000 men and nearly 3,500 tanks, in all sixty-seven rifle divisions; the West, Bryansk and Steppe Fronts on 10 July numbered a further sixty-five divisions.[28]

The German probes against the Voronezh Front began in the

late afternoon of 4 July, developing into a full offensive that night.
There was a hurried discussion between Zhukov and Rokossovsky
as to whether they should order the firing of the front counter-
bombardment and harassing fire programme or report to the
*Stavka* for instructions; Zhukov telephoned for Stalin's approval.
Stalin did not go to bed that night and, from time to time, he spoke
on the telephone to Zhukov, Vasilevsky and Vatutin. The next
evening Rokossovsky, whose troops were by then under great
pressure, telephoned Stalin to ask for reinforcements, but his
gratitude on being given another army was short-lived when
Stalin re-routed it a few hours later to Vatutin who, according to
the dictator, was 'in a grave situation'.[29]

Von Manstein had already begun to cut deeply into Vatutin's
defences. Rokossovsky has professed to believe that the fault lay
in the front's deployment; Zhukov doubts this view. Khrushchev,
blaming both Stalin and Zhukov, has described, or allowed others
to describe, his (Khrushchev's) own personal influence 'not merely
with his own front but much further afield . . . as an inspiration and
a guide'. Khrushchev said that, on 6 July, Stalin and Zhukov were
against the digging in of tanks and that both the Voronezh Front
military council and Vasilevsky had great difficulty in persuading
Stalin to permit it.[30] Vasilevsky and Ivanov, Vatutin's chief of
staff, say otherwise, however, and German air photo reconnaissance
has disclosed the presence of over eighty Red Army tanks dug-in in
that area before 4 July. At 1820 hours on 6 July, Vatutin telephoned
Stalin to describe the growing German panzer threat. Vasilevsky,
who was present with Vatutin, recommended to Stalin that two
tank corps should be hastened to the threatened sector and that
Rotmistrov's 5 Guards Tank Army should be moved south.
Stalin then gave Vatutin his orders, confirming the allocation of
the tank army and 'demanding that the enemy be stopped *on the
prepared defensive positions*'. The members of the Voronezh military council should, he said, be with the forward troops; only
Vatutin was to remain at the field headquarters; Khrushchev
should join Chistiakov's army, Ivanov go to Kriuchenkin, and
Apanasenko to Shumilov, while Vasilevsky was to meet the
arriving strategic reserve force consisting of Rotmistrov's and
Zhadov's armies.[31] Even Rotmistrov appears to believe that the
dictator acted correctly in ordering a rigid defence on a given
line.[32]

Since Vasilevsky had moved over to the South-West Front, Zhukov was ordered by Stalin, on 12 July, to fly to the area of Prokhorovka, where the 800 tanks of Rotmistrov's army were engaging about 500 tanks of the SS panzer corps, to co-ordinate operations between the Voronezh and the Steppe Fronts. The counter-offensive against the Orel grouping in the north began that day, but Hitler had already decided that *Zitadelle* offered no prospects of early victory, and, on 13 July, he ordered that the German offensive be broken off as he intended to move a number of divisions to Western Europe.

Stalin had earlier ruled that the front commanders should themselves decide when the time was opportune for the counter-offensive.[33] But when the defensive battle was actually at its height it was Stalin who took control; he liked his situation reports direct from the man on the spot and, not content with telephoning Zhukov, Vasilevsky and Voronov, he was in continuous touch with the front commanders. As early as 9 July he had been pressing Zhukov that the Bryansk Front might begin the counter-offensive, and, from 12 July onwards, so Zhukov has said, Stalin was co-ordinating all the offensives.[34] By 15 July, when the Voronezh and Steppe Fronts had gone over to the attack, Stalin was goading everyone forward, so that Zhukov and Vasilevsky had the greatest difficulty in persuading the 'heated and grudging' Supreme Commander that occasional pauses were necessary for preparation and resupply.[35] On 5 August an artillery salute was fired in Moscow in honour of the taking of Orel and Belgorod, the first of the many salutes to be fired during the war.

The Supreme Commander had reverted to his earlier strategy of attacking frontally from Velikiye Luki in the north to the Sea of Azov in the south. When, in early August, Zhukov had suggested that the withdrawing enemy should be enveloped, the dictator replied that 'the Germans are still too strong for that'; nor would he change his opinion when Zhukov returned to the theme later in the month.[36] Meanwhile the Supreme Commander tried to keep close control of operative detail, telling Popov on 17 July to keep his tank army well clear of the built-up area of Orel, and criticizing Vatutin on 6 August for failing to concentrate two of his armies on a narrow frontage of assault. Nor did Zhukov escape direction and censure, for, three days later, Stalin sent him a telegram detailing the action to be taken to envelop Kharkov. When the Voronezh Front failed to envelop the Kharkov grouping, suffering heavy casualties in the enemy counter-attack, Stalin, on 21 August, dictated to Shtemenko a strongly worded telegram to both Vatutin and Zhukov, blaming them for 'dissipating their forces by attacking everywhere to cover as much ground as possible', the faults which Zhukov later attributed to Stalin.[37]

On 17 August, when calling at a forward army headquarters, Vasilevsky found the following teleprint awaiting him:

> Marshal Vasilevsky. It is now already 0330 hours 17 August and you still have not seen fit to send to the *Stavka* a report on the outcome of operations on 16 August and your appreciation of the situation . . . Nearly every day you forget this duty . . . Again you have been pleased to ignore your responsibility to the *Stavka* by not reporting. It is the last time that I give you notice that in the event of your allowing yourself to forget your duty you will be removed from the post of the Chief of General Staff and recalled from the front. J. Stalin.[38]

Vasilevsky has said that he was much shaken, for he had never before failed to report or received a reprimand on this score, although the report on the night of 16 August had, admittedly, been delayed for several hours. Vasilevsky immediately telephoned Antonov in Moscow, to learn that Stalin had been agitated by the poor results of the offensives and had tried in vain to get in touch with the Chief of General Staff. Antonov confirmed that Stalin had actually dictated the telegram to Antonov after receiving Vasilevsky's report. Vasilevsky subsequently concluded that all *Stavka* representatives were subjected to Stalin's discipline and rigorous control, and added, somewhat philosophically, that 'the absence of any indulgence towards us was in the interest of the conduct of the armed struggle'. For, said Vasilevsky, 'the Supreme Commander followed the course of front operations very attentively and held the direction of the troops firmly in his own hands'. On 19 August Vasilevsky was in trouble again when he telephoned Stalin from Malinovsky's headquarters, asking for a six day delay in the offensive in order to regroup. Stalin was dissatisfied and once again 'the conversation was unpleasant', with 'not entirely justified reproaches' being levelled at both Vasilevsky and Malinovsky.[39]

On the morning of 23 August the Steppe Front occupied Kharkov. Konev immediately tried to telephone Stalin, only to be told by Poskrebyshev that the Supreme Commander always slept at that hour. Ignoring Poskrebyshev's instructions, Konev telephoned Stalin direct and, after long ringing, Stalin eventually picked up the receiver. Stalin was apparently not irritated at having been woken, and Konev's reward was a 'first category' 224 gun salute.[40] This desire by front commanders for recognition was to develop into a race to occupy cities; and Stalin, who took a personal interest in the framing of the *Sovinform communiqués* and the firing of the salutes, may have intended that it should. In September Rokossovsky felt himself robbed of a rich prize and complained in vain when his left front boundary was moved to the north, as a result of which Kiev fell within the zone of the Voronezh Front.[41]

There was no pause between the defensive and offensive phases for *Rumiantsev,* and, according to Shtemenko, there was no master plan for the operation, since this developed according to circumstances, recommendations by Zhukov and the front commanders being referred back to Moscow for confirmation or variation.[42] Thereafter Stalin would appear to have been in control, for Zhukov was only one of a number of *Stavka* representatives and front commanders who were formulating plans and proffering advice. Nor does Zhukov appear to have been in Stalin's confidence when grand strategy or the command and control of the Red Army and its reserves were decided, so that his designation as Deputy Supreme Commander was, in this respect, a misnomer. Zhukov appears to have relied on the occasional staff briefing by Antonov and on what he could extract from the general staff representatives when they visited him in the field, for any information outside of the Voronezh and Steppe Fronts.[43]

On 25 August at a joint GKO/*Stavka* meeting Stalin demanded immediate measures to prevent the enemy stabilizing his positions on a new East Wall line, and at the same time to halt the destruction by the enemy of the industrial and agricultural resources in the area through which he was withdrawing. An operation was to be mounted involving a rapid approach march and a breaching of the obstacle belt on a wide front. Zhukov was to stay with the Voronezh and Steppe Fronts while Vasilevsky acted as the *Stavka* representative with the South-West and South Fronts; Voronov remained with Sokolovsky's West Front and co-ordinated its operations with Eremenko's Kalinin Front, in what was to become the Smolensk operation. The Bryansk Front was shortly to be withdrawn. Later that same evening, Stalin examined Zhukov's requests for men and materials to reinforce the Voronezh and Steppe Fronts; and, said Zhukov, 'after comparing the list with his own figures of availabilities he took up a pencil and slashed the request by thirty to forty per cent'.[44]

On 3 and 5 August Stalin is said to have visited the headquarters of the West and the Kalinin Fronts, the only time during the course of the war that he entered a theatre of operations.[45] Stalin came no further forward than Yukhnov, Sokolovsky and Voronov being ordered to return to the rear area to meet him; they found him in an unsightly little *dacha* and concluded that the setting was being staged for a propaganda film.[46]

At the end of August when Voronov was told to check the readiness of the Kalinin Front for the Smolensk offensive, he thought that the preparation had been inadequate and was out of keeping with Eremenko's display of confidence; so he instructed the military council to ask Moscow for a postponement. Both Eremenko and Leonov, the political member, refused. Voronov has said that he himself was reluctant to telephone Stalin, as in the past he had often been a petitioner for others and had earned in return the dictator's unpleasant abuse. But in the end he was obliged to do so, and he was fortunate in that Stalin was preoccupied with some other matter and irritably agreed to put off the date. Eremenko's subsequent actions were to surprise Voronov and anger Stalin. For, if Voronov is to be believed, he had to veto Eremenko's decision not to inform his commanders and troops of the six day postponement, but to put off the attack day by day, 'so as not to unwind his subordinates'. When the offensive did start, Eremenko refused to let his staff inform Moscow – even when asked – of the extent of his success, because he wanted to do this personally at the end of the day.[47]

On 8 September a *Stavka* order promised the award of the Order of Suvorov to commanders who forced the Desna, and the title of

Hero of the Soviet Union to those officers and men who were first across the Dnieper. The approach march of 120 miles began on 18 September. On the night of 24 September two parachute brigades were dropped beyond the river line, but since these were scattered over a wide area the operation was a failure. The ground troops did, however, seize numbers of small bridgeheads to the north and south of Kiev, the largest of which was near Bukrin, fifty miles below the Ukrainian capital. Both Zhukov and the general staff were convinced that the main offensive would have to be shifted from Bukrin, for surprise had been lost and the wooded and broken ground there was unsuitable for the use of tanks. Stalin, however, was unwilling to listen to argument. He was still angry by the failure of the parachute brigades and had drafted a special order censuring the incompetence of its organizers. He told Zhukov to continue the break-out 'for the front was giving up the Bukrin attacks before it had really tried'. Fighting continued into October, still without success. The Supreme Commander, said Shtemenko, was very dissatisfied, and he reproached both Zhukov and Vatutin for lack of decision and drive, comparing their failure with Konev's good progress on the lower Dnieper. Not until 24 October would he agree to call off the Bukrin attacks and shift the main weight of the offensive to the Lyutezh bridgehead to the north of Kiev.[48]

Moskalenko was with Vatutin on the Bukrin bridgehead on 23 October, when Stalin called on the *V Ch*. Stalin expressed displeasure that the Bukrin offensive was still being continued and he made a detailed verbal appreciation of the tactical and operative factors – the enemy build-up on the ground and in the air, the broken country, which, though favouring the German defence, was unsuitable for tank troops. He wanted Vatutin to consider moving part of his force by night northwards to Lyutezh. Moskalenko said that, at the time, he marvelled at the thoroughness with which the *Stavka* analyzed the local situation.[49] The reasoning thus attributed to Stalin forms the first paragraph of the directive of 24 October sent over Stalin's and Antonov's signatures, this being a sharp reprimand to Zhukov and Vatutin for their failure in reading ground and in appreciating troop characteristics. For, when it so suited him, Stalin adopted as his own the opinions of those who had disagreed with him, and attributed to his opponents the discredited arguments which had stemmed from himself.

On 6 November Zhukov and Vatutin sent a joint telegram to Stalin announcing the occupation of Kiev, but this did not save the front headquarters from the rigorous inquiry which led to the dismissal of Ivanov, its chief of staff. Shtemenko believed that Ivanov was removed because he failed to report the loss of a major town.[50] In fact, the front was also charged with lack of control, for Vatutin wrote a personal letter to Antonov, defending the front signal organization and detailing the whereabouts of the members of the military council and the deputy commanders during the battle. Vatutin defended Ivanov and asked Antonov to show the letter to Stalin. By 1972, however, Moskalenko had become Stalin's champion, for he concluded that Antonov, not Stalin, was responsible for Ivanov's removal.[51]

On 20 October 1943 the designation of all the fronts in the Ukraine was changed to Ukrainian Fronts numbered consecutively from north to south, so that the Voronezh, the Steppe, the South-West and South Fronts became 1, 2, 3 and 4 Ukrainian Fronts. The Central Front became the Belorussian Front.

The more forceful front commanders, particularly those who enjoyed a measure of Stalin's confidence, appear to have been uninhibited by the presence of *Stavka* representatives in maintaining their link with Stalin. Rokossovsky put his own plan for the taking of Kiev not to Zhukov but direct to Stalin.[52] At about this time, Konev telephoned Stalin, again not Zhukov, to report that it was essential that the right wing of Malinovsky's 3 Ukrainian Front mount an immediate offensive to prevent the enemy escaping from encirclement near Krivoi Rog.[53] Nor did Stalin always deal with the *Stavka* representatives. For when one of Zhukov's two fronts was in difficulties and Vatutin lost Zhitomir to a German counter stroke on 18 November, Stalin telephoned Rokossovsky, Vatutin's right hand neighbour, instructing him to go at once to 1 Ukrainian Front and, if necessary, assume command of that formation and halt the enemy advance.[54]

In mid December Zhukov and Vasilevsky had been recalled to Moscow to prepare, together with the general staff, the detail of the new offensive by the four Ukrainian fronts, which was to destroy the enemy salient in the Dnieper bend and take the Red Army into Galicia and Rumania. This, according to Zhukov, took

**23** N. D. Iakovlev, the Deputy Chief of the Main Artillery Directorate (GAU) responsible to Stalin for combat equipment.

**24** Admiral N. G. Kuznetsov, the Commissar for the Navy.

**25** Rokossovsky, said to be of Polish-Russian parentage, was a tsarist cavalry NCO and Red cavalry corps commander, later imprisoned during the purges. From 1942 onwards he was a front commander.

**26** Voronov joined the Red Army artillery in 1918, by 1937 becoming the Director of Artillery. From 1942–45 he commanded groups of fronts.

five days from the conclusion of the main *Stavka* conferences during which Stalin reversed his earlier order forbidding encirclement operations.

The offensive began on 24 December and quickly made ground to the west and south-west. On the extreme left, however, Tolbukhin's 4 Ukrainian Front became bogged down in front of the enemy Nikopol bridgehead, and it became obvious to Vasilevsky that to continue the attacks would lead to enormous casualties with no gain. He telephoned Stalin in Tolbukhin's presence suggesting that 3 Ukrainian Front should be reinforced, so that the bridgehead might be outflanked. Once more Stalin abused them, but Vasilevsky could do no more, he said, than maintain his opinion; Stalin's excited voice involuntarily aroused Vasilevsky's resentment. In the end Stalin 'threw down the phone'.[55]

A day later, however, Stalin had regained his composure. Vasilevsky had taken up temporary residence with Leliushenko's army in front of the bridgehead, when, on 16 January, he was called to the telephone by Stalin. Vasilevsky took Leliushenko with him. Leliushenko, overhearing part of the conversation, was able to gauge the situation by the unruffled and measured tones. Stalin then wanted Leliushenko on the line. When asked for his appreciation, Leliushenko told the dictator that the frontal attack by his army held little prospect of success unless made in conjunction with a second offensive by 3 Ukrainian Front to the north. Stalin listened in silence. Action on these views was not long delayed, however, for the next morning Leliushenko received orders to hand over a proportion of his armour to 3 Ukrainian Front and prepare new plans for his remaining forces.[56]

Further to the west the flanks of Vatutin's and Konev's fronts had, on 28 January, encircled two German corps at Korsun. Information about the progress of an enemy relief thrust quickly came to Stalin's ears, and, at midday on 12 February, he spoke to Konev on the telephone angrily asking for confirmation that the enemy was beginning to break out through the 27 Army sector, part of Vatutin's 1 Ukrainian Front. Konev replied that 'Comrade Stalin should not worry himself, as he [Konev] had taken all necessary measures to prevent the enemy's escape', moving Rotmistrov's tank army into the area to provide a pivot between 1 and 2 Ukrainian Fronts. Stalin was surprised and pleased at this unusual initiative and said that he would consult the *Stavka*. He telephoned Zhukov, rousing him from his sick bed, and berated him for not knowing the detail of the local situation. According to Zhukov's version, Stalin said that Konev wanted the responsibility for the destruction of the enemy corps to be given to 2 Ukrainian Front. Zhukov opposed this course. Stalin merely hung up. Fifteen minutes later Stalin spoke again to Konev telling him that all troops in action against the encircled enemy would be placed under his command. Konev said that he protested against having to accept 27 Army, for the army communications and rear services ran through the 1 Ukrainian Front organization at Belaya Tserkov and Kiev. Stalin, however, brushed these objections aside, saying that Vatutin could remain responsible for both communication and supply, but that [*manes* Kameneva] Konev could pass his signal traffic to 27 Army through 1 Ukrainian Front headquarters.[57] The telegraphed directive was issued a few hours later. Vatutin, in his turn, complained to Zhukov against being robbed of the opportunity of gaining a Moscow saluted victory.[58]

Konev subsequently contradicted Zhukov's version of events, and, presumably motivated by malice, has published a signalled reprimand from Stalin to Zhukov, dated at 1645 hours that day, saying that the enemy breakthrough had occurred since the command weaknesses of 27 Army had not been rectified on the spot, and because Zhukov had not taken decisive measures to destroy, in accordance with Stalin's orders, the enemy Stablev grouping. On 18 February 1944, 2 Ukrainian Front was saluted by the guns of Moscow, nothing being said of Zhukov's and Vatutin's part in the victory; Konev was promoted to marshal of the Soviet Union, the third since the beginning of the war, for Zhukov and Vasilevsky had already been granted that rank in January and February 1943. Rotmistrov became a marshal of tank troops.

Vatutin had, however, remained responsible for blocking the path of the relief thrust of the incoming German armour during the Korsun battle. In this connection Novikov, the Commander-in-Chief of the Red Air Forces, has told how he was unexpectedly summoned to the Kremlin on 13 February. As he entered the dictator's room, Stalin, sitting on a divan and smoking his pipe, raised his right hand to his head as a sign of welcome. Rising, he walked up and down the room in silence and, approaching Novikov, looked him in the face and asked whether it was possible for aircraft to halt the advance of tanks. The question was unexpected, but Novikov had worked two years with Stalin and, so he said, 'already had his measure'. A direct 'Yes' or 'No' was called for, for Stalin wanted rapid and clear decisions and could not endure verbosity, or flabbiness and vagueness in thought. In reality the answer to the question depended on the circumstances, but Stalin would never allow others to cross-examine him. Without a moment's hesitation Novikov replied that they could. Stalin did not disguise his satisfaction and told Novikov to fly to Vatutin immediately. Khudiakov, the Chief of Air Staff and the man on the spot, sent by Novikov to co-ordinate the two air armies there, had obviously, said Novikov, fallen foul of the Supreme Commander, for Stalin gave his customary order, 'that he did not need such a man and that he was to be removed'. Novikov said that he attempted to defend Khudiakov but was quickly silenced by the sharpness of Stalin's reply, 'You fly to Vatutin and see that you stop those tanks'. That, said Novikov, was the end of that. The next two days were the most tense of his life, but he was rewarded by promotion to the rank of chief marshal of air troops.[59]

On 18 February Stalin restored Zhukov to his post as the *Stavka* representative and co-ordinator of 1 and 2 Ukrainian Fronts, but, on 1 March, the day after the fatal wounding of Vatutin by Ukrainian nationalists, Zhukov was appointed to command 1 Ukrainian Front, and the control over 1 and 2 Ukrainian Fronts reverted directly to Stalin.

Djilas visited Konev's headquarters at about this time and was shocked at the drinking party arranged in the Yugo-Slavs' honour. Konev, callous and taciturn, gave Djilas a verbal picture of the more senior Soviet military leaders: Voroshilov, he said, was a man of inexhaustible courage but incapable of understanding modern warfare; Budenny never knew much and he never studied anything – he was, in Konev's view, completely incompetent; Shaposhnikov he dismissed as a technical staff officer; but Stalin was 'universally gifted, brilliantly able to see the war as a whole and this made it possible for him to direct it so successfully'.[60]

Tolbukhin's 4 Ukrainian Front had already reached the mouth of the Dnieper, isolating the enemy 17 Army in the Crimea. At first there had been a difference of opinion in Moscow as to whether priority should be given to the reoccupation of the Crimea, or whether the peninsula should merely be sealed off at the Perekop isthmus, so freeing the larger part of 4 Ukrainian and the North Caucasus Front for service elsewhere. The general staff, said Shtemenko, was very conscious of the precedents of 1920, when Wrangel had attacked from the Crimea into the Kuban and the Taurida plain in the rear of the Red forces engaged against the Poles.[61] So no doubt was Stalin, for he regarded an enemy held Crimea as a threat to the Soviet forces in the western Ukraine. Vasilevsky, on 22 September, had given as his opinion that the main offensive should be made by Tolbukhin's forces from the north, down the Perekop isthmus and across the shallow and brackish Sivash. In addition part of the North Caucasus Front was to be put across the Kerch narrows, and this, together with the left wing of 4 Ukrainian Front, would attack on converging axes. This course was approved by Stalin, who decided to send Voroshilov, together with Shtemenko, to Petrov 'to have a look round and see what could be done'.[62]

Shtemenko has portrayed Voroshilov as a man of education and culture, a description at variance with the impression which Voroshilov made on western observers. But Shtemenko is agreed with Meretskov that Voroshilov was something of a showman, exuding cordiality and *bonhomie*, making a parade of his courage and thinking that he would be better received by the Terek and Kuban Cossack infantry by riding out to inspect them on a horse. Petrov had complained about the naval support provided by Vladimirsky, and Voroshilov presided over the co-ordinating conference held on 25 December to settle their differences. When Shtemenko proposed to forward the minutes of the meeting to Stalin as part of the routine reports, Voroshilov, said Shtemenko, 'thought otherwise and had the proceedings drawn up as a protocol, insisting that the ten representatives should all sign it'. The ladder of signatures angered Stalin, who likened it to the minutes of a meeting of a collective farm; he was surprised, he said, that all the participants had not taken a vote before coming to a decision.

Petrov's troops made a second successful sea-borne assault on 10 January and widened the beach-head. Yet Stalin, presumably acting on complaints from the navy and without consulting or informing anyone on the spot, decided to replace Petrov. The first that Voroshilov and Shtemenko knew of Petrov's replacement was the arrival of Eremenko's train in the Kuban; Petrov, who had only been promoted to the rank of general of the army three months before, was downgraded to a colonel-general. Voroshilov was recalled to Moscow for briefing, prior to being appointed to join Vasilevsky as a *Stavka* representative to 4 Ukrainian Front with a special responsibility as a co-ordinator between Tolbukhin and Eremenko in the successful campaign which was to end in the complete destruction of 17 German Army and the reoccupation of the Crimea.[63]

Hull, Eden and Ismay had been attending the conference held in Spiridinovka Street from 19 October until 1 November, 1943, together with Molotov, Litvinov, Vyshinsky, Voroshilov and Gryzlov, whose main interest was centred on whether the Anglo-American forces would invade northern France in the spring of 1944. Ismay and Deane made the presentation disclosing the invasion plans, the Russians, according to Ismay, listening attentively but giving no indication of their feelings one way or the other.[64] Voroshilov and Gryzlov did not, however, conceal their suspicions when the time came for questions.[65] In the political field, Hull and Eden had been instructed to arrange a meeting of the three heads of governments, but Stalin refused to leave Russia on the grounds that his presence was indispensable to the conduct of the fighting there. At the time, Eden was sceptical, but afterwards conceded that Stalin might have been speaking the truth, for on one occasion during the Kremlin talks Birse overheard the dictator on the telephone directing operations in the Crimea.[66] On 27 October Eden and Ismay had to return to the Kremlin on Churchill's telegraphed instructions, to explain that, due to unforeseen difficulties in Italy, the invasion of France might have to be postponed from the spring to the summer. To Ismay's surprise Stalin appeared 'perfectly happy once he had received Eden's assurance that a short postponement and not a cancellation was involved'.[67]

In the early hours of 25 November Stalin, together with Molotov and Voroshilov and accompanied by his personal NKVD bodyguard, boarded his train in the sidings near Kuntsevo *en route* for Stalingrad and Baku, from whence he was to fly to Teheran.

Shtemenko, carrying a set of marked-up maps covering the whole of the fighting fronts, was with the party as the general staff liaison officer responsible for briefing Stalin on the battle on the eastern front and passing Stalin's orders to Moscow for onward transmission to the front commanders. The special train stopped at scheduled halts from Michurinsk onwards, where there was access to the NKVD *V Ch* telephone circuit, Shtemenko's compartment being plugged in to the terminal at each of these stops so that he could speak to Gryzlov in Moscow and mark up his maps with the latest situation. At Teheran Shtemenko and his cipher officer were given a single room in Stalin's villa adjoining the signal centre, but that evening Stalin himself appeared in the office, ordering that it be changed since it was too small and dark. The effect, said Shtemenko, 'was immediate'. Shtemenko continued his morning and nightly briefings, and the drafts of all military orders requiring Stalin's signature, telegraphed or telephoned from Antonov, were presented to the dictator; the authorized version was then signalled back to Moscow, the original document bearing Stalin's signature being retained for safe keeping by the cipher officer. Stalin spoke to Antonov in Moscow during the Teheran conference and on one occasion had a direct signal conversation with Vatutin and Rokossovsky.[68]

At the first plenary meeting on 28 November Stalin appeared wearing the uniform of a marshal of the Soviet Union. Birse thought the dictator more care-worn than when he had last seen him in Moscow, but at the same time more affable.[69] His interventions were made in a quiet voice, without any gestures, but at the same time were direct and decided; sometimes they were so abrupt as to be rude. He left no doubt in anyone's mind, said Ismay, that he was master in his own house.[70] Deane noted that, in contrast to the British and American groups, each of which numbered twenty or thirty and had a strong military representation, Stalin had with him only Molotov, Voroshilov and Pavlov, his interpreter, and, as far as the Americans could tell, these three completed his entourage. Although, from time to time, Stalin had whispered consultations with Molotov and Voroshilov, Stalin was the sole spokesman; and, said Deane, there could be no doubt of his authority as there was never the slightest indication that he would have to consult his government.[71] Stalin said that he saw no point in separate chiefs of staff consultations, for that was his business and that was what he had come for; only reluctantly would he agree to be represented on the military committee, for he explained that he had brought no military experts with him; Voroshilov, however, 'would do his best'. His other comments were blunt, terse and to the point. On one occasion he capped Churchill's oratory by asking whether the British were only 'thinking' of *Overlord* in order to satisfy the Soviet Union; at another, after a particularly long speech from Churchill, he asked: 'How long is this conference going to last?'.[72]

Brooke, who was in agreement with Ismay on the poverty of Voroshilov's capabilities, was of the opinion that Stalin had a military brain of the highest calibre. Never once in any of his statements, said Brooke, did Stalin fail to appreciate all the implications of a situation with a quick and unerring eye, and 'in this respect he stood out compared with Roosevelt and Churchill'.[73]

Roosevelt surprised and disturbed his own chiefs of staff by bringing up the possibility of a Mediterranean operation across the Adriatic through Yugo-Slavia into Rumania, to effect a junction with the Red Army in the area of Odessa; Churchill associated himself with this suggestion. Stalin then gave his own opinion of the strategy which his allies should adopt. It was unwise, he thought, to scatter forces in various operations throughout the Eastern Mediterranean, since *Overlord* should be the basis of all operations in 1944; it would be better to abandon even the capture of Rome, so that the bulk of the allied troops in Italy might be used to invade southern France. Stalin said repeatedly that he was quite sure that Turkey would not come into the war, as if to emphasize that the Black Sea would remain closed to Anglo-American naval forces.[74] At the committee meeting the next day, attended by Voroshilov, Leahy, Marshall, Portal and Brooke, Voroshilov continued to press Stalin's views, while Brooke insisted, stubbornly according to Leahy, that all available Mediterranean forces should be used in Italy and the East Mediterranean. At the military meeting on 30 November a measure of agreement was reached in that the date of the cross-Channel operation was put off until 1 June 1944, since this would fit in with the proposed date of the Russian spring offensives. Stalin accepted the date with satisfaction.

Stalin had supported the United States' plan that all available allied forces should be landed in France, and Brooke and Deane subsequently ascribed motives of self-interest to the Soviet leader's proposals. Apart from securing an obvious diplomatic advantage in siding with the Americans against the British, Stalin wanted, suspected Brooke, to keep his American and British allies away from the Black Sea left flank, out of the Balkans and clear of the East Mediterranean.[75]

Stalin made a number of observations which, although not relevant to the proceedings, were of interest. His opinion of Hitler, much the same as that given to Eden the previous month, was that he did not share Roosevelt's view that Hitler was mentally unbalanced; indeed Stalin thought Hitler a very able man; his weaknesses were that he was greedy and thought too much of prestige and could not relate military aims to capabilities.[76] Stalin said he was in favour of shooting '50,000, perhaps 100,000 German officers', and the impression which he made on Churchill and Birse was that he was not joking. The dictator elaborated on the fighting qualities of the Red Army, saying that it had fought heroically because 'the Russian people' would not have tolerated otherwise; 'those who did not fight bravely were killed'. In 1939, he went on, the Soviet forces had done very badly against the Finns, and in 1941, in spite of the extensive re-organization, it could not be said that the Red Army was a first-class fighting force. But it had improved steadily, and now, he felt, it was genuinely a good army.[77] The Soviet margin of superiority over the enemy, said Stalin, was about sixty divisions, which could be moved rapidly from place to place over the extended front to provide the concentrations necessary to breakthrough in the selected directions. The Germans, so Stalin thought, had 260 divisions in the east against the 330 Red Army divisions opposing them.[78] And it was at Teheran that Stalin first hinted that when Germany was defeated the Soviet Union might be prepared to take a hand in the war against Japan.

# 10

# *Into Central Europe*

Towards the end of 1943 the Red Army ground forces in the north and the centre of the Russo-German front were reorganized and redeployed. Popov's Bryansk Front handed over formations to Rokossovsky's Central Front at the beginning of October and moved to the area between Velikiye Luki and Lake Ilmen to form a new Baltic Front; on 20 October Rokossovsky's enlarged Central Front, consisting of ten armies, was redesignated as the Belorussian Front; Eremenko's Kalinin became 1 Baltic Front and Popov's Baltic was renumbered as 2 Baltic Front. On 24 February 1944 Rokossovsky's Belorussian Front was renamed as 1 Belorussian Front, and Kurochkin's North-West Front headquarters was sent south to take over the sector on Rokossovsky's left, where it was redesignated as 2 Belorussian Front. On 13 February the Volkhov Front was broken up and its formations shared between Govorov's Leningrad and Popov's 2 Baltic Fronts, Meretskov assuming the command of the Karelian Front from Frolov. On the 21 April 1944 a new 3 Baltic Front, under Maslennikov, was formed in the Pskov area, taking over troops which had formerly belonged to the Leningrad and the Volkhov Fronts.[1]

Although Sandalov, Popov's chief of staff, subsequently said that he could see little sense in this reorganization and that Antonov would give him no information as to the reasons for it, the truth of the matter was that Stalin sent Popov north because he wanted the threat removed from Leningrad and an early reoccupation of the Baltic States.[2] But the rapid success of the Ukrainian fronts created a new situation in the centre with an ever-widening gap between Rokossovsky and Vatutin along the southern edge of the Pripet Marshes. This gap had to be filled by Kurochkin's headquarters taking over Rokossovsky's left flanking army and two further armies allocated from the *Stavka* reserve. Sandalov's criticism that the High Command formed a new front headquarters under Maslennikov when the Volkhov Front headquarters had been available in the area, would appear to be justified, however, for, according to Shtemenko, Stalin listened too readily to Govorov's urging that the Leningrad Front alone should be entrusted with the offensive operations to the south-west of the city.[3] So Stalin decided to break up the Volkhov Front, softening the blow to Meretskov by telling him that he was the most suitable commander for operations against the Finns, and by allowing him to take his headquarters with him and superimpose it on that of the Karelian Front.[4] Later, when Govorov's Leningrad Front stretched from the Finnish sector north of Leningrad down to Ostrov, Stalin had second thoughts as to whether Govorov could in fact handle such an extended sector which faced in two directions. In a telephone consultation with Vasilevsky, he said that he was inclined, in spite of Govorov's objections, to cut the Leningrad Front in two once more, setting up a new 3 Baltic Front to be interposed in the area of Pskov.[5]

On 16 November 1943, Stalin had Bagramian, still commanding 11 Guards Army, recalled to Moscow. When Bagramian reported to Antonov and asked the reason for his summons, he was told that 'the boss (*khoziain*) is not in the habit of making his thoughts public'. Bagramian accompanied Antonov and Shtemenko to the Kremlin where he learned that his army was to be transferred from 2 Baltic to 1 Baltic Front and that he himself was to replace Eremenko as the front commander. It only remained, said Stalin, to post an experienced commander to 11 Guards Army; Chibisov, he thought, would be suitable. Antonev began to praise Chibisov's military virtues, but Stalin, quick to note Bagramian's silence, asked whether the new front commander had anything against Chibisov. Bagramian said that he thought Colonel-General Chibisov a most experienced commander, but pointed out that Chibisov had been a lieutenant-general when Bagramian was a colonel. Would it not be possible instead to have Galitsky. Not only did Stalin agree, but, summoning Poskrebyshev, he ordered him to prepare a *Sovnarkom* order promoting Bagramian from colonel-general to general of the army.[6]

In February 1944 the general staff worked out a plan, which was approved by Stalin, involving a joint thrust on Riga by Bagramian's 1 and Popov's 2 Baltic Fronts, in order to envelop Army Group North. Timoshenko co-ordinated the operation and Shtemenko accompanied him as his chief of staff. Since no progress had been made following two days of heavy fighting, Timoshenko referred the plan back to Stalin, asking in vain for permission to vary it. The offensive was resumed a week later, with no greater success, and it was eventually broken off on 18 March. Shtemenko drafted the report to Stalin explaining the failure, a failure which in all probability led the next month to the replacement of Popov by Eremenko. Shtemenko's description of Timoshenko during this period shows the marshal to have been suspicious and testy, still living the glories of the Civil War, jealous and contemptuous of the younger commanders and staffs. He was at first openly hostile to Shtemenko and assumed that he had been sent as Stalin's spy.[7]

Following the loss of the Ukraine, the German held territory in the centre protruded far to the east in the form of a balcony, the right flank of the salient running from west to east for a distance of nearly 200 miles along the southern skirts of the Pripet Marshes. The front line showed a similarity to that of July 1941 when the Germans had used the salient as a springboard to attack southwards into the Ukraine and launch the offensive on Moscow. It was considered necessary, therefore, to evict the enemy from the Belorussian bulge to eliminate this threat and, at the same time, open the way for the Red Army into the Baltic States, East Prussia and Poland.

The findings of a GKO commission of enquiry held the cautious Sokolovsky responsible for the Soviet lack of success in the earlier offensives north of the Pripet, and the general staff used the report to support its own suggestion that the West Front, because it was over-extended, should be broken up into two new fronts, and that these should be reinforced preparatory to a main offensive into Belorussia.[8]

Although Stalin had said that he would make his offensives coincide with the launching of the second front in Western Europe, he had yet to make up his mind as to his strategic objectives, where he would strike his main and subsidiary blows and their timing. Zhukov, Vasilevsky, Rokossovsky and Shtemenko have confirmed that Stalin sought out opinions on these matters not only from the Deputy Supreme Commander, the Chief of General Staff and members of the *Stavka*, but also from the front commanders, continuously talking to them in turn on the telephone.

When Rokossovsky wanted to press his views he talked directly to Stalin and not through Antonov, for, said Rokossovsky, Antonov rarely insisted on a point in the face of Stalin's objections, and his usual reply to Rokossovsky's requests was that 'Comrade Stalin would decide for himself'. Rokossovsky was in favour of a major offensive into Belorussia, and he outlined to Stalin how, in his opinion, this could be done. A massive armoured blow from the area of Kovel would bypass the Pripet Marshes from the south and strike northwards on Brest; simultaneously a second tank thrust could be made to the north of the Pripet in the direction of Minsk and Bobruisk. Rokossovsky thought that both of these thrusts should be made by his own 1 Belorussian Front, and he urged that, as a preliminary, the armies of Kurochkin's 2 Belorussian Front should be transferred to him. As chance had it, Kurochkin got into difficulties soon afterwards when he lost Kovel, and his front was broken up on 4 April and its formations were transferred to Rokossovsky or withdrawn to the *Stavka* reserve.[9] Stalin liked Rokossovsky's plan and ordered the general staff to examine it, but its sequences and timing were not adopted because of the difficulty in marshalling a large tank force near Kovel. The general concept of a 1 Belorussian Front thrust south of the Pripet from Kovel on Brest, exploiting north-eastwards into Poland, was, however, included in the design of a second offensive. It thus became linked to a Zhukov plan, in which 1 Ukrainian Front was to wheel north on Lvov prior to advancing across southern Poland.[10]

On 12 April Stalin confirmed the general staff plan, based in part on Rokossovsky's and Zhukov's recommendations; the West Front was to be broken up into newly formed 2 and 3 Belorussian Fronts, which, together with 1 Belorussian Front, would provide the main striking force for the Belorussian operation north of the Pripet. The second offensive by 1 Ukrainian Front and the left wing of Rokossovsky's 1 Belorussian Front to the south of the Pripet, would follow immediately after the Belorussian operation.

Petrov had been temporarily restored to favour and given the command of the new 2 Belorussian Front. The Commander of 3 Belorussian Front was to be Cherniakhovsky, a former army commander only thirty-eight years old, promoted by Stalin in response to a recommendation by Zhukov, and appointed a front commander at the beginning of April following a Stalin telephone conversation with Vasilevsky in the Crimea.[11] Since Cherniakhovsky considered that he would need a tank army to smash the enemy reserves in the area of Minsk and Borisov, a conspiracy was entered into whereby Cherniakhovsky was to initiate a formal request to the *Stavka*, on the understanding that the general staff would support it when it was considered. In the event this came to nothing and Stalin was not apprised of Cherniakhovsky's views until the final presentation was made to the dictator.

The general staff was out of favour with Stalin through recommending the suspension of offensive operations over the whole of the Russo-German front, in order to rest the troops and prepare for the summer offensive. At first Stalin said that preparations for the summer operations should not be allowed to interfere with the attacks then in progress, although he was aware that the front commanders were against this course. Not until 15 April would he agree to calling off offensive operations in the north and west; and, since Red Army troops were still making some gains in the south, he instructed the general staff 'to be in no hurry to suspend the attacks, but to bring the Ukrainian fronts over to the defence gradually as they lost momentum'. The last of the orders calling off the offensives was issued on 7 May.[12]

Zhukov was summoned for consultation on 22 April, and, on arriving at the capital, Antonov briefed him on the supply and reinforcement position, at the same time warning him not to reveal to Stalin that he had done so, since the dictator had forbidden that such information be divulged. At the afternoon meeting attended by Zhukov, the general staff and the arms directors, Stalin surprised the meeting by proposing that the 1 Ukrainian Front thrust from the south should provide the opening to the Belorussian campaign, so drawing the enemy reserves southwards; but he quickly dropped the idea when Antonov brought his attention to the good lateral roads available to the enemy. Zhukov and Antonov were ordered to spend the next six days in drawing up outline plans, during which time Vasilevsky and the front commanders were to be asked for their further views.[13] At the beginning of May Zhukov gave up the command of 1 Ukrainian Front to Konev, in order to be free to concentrate his attention on Belorussia. Malinovsky replaced Konev, and Tolbukhin took Malinovsky's vacant command; 4 Ukrainian Front was to be taken into reserve.

Vasilevsky has said that when he was in the Ukraine and the Crimea he was continually consulted by both Stalin and Antonov. The general staff, he said, did not really get down to working out the operational plan of the Belorussian campaign until April, and it was envisaged that Army Group Centre could be destroyed by two mighty blows on the flanks of the salient, one from the north towards Borisov and Minsk, the other from the south to Bobruisk and Minsk. Both he and Zhukov were summoned to Moscow from time to time for talks with Stalin, Antonov being present, but often Stalin discussed the details of individual plans with them by telephone; during these conversations he would refer to talks which he had had with front commanders, 'particularly with Rokossovsky'. During the month of April Vasilevsky was repeatedly reminded by the Supreme Commander that the Ukraine operations must be completed that month, come what may, in order that the Chief of General Staff might devote his full attention to the Belorussian operation. On the night of 29 April, shortly before the successful storming of Sevastopol which ended the fighting in the south, Stalin had a long telephone conversation with Vasilevsky, in which he expressed himself entirely satisfied with future plans and with the progress to date. But then, when the subject passed to a new postponement of the Sevastopol operation by only a few days, Stalin, according to Vasilevsky, 'entirely lost his mental equilibrium'.[14]

If Vasilevsky is to be believed, the liaison between Stalin and himself was close even though he was at that time in the Crimea. Daily, sometimes hourly, consultations went on over the *V Ch* telephone, Stalin asking him for his views on operational planning, reorganization and senior appointments. Vasilevsky gives the credit for the closeness of the relationship between himself and Stalin, and for the efficiency with which business was conducted, to Antonov and the general staff in Moscow, for they briefed him regularly day by day on events in all the battle areas, so that the

Chief of General Staff usually understood the problem before the Supreme Commander consulted him. Vasilevsky shared Shtemenko's high opinion of Antonov's ability, and he praised the systematic efficiency and good order in the general staff, which, he said, still reflected the personality of Shaposhnikov its founder.[15]

It was decided that the first major offensive would be that against Finland, at the same time as the opening of the second front in Western Europe. The great offensive into Belorussia would then begin at the end of the third week in June. As soon as the enemy Army Group Centre was fully engaged, its neighbour to the south, Army Group North Ukraine, was to be attacked south of the Pripet Marshes in the Lvov offensive. Then finally, towards the end of the summer, the Soviet left wing, on the Balkan flank, was to mount another massive campaign into Rumania, Bulgaria and Hungary. In May and June a number of deception measures were undertaken, indicating troop concentrations in the areas of Pskov and Kishinev. Meanwhile all the Soviet tank armies were left in the south.[16]

---

In mid February when the unwilling Meretskov had been transferred to the Karelian Front, Stalin had told him that Frolov had done good work, but that he and his staff had been on the defensive so long that they no longer had the mentality needed to mount an offensive. In any event, the Karelian Front had become a perpetual mendicant (*vechnym prositelem*) always whining for more.[17]

Stalin had still not determined how the Finnish War was to be fought, for, at the end of March, Antonov told Shtemenko to go to the Kuntsevo *dacha*, 'so that the boss might look at the maps and operational plans for the northern flank'. Having studied the maps, Stalin asked questions about the strength and state of the troops there; he walked up and down the room, reasoning with himself while Shtemenko noted down the purport of his ideas. Stalin thought that if the Leningrad Front mounted simultaneous operations in the Karelian Isthmus, then the Karelian Front, in the huge open territories to the north, could strike two operational blows in sequence, the first against the Finns and the second against the Germans.[18]

In the weeks that followed, Stalin's attention was continually occupied with 20 German Army in Lapland, for he was repeatedly to warn Meretskov not to weaken the Red Army forces facing it.[19] Meretskov had the greatest respect for Stalin but little for his own military superiors and subordinates; he was demanding and tactless, and he took a pride in that his own staff found it difficult to work with him. Although closely acquainted with Stalin, he frequently misjudged him.

Meretskov had been at work for nearly three months organizing operations in the far north against the enemy in Lapland when the priorities were suddenly changed by Moscow and he was ordered to prepare an immediate offensive across the Svir against the Finns in Southern Karelia. Meretskov came to the capital on 30 May bringing with him panoramic aerial photographs and a model of the Finnish defences, and he insisted on taking these with him into Stalin's room, against the advice of the general staff who warned him 'that Stalin did not like to be presented with unnecessary material and could not bear predictions about the enemy'. Meretskov made matters worse by introducing his models before making his address, so that he was quickly cut short by Stalin who said that the front commander was hypnotized by the enemy's defences and was trying to frighten the *Stavka* with toys; the dictator was, he said, beginning to have doubts as to whether Meretskov was the man for the task. Meretskov then came out with his request for heavy tank regiments; he was silenced by accusations of blackmail. Yet, when the meeting was about to break up and Stalin's anger had cooled, he wished Meretskov luck and advised him in future not to be afraid of the enemy.[20] Meretskov had always been one of Stalin's favourites.

Meretskov went direct to 7 Army to prepare for the coming attacks, but was recalled to the Kremlin on 9 June for further planning talks. Stalin told him that he could have ten days to complete his preparations, and, as it would be impossible to redeploy the Karelian Front in time, he would be allocated additional outside forces for the operation. Stalin was ready to meet Meretskov's request for two infantry corps and additional tanks, but when Meretskov asked for yet another infantry corps he was subdued by the strong objections from Zhukov and Vasilevsky. After the two marshals had left and Meretskov had accompanied Stalin, at the dictator's invitation, to watch the firework display and gun salute in honour of the Leningrad Front, Stalin told

Meretskov, on parting, that he would in fact let him have the additional infantry corps.[21]

The Leningrad Front's success had been greater than expected for it was already preparing to storm the third and last line of defence near Viborg. On the night of 17 June Stalin spoke by telephone to Govorov, in Vasilevsky's and Antonov's presence, to hear the latest situation report, before discussing with Vasilevsky the objectives to be taken after Viborg. He then rang Meretskov and, after pointing out that Govorov's success must lighten the Karelian Front's task, he demanded that the offensive should start not later than 21 June.[22]

Matters were still not going smoothly for Meretskov. It had been agreed earlier that 7 Army would make its main river crossing below the fifty foot high dam of the Svir-3 hydroelectric station, but after looking at the ground Meretskov had come to the conclusion that he must first control the area of the dam to prevent the enemy opening the flood-gate. In consequence, he introduced certain minor changes to the original plan. Immediately afterwards, he and his front military council were hauled back yet again to the Kremlin, personally to explain their actions. In recounting this incident, Meretskov said that 'it was just like Stalin to call the front commander to Moscow to explain modifications . . . for summonses of this sort were not infrequent'. Stalin insisted on personal contact because, Meretskov suspected, he liked to size up people by talking to them; moreover, in this way he could find out more about the local situation than by reading reports. Stalin had, said Meretskov, a marked ability to acquire knowledge from others, 'so that he learned his military expertise from his generals'. Stalin was closely interested in all policy and general matters, but his weakness, thought Meretskov, was 'that he would, on occasions, go into the minutest details, when experience must have shown him that it was impossible to plan and make contingency arrangements for the entire course of an operation'.[23]

Novikov had been detached to the north to co-ordinate the 200 aircraft of the Baltic Fleet and the 1,000 aircraft of the Leningrad Front. Stalin had earlier asked Golovanov, the Commander of the Long Range Air Force (ADD) directly subordinate to the Supreme Commander, whether night bomber divisions of Il 4 and Tu 3 aircraft might not be used to augment the air support by day. Golovanov thought not, and Stalin had thereupon asked for Novikov's opinion. Novikov, whom even Zhukov characterized as always 'highly optimistic', disagreed with Golovanov and requested Stalin to allocate two long range air divisions to him for daylight use during the Karelian operation, since the Finnish interceptor force was already much weakened. During the battle, when Stalin telephoned asking to be briefed on the air situation, he did not forget to ask Novikov how the two air divisions had fared, and their success established a precedent for the daylight use of ADD formations in a tactical ground support role in Belorussia.[24]

---

The plan for the Soviet Belorussian campaign was based on a double envelopment made on Minsk, which lay over 100 miles in the German rear, the right pincer from the north-east being provided by Cherniakhovsky's 3 Belorussian Front supported on its right flank by Bagramian's 1 Baltic Front, and the left pincer from the south-east being formed by Rokossovsky's 1 Belorussian Front. Meanwhile Petrov's 2 Belorussian Front, which was sandwiched between 1 and 3 Belorussian Fronts, was to make a series of frontal attacks to pin Army Group Centre.

Rokossovsky's plan had been based on two powerful blows and a two-pronged advance, one to the east and one to the west of the Berezina, this unusual solution having been forced on him by the relatively few areas in the Pripet which afforded good going. An author with the odd name of Nepomniashchy, writing in 1964, has described how Stalin disagreed with this dispersion of forces into two tactical blows, and twice ordered the front commander to retire from the Kremlin study to reconsider the matter; Molotov tried to persuade Rokossovsky not to oppose Stalin. But in spite of this, said Nepomniashchy, Rokossovsky would not be moved and it was Stalin who finally gave way.[25] Batov, who was unlikely to have been present, repeated this story, and Rokossovsky himself said that the incident occurred on the night of 22 May.[26] Zhukov, however, says that the incident never happened, 'for the general staff accepted and Stalin authorized the plan without question'.[27] Zhukov is supported in part by Telegin, who was the political member of Rokossovsky's Belorussian Front.[28]

At the time the military opinions on the aims, methods and scope of the Belorussian operation were divided; even now the accounts of the participants still differ.[29] Since the enemy had little tactical and virtually no operational depth in Belorussia, there was little doubt that the breakthrough would be successful, but there was disagreement on what should happen thereafter. According to Shtemenko, the general staff wanted to strike deeply and swiftly into the enemy rear and was opposed even to the use of the word 'encirclement', for it reasoned that a series of envelopment battles would be costly in casualties and time, allowing the enemy sufficient respite to reform his front. This view, however, found little favour with Zhukov.[30] On 23 May Stalin sided with Zhukov when he ruled that the object of the campaign was to be the encirclement and destruction of Army Group Centre. Within the fronts the arguments on tactical detail continued.[31]

Stalin was apparently convinced that the largest armoured formation which could be employed in Belorussia was the tank corps, while in the wooded sectors nothing larger than a brigade or a regiment might be used. Cherniakhovsky, who was himself a tank officer, had urged that he must have a tank army, in addition to independent corps and brigades. The general staff did not care, however, to raise the subject with Stalin.

The first general staff plan for the Belorussian operation had been completed on 14 May and recorded in a short manuscript text, written by Gryzlov, together with a marked map. On 20 May at a preliminary meeting attended by Zhukov and Vasilevsky, who had just returned wounded from the Crimea, Antonov presented the outline of the operation to Stalin, who ordered that Rokossovsky, Cherniakhovsky and Bagramian, together with their military councils, should report to the Kremlin on 22 and 23 May for co-ordinating presentations. Petrov, the Commander of 2 Belorussian Front, was not invited. Stalin called the new operation *Bagration*, after yet another Russian prince and general, the descendant of the *Bagratidae* of the royal house of Georgia.

The *Stavka* meetings on those two days were attended by Zhukov, Vasilevsky, Antonov, Voronov, Novikov, Iakovlev, Vorob'ev, Peresypkin and Khrulev. On 22 May Rokossovsky's military council presented its plans and, since these had been worked out in parallel with the general staff, they were immediately approved by the Supreme Commander. On the following day, however, there were some changes, for Bagramian thought that the operation might have greater success if he attacked westwards towards Polotsk to drive a wedge between Army Groups North and Centre. The proposal was accepted by Stalin.

Cherniakhovsky arrived in Moscow on 24 May, and he and Makarov, the political member, went over their plans with Zhukov and Vasilevsky; these did not take into account the allocation of a tank army. On the following day when the plans were presented to the *Stavka*, the moment appeared propitious to raise the question and Stalin agreed that Rotmistrov's 5 Guards Tank Army should be transferred from Malinovsky to Cherniakhovsky. Cherniakhovsky was to produce a new plan that night. Before dawn, Cherniakhovsky, Makarov and Shtemenko drove out to Stalin's far house on the Dmitrov road, where the dictator listened to their revised plan and confirmed it without comment.[32]

Vasilevsky said that the plans were built up by discussion and amendment, the general staff being ordered to correct and re-correct, each of the corrections being taken back to be confirmed by the Supreme Commander. On 30 May Stalin confirmed what was believed to be the final plan, and the date of the start of the offensive was provisionally set as 19 June. That evening, Stalin, as he had done frequently on such occasions in the past, emphasized that since the central planning was complete, it was the task of the GKO, the *Stavka* and the general staff, to go out into the field and help the commanders to get the troops ready. The dictator thought that there were quite enough people in the general staff and Commissariat of Defence for day to day work and would prefer that Zhukov and Vasilevsky did not outstay (*zasizhivalis'*) their welcome in the capital.[33] Zhukov would be responsible, as the *Stavka* representative, for Rokossovsky's 1 Belorussian Front making the main thrust in the south, while Vasilevsky would co-ordinate Bagramian's and Cherniakhovsky's offensive in the north. Before leaving for the fronts, Zhukov and Vasilevsky visited the dictator again to receive his final instructions; he warned them both that they must keep him closely informed of all developments.[34]

Shtemenko had been appointed as the *Stavka* representative with 2 Belorussian Front, being responsible in the first instance to Zhukov, and it was his unpleasant duty to replace, on the Supreme Commander's orders, its commander Petrov by Zakharov.

According to Shtemenko, Stalin was prejudiced against Petrov, who was unfortunate in having Mekhlis as the political member of his military council. Gorbatov described Mekhlis at about this time as being 'subdued, but still indefatigable, severe, inflexible, and extreme, and so mistrustful that he would not allow anyone else to write his messages for him'. Mekhlis continued, however, to write private letters to Stalin, and in one of these, so Stalin told Antonov and Shtemenko, he had described Petrov as being flabby and incapable and always under the doctor's care.[35]

Extracts from both Zhukov's and Vasilevsky's time-tables and diaries during this preparatory phase have since been published. On 5 June Zhukov was with Rokossovsky discussing the plans with heads of arms, and visiting the army commanders; the next morning he made his telephone report to Stalin asking him to ensure that Kaganovich and Khrulev completed the transportation plan in good time. On 6 June he set out to see the forward corps in Gorbatov's sector and, for the second time that day, reported the situation to the dictator. On 7 June, accompanied by his entourage of the front military council and members of the staff, he motored from Rogachev, arriving unannounced in the forward area of Batov's army. If Batov's 1962 account is to be believed, the hectoring Zhukov was much out of temper and entirely unreasonable, for without good cause he summarily ordered the removal of a corps commander and the committal of the commander of an infantry division to a penal company.[36] On 8 June Zhukov, accompanied by the artilleryman Iakovlev, toured 2 Belorussian Front forward area, together with Zakharov and Shtemenko.

On 10 June Zhukov and Rokossovsky were again in the forward areas and, when the Deputy Supreme Commander spoke to Stalin that day, he suggested that the whole of the long range air force should be allotted for operational and tactical air support in Belorussia and, when Stalin agreed to this, asked that Novikov and Golovanov should report to him by 11 June. On 11 June Zhukov was still complaining about the supply deficiencies. So day followed day, telephone reports being made direct to Stalin twice daily. On 19 June the conversations took a more optimistic note, Zhukov considering that preparations should be complete by 21 June. On 19 June Novikov, Khudiakov and Golovanov, together with the commanders of the two tactical air armies, began to prepare a joint artillery air support programme with Iakovlev, covering Rokossovsky's and Zakharov's fronts.[37]

The arrangements were excellent, but, according to Shtemenko, the two marshals, Zhukov and Vasilevsky, had taken everything for themselves. Vasilevsky had been assigned 350 long range aircraft as 3 Belorussian Front's share and 2 Belorussian Front got nothing. Shtemenko complained repeatedly to Zhukov, who eventually made what Shtemenko called some paper allocations, but as no representative of the long range air force ever appeared at Zakharov's headquarters, no use could be made of them. In the event, Zhukov was granted permission to postpone Rokossovsky's offensive by one day, as a result of which a number of his air formations were switched to support Zakharov for a period of twenty-four hours.[38]

Vasilevsky, who was with the 3 Belorussian and 1 Baltic Fronts, had with him Iakovlev's and Novikov's deputies, Chistiakov and Falaleev. Like Zhukov, he spent his time in visiting fronts and armies, and had long telephone conferences with Stalin. On 8 and 9 June Vasilevsky expressed his disquiet at the slow rate of arrival of reinforcements; on 11 June he spoke to Kaganovich telling him that the reinforcement and supply build-up and the move of Rotmistrov's army from the south must be completed by 18 June, and on the same day he warned Stalin that it was possible that the fronts would not be ready on time. Rotmistrov himself had come on ahead and it was, presumably, because of his reconnaissance reports that Vasilevsky began to have doubts about the wisdom of using the Orsha axis, and he reported these to Moscow on 17 June, suggesting that the tank army should be used north of Orsha where the enemy's defences were weaker. In reply Stalin made Vasilevsky responsible for selecting the axis and the timing for Rotmistrov's force. But until these were satisfactorily resolved Stalin proposed to keep 5 Guards Tank Army under his own hand by retaining it in the *Stavka* reserve.[39]

On 17 June Vasilevsky was still complaining about the lack of schedule on the railways, but matters improved thereafter, Stalin, as Shtemenko worded it, 'apparently having managed to exert his influence over the transport people'. That day Vasilevsky was recalled to Moscow and he and Antonov went to the Kremlin that night. After a discussion on Finland, Stalin turned to Belorussia.

First he told Antonov to report on the latest information coming from Normandy; and, after what Vasilevsky called 'an exchange of opinions', Stalin decided on the evening of 18 June as the latest report time for the preparations of the Belorussian offensive.

On the night of 18 June Vasilevsky and Antonov returned to Stalin's office, to make the final general staff presentation. Zhukov was still in Belorussia. During Vasilevsky's briefing, 'Stalin, as always, interested himself in the detail concerning the disposition, preparedness and security of the troops, and even in the working of the front command'. Stalin decided to postpone the offensive until 23 June. But then, while Vasilevsky was still in Moscow, Zhukov asked the Supreme Commander that Rokossovsky should be allowed a further day's preparation. Stalin asked for Vasilevsky's opinion. The Chief of General Staff consulted Cherniakhovsky and Bagramian on the telephone, and the three of them came to the conclusion that the postponement in the south would benefit the main offensive in the north since they, like Shtemenko, hoped to get some of Zhukov's share of Golovanov's long range air force for the interdiction tasks of 23 June.[40]

Peresypkin had been sent by Stalin out to the fronts, and he has since given some detail of the signal facilities of Cherniakhovsky's 3 Belorussian Front headquarters, based on a fleet of nineteen vehicles carrying Baudôt and ST-35 teleprint telegraph, telephone and radio, together with short wave radio telephone.[41] It was at about this time that the high frequency (*V Ch*) telephone appears to have been used on a radio link, for Konev has said that he was given 'a mobile *V Ch* station with a direct channel', to the Moscow circuit.[42]

On 22 June Stalin called Konev and Krainiukov to Moscow to outline their plans for the offensive into south-east Poland, and Krainiukov has described how members of the Politburo, the *Stavka* and the general staff had been summoned to Stalin's office to hear the presentation. Neither Zhukov nor Vasilevsky appears to have been there. Konev explained how he proposed to strike Army Group North Ukraine two major blows, a double envelopment aimed at encircling and destroying the enemy grouping near Brody. This plan had already been accepted in principle by Stalin and the general staff. Stalin, however, suddenly harked back to Zhukov's original concept, wanting to know why two separate blows should be aimed at the enemy; perhaps it wouldn't come off; why not one mighty shattering blow at Lvov. Stalin walked up and down reasoning with himself before finally accepting Konev's plan. The discussion continued and, according to Krainiukov, Stalin did not press his views; he closed the meeting by telling the military council that he would want to hear the plan again in its final form after the detail had been worked out, and he reminded the front commander that he was personally responsible for the success of the operation, which must be conducted without a flaw (*bezuprechno*).[43]

The Belorussian operation is said to have been mounted by 120 divisions of the 166 divisions forming the four fronts, and numbered over 5,000 tanks and 6,000 aircraft, not including the 1,000 aircraft of Golovanov's long range air force.[44] Busch's Army Group Centre comprised 38 infantry and two panzer divisions.[45] The violence of the Red Air Force bombing and machine-gun attacks paralyzed Army Group Centre so that the Red Army success was immediate and, since Hitler forbade any withdrawal by German troops, the Soviet front commanders retained the initiative throughout. By 28 June Soviet tanks were already over the Berezina and to the west of Lepel, and about 100,000 enemy had been cut off to the east of Minsk. Between 5 and 11 July the Soviet command began the destruction of this great pocket, without halting the rapid westward movement of its tank forces, so that, of the whole of Army Group Centre, only the wings remained, leaving a gaping hole in the German front; about 28 German divisions had been lost and the total casualties were put as high as 300,000 men.[46] The defeat was as great as that of Stalingrad.

On 6 July Burrows and members of the British Military Mission were taken on a three day visit to 3 Belorussian Front, the only time that Burrows had been permitted to go into a war theatre. The Soviet intention, so Burrows told London, was to impress on their allies the magnitude of the victory. Burrows had been for long a severe critic of Soviet obstructionism and was contemptuous of Slavin, the general staff liaison officer; he was all the more surprised, therefore, by the friendliness of Vasilevsky, whom he had not met before. Vasilevsky said that the Soviet success had been mainly due to the Red air force and artillery but he detected some deterioration in the fighting value of the Germans, who had 'a blockhouse mentality' and were nervous of their rear because of the partisans. The captured senior German officers with whom Burrows talked, said they had been surprised at the skill of the Soviet High Command. Burrows, an experienced observer, was amazed at 'the considerable disorder' in which the Red Army advanced, but, so well had Slavin done his work and so reticent were his hospitable Russian hosts, that Burrows was unaware of the appointments held by many of the officers with whom he talked; he conjectured, rightly, that F. F. Kuznetsov might be the Director of Military Intelligence, but he was convinced that the military commissar Makarov was Cherniakhovsky's chief of staff, so much was he in the front commander's confidence.[47]

Further to the south, on 6 July, Zhukov was with Batov's army, abusing its military council, so Batov said, in case Vasilevsky should be in Vilna before Zhukov had taken Baranovichi. The next day Stalin telephoned, ordering the Deputy Supreme Commander to return to Moscow.

Shortly after midday on 8 July Zhukov and Antonov joined Stalin at his summer *dacha*. Stalin wanted Zhukov's and Antonov's opinion as to whether Konev and Rokossovsky were strong enough to reach the Vistula unaided. Zhukov thought that the task was well within their capabilities and he suggested that Konev's front, which numbered 1,200,000 men, 2,000 tanks and 3,000 aircraft, was unnecessarily large, and could afford to transfer formations to Vasilevsky so that he might cut off Army Group North against the Baltic and occupy East Prussia. Vasilevsky, according to Zhukov, had already made a similar request to the Supreme Commander. Stalin, however, took the view that the enemy would defend East Prussia to the last and that Vasilevsky might get bogged down there. It would be preferable, he thought, to make sure of over-running the area of Lvov, and what he called the eastern regions of Poland.[48] Presumably the obtaining of a foothold in south-east Poland was, for political reasons, of greater priority.

Zhukov had been made responsible for the offensive south of the Pripet, the co-ordination of Konev's Lvov operation with the thrust of Rokossovsky's left wing from the area of Kovel. On 9 July Stalin and Zhukov jointly considered Rokossovsky's plan to strike with his reinforced left to the south of the marshes, destroy the enemy Lublin grouping, and advance on a broad front securing bridgeheads across the Vistula, at the same time thrusting north-wards on Brest, round the western edge of the marshes. Then, on 10 July, Zhukov studied Konev's plan before leaving the next morning for 1 Ukrainian Front, where he sited his command group near the inter-front boundary between Konev and Rokossovsky. The customary higher commander and staff planning rehearsals were held in the area of Kovel immediately before the attack, these being attended by Zhukov, Rokossovsky, Novikov and Peresypkin.[49]

Konev's attacks began on 13 July and four days later, when Rokossovsky joined in the general offensive, Konev's three tank armies had already entrapped a German corps of over 40,000 men at Brody. By 21 July, however, Konev's tanks were unable to make any ground towards Lvov, and the next day Zhukov agreed with Konev that a tank army should outflank Lvov from the north. Meanwhile the troops on Konev's right flank continued to move north-westwards on Sandomir.

In the early morning of 23 July, Konev told Zhukov that he had just received a telephone call from Stalin, asking what he and Zhukov 'were up to (*zateiali*) going for Sandomir'. The priority task, said Stalin, was to take Lvov. Zhukov was to telephone Stalin. The opportunity presented itself almost immediately afterwards when Rokossovsky's armoured troops took Lublin, Zhukov hastening to report the good news. Stalin was still resting in his Kremlin flat, but had already heard about Lublin. Khrush-chev, said Stalin, had been opposed to Zhukov's and Konev's tank raid and had told him about it. The whole trouble, continued Stalin, was that the two marshals were in too much of a hurry to get to the Vistula – after all it would not run away from them. They had better take Lvov first.[50] The general staff, so Shtemenko subsequently said, shared Stalin's view that Zhukov's tendency to undertake broad but inadequately supported offensives had to be checked.[51]

On 27 July, when the enemy had evaucated Lvov, a *Stavka* directive ordered Konev to secure a bridgehead over the Vistula by nightfall the next day, prior to seizing Sandomir. On 30 July Konev was across the Vistula having covered over 130 miles in nineteen days. Rokossovsky's advance immediately to the north,

**NORTHERN EUROPE**
(Frontiers as in 1923)

0       200

Miles

had been even more rapid. The Pripet Marshes had been left far behind and the forward troops were within twenty miles of Warsaw. The long advance from Galicia into southern Poland had, however, given rise to a long and exposed Carpathian flank to the south of 1 Ukrainian Front. At the end of July when Konev had asked for a separate command to take over responsibility for his two flanking armies in the south, Stalin had replied that, as Petrov and the 4 Ukrainian Front headquarters were held in the *Stavka* reserve, they could report on 4 August and become operational the next day.[52] Mekhlis was ordered to join the new headquarters.

On 27 July there had been a *Stavka* meeting to discuss future strategy, attended by Stalin, Zhukov, Vasilevsky, Antonov, Shtemenko and Gryzlov; the question of an advance into East Prussia was brought up yet again. Stalin ruled that operations in the north should be undertaken systematically and in sequence, the area of the Baltic States being encircled and chopped off from East Prussia, following which East Prussia would be enveloped and cut off from the rest of Germany. Stalin told the meeting that several generals had complained about those *Stavka* representatives 'who took the conduct of operations out of the hands of the front commanders'; Zhukov gave his opinion that *Stavka* representatives should have the right to do this, and, as Shtemenko commented, 'Zhukov, with his powerful personality, did so anyway'. A compromise was announced in a special decree of 29 July, whereby only Zhukov and Vasilevsky were permitted to take over control of field operations.[53]

Lvov, as the western allies were yet to learn, was regarded in Moscow as Ukrainian and not Polish; Lublin, however, was recognized as being inside Poland, and there, as Rokossovsky said, the Polish National Liberation Committee assumed control. On 1 August Bor-Komorowski, the Commander-in-Chief of the London supported Polish Home Army (AK), began the ill-fated insurrection against the Germans in Warsaw. The AK leaders in the areas held by the Red Army were being hunted down and arrested, but Stalin was apparently unwilling to involve the Red Army in openly fighting Polish patriots. At first Stalin pretended to his western allies that there was no rising in Warsaw, then that the AK was friendly to the Germans, and finally, claimed that its

leaders were both criminal and irresponsible in needlessly sacri-
ficing Polish lives. On 16 August Moscow informed the British
Government that it proposed to have nothing to do with the affair,
and, three days later, Moscow refused a British and United States
request for air-landing facilities on Soviet soil so that the insurgents
might be supplied by air with arms, ammunition and medical
supplies. On 22 August in a message to Churchill Stalin referred
to the AK as a group of criminals.[54]

After Soviet protestations of friendliness and gratitude, the
local Vilna AK leaders had been invited on 17 July to a staff
conference with Cherniakhovsky, only three days before Deane
and the United States mission arrived there. The Poles were not
seen again. Yet Rokossovsky complained that the AK leaders
near Lublin were shy of his offers of help. Though the Kremlin
protested afterwards that it had been informed of the rising only
after it had begun, it is also true that it had dropped manifesto
leaflets from the air, inciting the Poles to take up arms against the
Germans and that, on 29 July, Moscow radio was calling on Warsaw to do the same.[55]

Rokossovsky, who knew of the uprising on 2 August, has absolved
the Soviet leadership of responsibility simply by postulating in a
single sentence that the problem was his own, saying that 'certain
critics in the western press did at one time accuse the 1 Belorussian
Front and its commander of deliberately not supporting the
Warsaw insurgents'.[56] If Rokossovsky is to be believed 'Stalin
wanted to give all possible help to the insurgents and ease their
plight'. An earlier communist view of capitalist Poland was that
expressed in Lenin's instructions to Skliansky.[57] Time was to
show that Stalin had no intention of restoring the former Polish
government, for, as he told Zhukov in March 1945, the Soviet
Union 'could not permit Churchill to establish a *bourgeois* alien
Poland on its borders'. Concern over the fate of the AK supporters
was hardly likely to move a man who had already purged Poland
in 1939, destroying or transporting its leaders, intellectuals, priests,
landowners and much of its working class and peasantry, in their
tens of thousands, and who intended to do it yet again as soon as
Poland was overrun.

At the end of September Stalin ordered that Warsaw should be
outflanked from the north, much in the same way as Tukhachevsky

had attempted in 1920. But the enemy artillery was so strong in the area that Red Army casualties mounted rapidly, forcing Rokossovsky to cancel the offensive; he immediately informed Stalin by telephone and the dictator confirmed the decision. Zhukov has a different version in that he said that it was he who telephoned the Supreme Commander and asked for permission to halt the offensive. Zhukov's report, or the way he delivered it, angered Stalin, and he ordered Zhukov and Rokossovsky to report to him in Moscow the next day. Molotov and Antonov were present there, and, according to Zhukov, the dictator was restless and displeased. He sat silent, leaving it to Molotov to question the wisdom of going over to the defence when faced with a beaten enemy.

When Zhukov was asked for other proposals for an offensive against Warsaw, he suggested encircling the capital from the southwest. Stalin became heated and told them to go to the waiting room 'and think some more'. Twenty minutes later Stalin recalled them to say that 1 Belorussian Front might go over to the defensive; future plans would be discussed later. Zhukov said that he and Rokossovsky left in silence, 'going their separate ways, each preoccupied with his own thoughts'. The next day Zhukov learned that he was to cease being the *Stavka* representative and coordinator of fronts and was to take over the command of 1 Belorussian Front from Rokossovsky, a decision which he associated in part with Stalin's displeasure.[58] Rokossovsky mentions nothing about this meeting but says that Stalin did not inform him about his transfer until 12 November.[59]

It is not impossible that Zhukov's account may have been meant to emphasize to the present day Polish reader that Stalin did his utmost for the Warsaw insurgents. On the other hand Zhukov may have been removed from his post as a *Stavka* representative, as he said, due to a difference of opinion with Stalin, not necessarily that which he described, for it can be deduced from his memoirs that he remained sensitive about the incident which was a blow to his dignity and self-esteem. He has assured his readers that he remained the Deputy Supreme Commander, which was indeed the case, and that all other *Stavka* representative posts were abolished at this time, this latter statement being untrue. For it was not until the end of the year that Stalin asked his commanders and staffs whether they considered the use of *Stavka* representatives still necessary. Zhukov, by then a front commander, replied that they were not, as the shortening frontages meant that fronts could easily be co-ordinated from Moscow. When the same question was put to Antonov, he 'as usual', said Shtemenko, rang Vasilevsky for his views. Vasilevsky thought that *Stavka* representatives should be retained in certain circumstances where the local conditions were complicated, particularly to the flanks in the area of the Baltic and in the Balkans. Stalin agreed with Vasilevsky, and Vasilevsky, Govorov and Timoshenko remained as *Stavka* representatives throughout the early months of 1945.[60]

Vasilevsky had remained in the area of the Baltic from June 1944, responsible for the co-ordination and supervision of 1 and 2 Baltic Fronts and 3 Belorussian Front. At the beginning of July when it appeared that the Red Army formations which had thrust forward in a great salient to the Lithuanian frontier were about to envelop the enemy Army Group North, the Supreme Commander issued a series of directives. Govorov's Leningrad and Maslennikov's 3 Baltic Fronts were to attack on both sides of Lake Peipus into Estonia, while Eremenko's 2 Baltic Front was to advance due west, supporting Bagramian's wheeling movement in the direction of Riga. On 6 July Stalin signed the directive to 3 Baltic Front, but two days later, when the general staff were making the customary briefing report, Stalin decided that as no one had been out to see Maslennikov, whom he described as a young commander with an inexperienced staff, Shtemenko should go, taking Iakovlev and Vorozheikin with him.[61] Eremenko and Maslennikov began to make ground westwards, but the situation was changed yet again when, on 27 July, Bagramian took Siauliai, a main road and rail communication centre, midway between Riga and Tilsit. A *Stavka* telephone and written directive was then sent to Bagramian ordering him to turn his main forces northwards on Riga, but, at the same time, to continue westwards with a subsidiary thrust on Memel to sever the coastal railway between Tilsit and Riga. By 31 July the Red Army reached the Bay of Riga near Tukums, but was driven back again when an enemy counter-attack re-established a narrow coastal corridor reconnecting Army Group North with Kurland.

Many Soviet historians consider that in its strategic concept the Baltic operation was one of the largest and most important of the

1944 campaigns.[62] Stalin was of the opinion that the Baltic area should be cleared before the main thrust on the Warsaw-Berlin axis could begin, because he regarded Army Group North as a threat to his flank.[63] Bagramian's rapid success presented the first opportunity to encircle Army Group North and pin it against the sea east of the Bay of Riga, and in order that Vasilevsky might devote his attention to this task he was ordered temporarily to relinquish his responsibility for Cherniakhovsky's 3 Belorussian Front and concentrate on co-ordinating the three Baltic fronts in a renewal of the offensive on Riga. The offensive, which began on 14 September, made good progress and, so Moscow believed, had some influence on Finland's decision on 19 September finally to withdraw from the war. The Germans began to pull back from the Narva area, Tallinn was evacuated on 22 September, and four days later the whole of the Estonian coast had been cleared.

By 24 September it had become obvious that the enemy was withdrawing the bulk of his forces from Estonia to Kurland, and in consequence Stalin no longer showed interest in closing the Riga gap. Since the enemy was also trying to envelop Bagramian's right flank from the west, Stalin decided to shift the main thrust in a 90 degree arc due west on Memel, both to envelop the enveloper and to cut off the whole of Army Group North in Kurland. Bagramian's 1 Baltic and Cherniakhovsky's 3 Belorussian Fronts were to provide the main force. Vasilevsky reassumed control as the *Stavka* representative of 3 Belorussian Front on 1 October and gave up Eremenko's and Malennikov's fronts to Govorov, who henceforth was responsible to Stalin as the *Stavka* representative for clearing the area of the Baltic States and islands, using 2 and 3 Baltic Fronts and his own Leningrad Front.[64]

According to Shtemenko, Stalin took a close interest in the preparation of the Memel operation, discussing with Vasilevsky all details concerning the grouping of the forces and the deception measures required to conceal the movement of nearly half a million men, 10,000 guns and 1,300 tanks from Bagramian's right to his left, over distances of up to 150 miles.[65] The operation began on 5 October and, after a six day engagement, Vol'sky's tank army reached the sea; Memel was invested and Army Group North was finally isolated in Kurland.

Further to the north Govorov had been ordered by a *Stavka*

**27** Shtemenko *(left)*, head of the operations directorate together with Antonov, the first deputy chief of general staff.

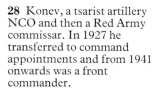

**28** Konev, a tsarist artillery NCO and then a Red Army commissar. In 1927 he transferred to command appointments and from 1941 onwards was a front commander.

**29** Purkaev, a Mordvin, was a tsarist junior officer of infantry who entered the Red Army in 1918. In 1939 he was military attaché in Berlin. Throughout the war he commanded armies and fronts.

**30** Rotmistrov entered the Red Army in 1919 becoming an instructor in mechanized warfare in 1935. In the war he was an armoured leader of note.

directive of 6 October to reduce the Riga enclave, then about 30 miles in depth. Govorov, whom Shtemenko described as grim, reticent and sombre, was, apparently, held in high regard by the troops; his career had not been easy, for it had always been held against him that he was once a White Guard artillery officer with Kolchak; in 1936 he had not been allowed to complete the course at the General Staff Academy, and it was said that in 1940 he was again under a cloud and in danger of arrest. In 1942, however, he was accepted into the party without candidate status, presumably at Stalin's nomination, and between 1943 and October 1944 he had risen rapidly in rank from colonel-general to marshal of the Soviet Union. In the field, south of Riga, he made a strong and favourable impression on Kazakov, the Commander of 10 Guards Army, by his thoughtful and taciturn manner and by the firm way in which he handled Eremenko, the Commander of 2 Baltic Front, refusing to allow him to reinforce defeat and insisting that Kazakov's army be regrouped south of the West Dvina.[66] Riga was cleared of the enemy who withdrew westwards into Kurland. Immediately afterwards, on 16 October, Maslennikov's 3 Baltic Front was disbanded.

Further attempts by the two Baltic Fronts to reduce the enemy Kurland group, consisting of no fewer than 26 German divisions, failed, and the Soviet High Command was forced to turn its attention to more important theatres and accept the existence of this isolated enemy force far in its rear. The enemy Kurland group remained in being until after the end of the war.

---

A department had been formed within the general staff responsible for publishing regular training bulletins summarizing 'the lessons learned at the front during the course of the fighting', and Stalin studied each copy as soon as it appeared. Its editor was Vechny, who was conscious that he had to rehabilitate himself in Stalin's eyes for the spring 1942 *débâcle* in the Crimea, where he had been Kozlov's chief of staff.

It was by his careful reading of this military periodical that Stalin became aware in the autumn of 1944, that Voronov had issued two regulations (*ustavy*) concerning field and anti-aircraft artillery, both countersigned by Zhukov, without the dictator's knowledge – Stalin called it 'without the authority of the *Stavka*'. When Stalin queried the matter with the general staff, Antonov knew nothing and was given two days to investigate. When the general staff report was made to the Politburo, Stalin's irritation was increased when he realized that his two illustrious marshals did not understand the difference between an *ustav* and a *prikaz*.

According to Shtemenko, who was present at the time, Stalin thought the matter over as he walked up and down. Then, turning to the Politburo members, he said that an order must be given out, but, 'since it would be improper for the general staff to do this to two generals of such rank', the Politburo itself would perform the duty. He then dictated an order, extracts from which are shown below.

> One. Marshal Zhukov, without sufficient checking, without calling for or consulting the people at the front, and without notifying the *Stavka*, confirmed and enacted the *ustav*. [At this point Stalin included definitions explaining the difference between an *ustav* and a *prikaz*.]
>
> Two. I reprove Chief Marshal of Artillery Comrade Voronov for his light-hearted attitude to artillery regulations.
>
> Three. I make it incumbent upon Marshal Zhukov to display circumspection in deciding serious questions.

Stalin then appointed a commission under Bulganin to investigate the matter.[67]

-----

Rumania had for long wanted to leave the war. In April and May 1944, secret peace talks were held with the Soviet Union's repretives in Cairo, and these contacts appear to have continued in Stockholm and in Bessarabia throughout the summer. Bucharest was not, however, a free agent, as there were 360,000 German field troops inside Rumania, forming, together with about 450,000 Rumanians, Friessner's Army Group South Ukraine. Since the Rumanian monarch and an influential part of the political and military leadership intended that Rumania should seek an armistice, there was little question of prosecuting the war with vigour. This political and military background, and the fact that Rumanian resistance was not to be reckoned with, are not, however, admitted in Soviet historical accounts, all of which depict the August 1944

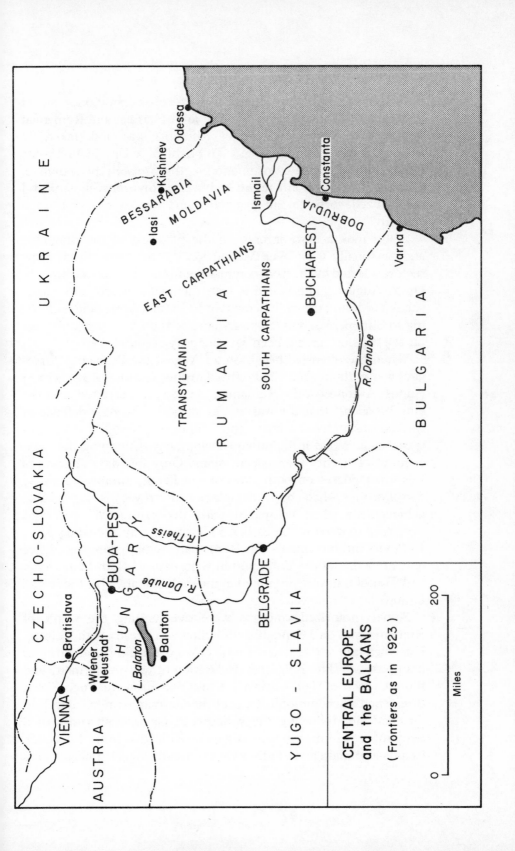

CENTRAL EUROPE
and the BALKANS

( Frontiers as in 1923 )

0          200

Miles

UKRAINE

AUSTRIA

VIENNA

Bratislava

Wiener Neustadt

CZECHO-SLOVAKIA

HUNGARY

BUDA-PEST

L.Balaton

Balaton

R. Danube

R. Theiss

YUGO - SLAVIA

BELGRADE

TRANSYLVANIA

RUMANIA

SOUTH CARPATHIANS

EAST CARPATHIANS

Iasi

MOLDAVIA

BESSARABIA

Kishinev

Odessa

Ismail

BUCHAREST

R. Danube

DOBRUDJA

Constanta

Varna

BULGARIA

campaign as a well planned and ably executed operation, a model of a victory of Soviet arms over the joint German and Rumanian forces. The Soviet invasion of Rumania was undertaken by Malinovsky's 2 Ukrainian and Tolbukhin's 3 Ukrainian Fronts under Timoshenko's co-ordination as the *Stavka* representative. Together the two fronts numbered over 90 divisions, six tank and mechanized corps, in all 939,000 men, 1,400 tanks and 1,700 aircraft.[68]

Stalin took a close interest in the planning of the campaign and personally went over Malinovsky's plans, even altering the sectors selected by the front commander for the main breakthrough. On 21 August Stalin is said to have dictated a directive to Timoshenko ordering the encirclement of 6 German Army, and, according to Shtemenko, only 24 hours later sent off his congratulations on the mission having been satisfactorily accomplished.[69]

When the offensive began on 20 August the Rumanian forces gave way without a fight and refused to obey German orders. On 23 August Antonescu, the Rumanian dictator, was arrested, and the king broadcast that the war was at an end. The Axis defence in Moldavia rapidly fell apart and Malinovsky's and Tolbukhin's spearheads joined in a double envelopment entrapping the main element of twenty German divisions. Only five days afterwards this great pocket on both sides of the Pruth, numbering nearly 200,000 men, had been completely destroyed, a remarkable achievement when compared with the protracted operations necessary to destroy the earlier 6 German Army at Stalingrad.[70] In Soviet military annals this Rumanian victory takes precedence only after that at the Volga and in Belorussia.[71] Both Malinovsky and Tolbukhin were promoted to the rank of marshal of the Soviet Union.

Soviet motorized columns were overrunning the whole of Rumania and, on 8 September, Zhukov was already with Tolbukhin when the 3 Ukrainian Front crossed the Bulgarian frontier unopposed.[72] The Bulgarian declaration of war on Germany and the approach of Tolbukhin's 3 Ukrainian Front to Yugo-Slavia threatened the communications of the German Army Group E in Greece, and, following the widespread partisan uprisings of 8 September, German troops began to withdraw from the Greek islands and mainland. Tolbukhin eventually wheeled northwards coming up on the left flank of Malinovsky's 2 Ukrainian Front which was moving north-westwards from Rumania into Hungarian occupied Transylvania. On 29 August Stalin signed a directive to Petrov's 4 Ukrainian Front, which was facing 1 Hungarian Army in the East Carpathian foothills, ordering it to go over to 'a firm defence, based on three entrenched systems echeloned to a depth of not less than twenty to twenty-five miles, with strong corps, army and front reserves in the main sectors'.[73] Since Petrov was by then flanking the withdrawing remnants of Friessner's forces and was well placed to put pressure on the enemy held Szekler salient from the north while Malinovsky attacked it from the south, 4 Ukrainian Front was, shortly afterwards, transferred to Timoshenko's control.

On 1 October a Hungarian delegation arrived secretly in Moscow to sign an armistice, but three days later the Germans became aware of the negotiations and seized all Hungarian communication centres. On 16 October, the day after Horthy had broadcast that the war was at an end, the Hungarian government was arrested and removed to Germany, for Hitler had decided to hold Hungary and the Transylvanian plateau for its oil, manganese and bauxite. In no other theatre was the German resistance so bitter in this final stage of the war.

Timoshenko's offensive, which had started on 6 October, moved across the Hungarian plain, reaching, on 28 October, a point about forty miles south of Budapest. On that day Mekhlis sent a personal telegram to Stalin from 4 Ukrainian Front telling him that the Hungarian forces were totally demoralized, from which Stalin concluded that the capital could be easily occupied. Together with the general staff he drew up a hasty plan whereby the German right, between the Theiss and the Danube, which was held by elements of 3 Hungarian Army still in the Axis service, was to be attacked. Stalin transmitted the plan to Malinovsky by telephone and demanded the immediate taking of Budapest; and, said Shtemenko, 'since Antonov was not aware of the local conditions, he was unable to represent to Stalin that Mekhlis's report was false'.[74] Malinovsky had asked if the offensive could be put off for five or six days, so that it might be properly prepared, but was told that he was to attack on the morrow. It was necessary, said Stalin, whatever the cost, to take the Hungarian capital immediately for political reasons.[75] Malinovsky then suggested a two day postponement until a mechanized corps could be brought up on 1 November; but Stalin would not allow even this, and he accused the front commander of stubbornness, and, after ordering him 'categorically to attack Budapest', abruptly hung up. A few minutes later Antonov rang Malinovsky, asking for the time of the attack, in order that he might report it to the Supreme Commander. Malinovsky named the date as 29 October and he subsequently blamed Stalin for the ill-judged haste which, although it brought Red Army troops to within a few miles of the city outskirts, failed to take the capital.[76]

The general staff soon came to the conclusion that Malinovsky's appreciation of the local situation was the correct one, but, said Shtemenko, 'as the decision to attack from the Theiss was made personally by Stalin, no one could alter it'. But Antonov suggested that Malinovsky should put his case to the Supreme Commander on 4 November and he promised to give it general staff support. This, however, availed Malinovsky nothing, for Stalin merely demanded that the offensive be renewed by not later than 7 November, and in a written directive he laid down the mechanized-cavalry group's tasks. Not until 24 November, following the receipt of a report from Timoshenko, would Stalin agree to call off the attacks in favour of an offensive which was to encircle Budapest from the north.[77] This new operation was to be made in conjunction with Tolbukhin's 3 Ukrainian Front which was by then entering South Hungary from Yugo-Slavia.

# II
# The Year 1945

Since Stalin had directed that Antonov should be the principal speaker when the Soviet military plans were presented to Churchill and Eden during their mid October Moscow visit, Antonov's draft was sent down to Kuntsevo to be checked and corrected. The dictator disagreed with Antonov's description of the aims of Soviet strategy, and he began to rewrite the offending paragraphs. The Soviet Union, he told Shtemenko, had a primary interest in occupying and holding Hungary as the centre of Europe; let us convince the allies, he continued, that we are much stronger on this Balkan flank than we really are; and we will tell them that the basis of our strategy in this theatre is to get into Germany from the south as quickly as possible, by first smashing Hungary.[1]

Antonov was particularly reticent in the presence of foreigners, but, on 14 October, Brooke found him most friendly and communicative. Antonov explained how the Red Army forces had been attacking on the Baltic and Balkan flanks where the going was softer, and how the capitulation of Hungary might open up possibilities for attacks on Germany from the south.[2]

That same evening the British delegation, together with Harriman and Deane, attended a military presentation in Stalin's Kremlin conference room. Brooke described to the meeting the allied operations in Europe and Burma, and Deane gave an address covering the Pacific War. This was followed by a description of operations in the Russo-German theatres, given by Antonov, who, according to Eden, was lucid and fluent but always looking to Stalin for confirmation.[3] He was continually interrupted by

Stalin, who, in Deane's view, was determined to impress Churchill with the tremendous accomplishments of the Red Army. Eventually Antonov's caution in revealing Red Army plans seemed to irritate Stalin, who took the pointer from him and outlined the proposed Soviet operations.[4] It was Stalin, whom Ismay described as 'much on the ball', who answered most of the questions put by the allied delegations.[5]

At six o'clock the next evening, when the talks were resumed, Stalin told the meeting that the Soviet Union would deploy 60 divisions in the Far East, 30 more than were already there, and it would take three months to do this after the war with Germany was ended. In reply to a question from Harriman, Stalin said that the Soviet Union would go to war against Japan three months after Germany's defeat, provided that the United States would assist in building up the necessary reserve supplies and provided that 'the political aspects of the Soviet Union's participation had been clarified'. He agreed that the Petropavlovsk naval base and airfields in the maritime provinces should be put at the disposal of the United States forces, but made it clear that the Americans would have to use the Pacific and not the Trans-Siberian route.[6]

Brooke asked Antonov whether the 60 Red Army divisions could be maintained by the Trans-Siberian railway, and said subsequently that 'Antonov undoubtedly knew the answer but was not certain what Stalin would require him to say'. Antonov looked at Stalin for guidance, but got no help; at a loss, he said that the railway could supply the force, and he was at once brushed aside by Stalin who launched into what Brooke called 'an astounding presentation of technical railway detail': the railway capacity was limited to 36 pairs of trains a day of which five pairs were required for railway maintenance and five for the civilian population in the maritime province. In Stalin's view the balance of 26 trains available to the military, with a lift of 600–700 tons each, would not be adequate for 60 divisions and the air forces in the Far East, and he quoted the example of Kuropatkin who was brought to a standstill through lack of supplies during the Russo-Japanese War. It was essential, concluded Stalin, to stockpile two to three months' maintenance reserves in the Far East before the start of operations. Brooke said that he was more than ever impressed by the dictator's military ability.[7] However, a military logistic planner, using Stalin's own figures, can easily deduce that the force would require a daily supply of little over 5,000 tons and that three months maintenance reserves could be stockpiled in 45 days. Antonov was therefore right and Stalin was wrong; but Stalin was determined to receive United States sea-landed supplies in the Far East, and, at the same time, deny the Americans the use of the Trans-Siberian railway.

The third military meeting on 17 October was attended only by Soviet and United States representatives. Stalin illustrated on a map the strategy he intended to use in his Far Eastern offensive, and then presented what Deane called his bill, a list for a two months' supply of food, fuel and transport based on a Far East force of one and a half million men, 3,000 tanks, 75,000 motor vehicles and 5,000 aircraft, in all the surprisingly high figure of over a million tons of goods. The deliveries were to be completed by 30 June 1945 and were additional to the supply programme already agreed under the current fourth protocol. At this meeting Stalin was agreeable to all the American counterproposals on the use of Soviet air and naval bases; joint planning could begin at once. But, said Deane, these promises were not met and the end result was that the Russians got their supplies and the United States got nothing. On 27 October Deane succeeded in obtaining a meeting with Antonov, but found that he was interested only in having confirmation that the supply programme was approved; and Antonov brushed aside the other points raised, saying that they were under consideration by the general staff. Deane's experience of dealing with Moscow led him to conclude that an American air force would never be based in Siberia.[8]

---

Shtemenko, more than 20 years after the event, described the strategic survey drawn up by himself, Antonov, Gryzlov and Lomov at the beginning of November 1944, recommending that the main offensives should be switched to Hungary and East Prussia so that the enemy would be obliged to reinforce his flanks at the expense of his centre. Then Zhukov's and Konev's fronts, side by side on the Vistula, would strike westwards in a swift offensive against Army Group A to a depth of up to 430 miles in 45 days, a distance which would take them to the west of Berlin and Dresden, 'the attack on Berlin being made quickly, and without a pause'.[9] Such a plan comes strangely from one who had censured Zhukov for so boldly outflanking Lvov.

In preparing the campaign plan for 1945 Stalin did not follow his usual practice of holding a general conference of all front commanders, but he summoned each front commander in turn to Moscow. The fronts' axes were decided at this time; Cherniakhovsky's 3 Belorussian Front was to strike for Königsberg; Rokossovsky's 2 Belorussian Front was to make two blows, one at Marienburg to envelop the East Prussian forces and the other at Allenstein, to assist Cherniakhovsky; Zhukov was to bypass Warsaw and advance on Poznan, while his left would co-operate with Konev's right. Konev and Petrov were to take Cracow in the initial offensive while Tolbukhin and Malinovsky were to clear Hungary and enter Austria. Stalin approved the plans in principle, said Shtemenko, and agreed that the offensive in the centre would probably begin about 20 January; no directives were issued however. Since the Supreme Commander had decided personally to control the four fronts which were advancing into Germany, Vasilevsky gave up his co-ordinating role for 3 Belorussian Front but took from Govorov the responsibility for 2 Baltic Front.

Zhukov was already at work with the general staff in late October and early November, primarily in connection with the central sector, and he was subsequently critical of Stalin for rejecting his earlier advice to give priority to the destruction of the enemy in East Prussia. From November onwards Zhukov concerned himself only with the projected operations for the 1 Belorussian Front. Contrary to what Shtemenko has said, Zhukov has made it clear that there was no question of striking directly for Berlin, for Stalin had agreed only to the first phase, that is to say the offensive into East Prussia by Cherniakhovsky and Rokossovsky, while Zhukov thrust towards Poznan and Konev reached the Oder between Glogau and Ratibor. It was even considered possible, said Zhukov, that 1 Belorussian Front might have to move a considerable part of its forces northwards to support Rokossovsky, for the entire 2 Belorussian Front was spearheaded against (*natselen protiv*) the East Prussia grouping.[10]

Rokossovsky's account of his mission reads yet differently. He had been aggrieved at losing the command of 1 Belorussian

Front, and Stalin's purpose in summoning him to Moscow, on or about 17 November, was, so Rokossovsky said, to assure him that 2 Belorussian Front was a main and not a secondary front. Stalin personally outlined Rokossovsky's task, saying that he was to advance on a north-westerly axis, ignoring the East Prussia grouping which was Cherniakhovsky's responsibility; indeed no mention was made of any co-ordination with this right hand neighbour, although, as Rokossovsky added, 'subsequent events forced the 2 Belorussian Front to turn a large number of troops to the north'. On the other hand, special emphasis was placed by Stalin on the necessity for co-ordination with Zhukov on the left, and Stalin drew a red arrow on the map to demonstrate how Rokossovsky was to attack the flank of the enemy in front of Zhukov 'if 1 Belorussian Front's advance should slow down'.[11]

Vasilevsky has attempted to put these differences into perspective. He had been recalled to the *Stavka* at the beginning of November and immediately started work, where Zhukov had left off, on the plans for the winter and spring offensive. Several members of the GKO and Politburo were involved in the planning, which, said Vasilevsky, took place under Stalin's direction. Opinions had been divided as to what action should be taken against the enemy in East Prussia, but, emphasized Vasilevsky, in the plan accepted by the Supreme Commander the aim was *to destroy* Army Group Centre. In the first stage, 2 and 3 Belorussian Fronts were to envelop the enemy, cutting him off against the sea, and in the second, while 1 Baltic and part of 3 Belorussian Fronts were rolling up the encircled enemy, 2 Belorussian and 1 Belorussian Fronts would overrun Pomerania. Vasilevsky has reiterated the established planning sequence. When the plans had been drafted by the general staff and the front military councils, they were presented to Stalin for approval. The front commanders were then summoned to Stalin and the plans were presented and examined yet again. Vasilevsky admitted that he was back in the Baltic area when Rokossovsky was interviewed, but he obviously doubts Rokossovsky's account of the talk with Stalin, for, said Vasilevsky, Stalin did not mince matters or words, always speaking with firmness and bluntness (*tverdost' i nepokolebimost'*) and there was never any doubt that all his verbal orders were confirmed in writing without the slightest material change.[12]

Vasilevsky's explanation does not, however, refute Rokossovsky's contention that the *Stavka* plan was a bad one. The *Stavka* directive of 28 November gave Rokossovsky the principal task of sealing East Prussia from the south-west by a thrust on Marienburg, and a secondary, in co-operation with Zhukov, to destroy the stronghold of Modlin on the inter-front boundary. Not until 20 January did Rokossovsky learn, so he has said, that he would have to turn four armies northwards to break up the enemy grouping in East Prussia.[13] He certainly remained responsible for supporting Zhukov's right flank, and, as events proved, Zhukov did not hesitate to complain to Stalin when Rokossovsky lagged behind.[14] This *affaire de rien* between the Soviet marshals cannot be resolved by their reproduction of incomplete, contradictory and possibly out of context directive extracts. The truth of the matter appears to have been that Rokossovsky came to be given two separate missions on widely divergent axes by Stalin, tasks which should have been entrusted either to two separate fronts or, more logically, have involved the transfer of Rokossovsky's right flank armies to Cherniakhovsky. In this particular instance Rokossovsky was not directed to hand over his armies to Cherniakhovsky until 10 February.

When Konev had been called to Moscow in November to discuss his final plan, members of the GKO were present. As usual the address and explanations were given by the front commander, although the details of the operation were already known to Stalin. Konev has said that he well remembered how Stalin discussed the plan in detail and emphasized the economic importance of the industrial region of Silesia by pointing it out on the map with his finger and repeating the word 'gold'.[15]

Although preparations for a Soviet offensive were ready in early December, the Red Army lay inactive, and in German quarters the erroneous view was expressed that the delay was deliberate, in that the Kremlin was trying to bring pressure on its western allies to recognize the Lublin Poles as the *de jure* government.[16] In truth, Moscow was unwilling to begin an offensive in the heavy mud and poor visibility, since these would make it impossible to exploit the Soviet fire, armoured and mechanized superiority. As early as 14 December Stalin had told Harriman that he was awaiting a spell of fine weather before starting any major action, and the fact that the Red Army had long been ready and was waiting for clear and frosty weather had been noted in German war diary entries at the time.[17] On 6 January Churchill had sent a personal communication to Stalin asking whether a renewal of the Vistula offensive could be counted on during January, the Ardennes battle being, in Churchill's words, very heavy; in reply Stalin explained that he was awaiting a change in the weather but promised an offensive not later than the second half of January.[18] On 8 January, however, there were definite indications that Poland was about to have cold and hard weather and this was confirmed by the meteorological reports the next day. On 9 January Antonov spoke in Stalin's name to Konev on the *V Ch*, ordering the offensive to begin three days later. The cold spell lasted for only nine days, but was sufficient to take the Red Army to the Oder.

On 15 January, Tedder, the Deputy Supreme Commander to Eisenhower, had a meeting with Stalin at which they discussed details of impending operations, including the targets of the western air operations, and Stalin assured his listener that he had begun his own offensive early, on 12 January, in response to Churchill's request, and that operations would continue for about two and a half months, their objective being the line of the Oder. A second offensive would then be mounted about the end of May.[19]

Vasilevsky was recalled to Moscow to remain in the capital while Stalin and Antonov went to the Crimea for the Yalta conference, his *Stavka* representative duties in the area of the Baltic having been assumed by Govorov.[20] When Stalin and Molotov called on Churchill at Yalta on the afternoon of 4 February, Churchill suggested, without the agreement of his own chiefs of staff, that a British force should be sent from Italy through northern Yugo-Slavia to operate on the Soviet left flank, a suggestion which, according to Shtemenko, was most unwelcome to Stalin.[21] Stalin gave his view that the war might go on until the summer and that it was desirable that there should be some co-ordination of the offensives between east and west. Co-ordinating discussions were accordingly held on 5 and 6 February between Antonov, Kuznetsov and Khudiakov and the United States and British chiefs of staff. On the Soviet side Antonov was the main speaker. Since the British and Americans were not in complete accord and Antonov was unwilling to commit himself without reference to Stalin, little was effected.[22]

Konev had begun his attacks on 12 January and the other fronts went over to the offensive in the course of the next three days. The German defence could not hold, because it was tied rigidly to ground, had no mobile reserves and lacked operative depth. On 17 January a *Stavka* directive laid down a time programme for the taking of the objectives, Zhukov to be on the Poznan line before 4 February, Konev to be on the Oder by 30 January, and to take Cracow, together with Petrov, by 22 February.

On 25 January Zhukov telephoned Stalin to say that the enemy was demoralized, and, since the enemy grouping to the north in East Pomerania was no immediate danger, there was nothing to prevent a westward advance and the seizing of a bridgehead across the Oder at Küstrin. Stalin was at first doubtful of the wisdom of Zhukov's suggestion since such a thrust would be unsupported by Rokossovsky or Konev, but after some days he agreed that Zhukov should advance to the Oder, on the firm understanding that 1 Belorussian Front should protect its own right flank.[23]

While Stalin was considering the Küstrin proposal, Zhukov had, on 26 January, put forward an even more ambitious plan. He suggested that 1 Belorussian Front should cross the Oder on 1 February from the line of march, with a view to striking to the north of Berlin. Two days later Konev, not to be outdone, sent his plan to the *Stavka*, asking that he should be permitted to advance into Brandenburg with the aim of reaching the Elbe before the end of February, taking Berlin by a double envelopment in conjunction with 1 Belorussian Front. According to Shtemenko these plans were approved in principle on 27 and 29 January. Yet subsequent events showed that Stalin attached no importance to them.[24] On 31 January, as 1 Belorussian Front was about to pass over the Oder near Küstrin only fifty miles from Berlin, Zhukov and Telegin sent a signal to Stalin complaining of the vulnerability of their troops. To this message they received, in Zhukov's words, neither prompt reply nor material help. This was not surprising in view of Stalin's warning given only a few days before.

On 4 February, Zhukov, Malinin and Telegin signed a directive to their armies and staffs warning them to be in readiness by 9 February to resume the offensive towards Berlin, which, according to their estimate, would be taken seven days later.[25] If Chuikov is to be believed, Zhukov had that day called a conference of his army commanders; Chuikov sat next to Zhukov, close to the telephones, so that he became an involuntary listener to a telephone conversation between Stalin and the front commander. Stalin wanted to know where Zhukov was and what he was doing, and when told that the conference was planning the strike for Berlin, the dictator told him that he was wasting his time; he must first consolidate on the Oder and then turn his force northwards to destroy, in conjunction with Rokossovsky, the enemy's flanking force in Pomerania. Thereupon Zhukov postponed indefinitely the offensive against Berlin. Chuikov subsequently said that he was at a loss to understand why Zhukov had agreed with Stalin 'without a murmur'. 'Everyone', said Chuikov, 'just waited for Stalin to say what should be done next'.[26]

Chuikov is a retrospective 'if only' man. The rapid advance of 300 miles across Poland was, he admitted, a remarkable achievement; but, he continued, if only the *Stavka* and fronts had got the necessary supplies to the Oder, if only the air force had the use of forward airfields and if only the bridging had been where it was wanted on the river bank, then the four Soviet armies would have reached Berlin. Telegin has marvelled that Chuikov first saw fit to raise this matter twenty years after the event.[27] There was nothing to have prevented Chuikov writing a private letter to Stalin at the time giving his views. Others did, and at least one illustrious general is known to have paid the extreme penalty. Zhukov has denied Chuikov's story, saying that 'there was no such conference on 4 February'. Shtemenko similarly dismisses Chuikov's account, telling his readers that, at the time, Chuikov was for ever complaining to the front about the lack of ammunition and transport.[28]

On or shortly after 4 February the projected axis of 1 Belorussian Front was turned from Berlin to Kolberg on the Baltic, and Zhukov subsequently defended the decision, although this must have been Stalin's and not his own. The general staff was apparently on the side of caution, for it was rightly believed that the new enemy Army Group Vistula was about to mount an offensive from Stargard into Zhukov's right flank; and although this danger was in fact much exaggerated, neither the general staff nor the front commander could have gauged this at the time.

Zhukov had obtained Stalin's permission to remain on the

defensive until his right hand neighbour Rokossovsky started to thrust northwards to cut the enemy East Pomeranian grouping in two.[29] Rokossovsky pressed Vasilevsky, who was in Moscow, that Zhukov's offensive should begin on 24 February, and the Chief of General Staff, according to Rokossovsky, 'promised he would attend to this'.[30] Co-ordination was presumably lacking, however, for Rokossovsky had to commit all his forces to the initial action, and his anxiety was increased when he found that his left was uncovered since Zhukov was not supporting him and that enemy forces were concentrating in Neustettin on the exposed flank. When Rokossovsky complained to Moscow on 26 February a puzzled and suspicious Stalin eventually came on the line. He asked whether Rokossovsky thought that Zhukov 'was playing some crafty game (*khitrit*)'. Rokossovsky did not think so, but said that the fact remained that 1 Belorussian Front was not advancing. Stalin inquired whether Rokossovsky could not take Neustettin using his own troops, for if he did, a Moscow salute would be fired in his honour. Rokossovsky would try, and meanwhile Stalin, who 'sounded quite pleased', promised to hasten Zhukov's offensive. The co-ordination between the fronts appears to have been effected through Stalin or Vasilevsky in Moscow. Only personal and relatively unimportant messages and those which were so impolitic as to make their transmission through Moscow unwise, went directly between the fronts. On 8 March, for example, when the *Stavka* ordered Zhukov to loan a tank army, Zhukov telephoned Rokossovsky, warning him that he wanted the army back 'in the same condition as when it was dispatched'.[31]

Stalin had 'expressed a wish' that the Chief of General Staff should go to East Prussia, for it was essential that the enemy there be destroyed quickly 'in order that troops might be transferred to the Berlin axis, while two or three of the better of the armies could be sent to the Far East'. Vasilevsky, said Stalin, should be ready to take over as Commander-in-Chief for the war against Japan. Vasilevsky 'in thanking Stalin for his continued confidence' had asked to be relieved of his post as Chief of General Staff, a post from which he had been a virtual absentee since the beginning of 1943. Vasilevsky recommended that Antonov should take the appointment, although he knew that Antonov did not want the post. Stalin, according to Vasilevsky, showed surprise and asked whether the loss of the appointment would not cause Vasilevsky offence; Stalin would, in any event, think about it.

On the night of 18 February Vasilevsky was at the Bolshoi Theatre when he was called to the telephone by Stalin, who told him of the death of Cherniakhovsky at Mehlsack. The *Stavka*, said Stalin, intended to appoint Vasilevsky to the vacant command. The next evening he was again with Stalin from whom he received, 'during an exceptionally warm talk, much valuable advice'. Vasilevsky particularly remembered being handed two sealed letters by Poskrebyshev. One was merely a letter appointing him to the command of 3 Belorussian Front from 21 February. The other envelope contained a GKO decree changing the 10 July 1941 composition of the *Stavka* to Stalin, Zhukov, Vasilevsky and Bulganin, the three latter being deputy commissars for defence, together with Kuznetsov and Antonov. Vasilevsky involuntarily commented to Poskrebyshev that, as the Chief of General Staff and deputy commissar of defence and the co-worker and co-signatory with Stalin for most of the war, it had not been necessary for him to be appointed as a member of the *Stavka*; why, asked Vasilevsky, had it been considered timely to appoint him now. Poskrebyshev could volunteer nothing by way of reply.[32]

Although the enemy-held territory in East Prussia had been compressed in ten days to half its former size, the failure to reduce Königsberg was taken hard by Stalin; Bagramian's 1 Baltic Front was held to be responsible and was downgraded to a group and incorporated into Vasilevsky's 3 Belorussian Front. The Soviet offensive was postponed until 13 March. Meanwhile Vasilevsky decided, with Stalin's agreement, to alter the earlier priorities and attack the southern grouping about Heiligenbeil before dealing with Königsberg and the enemy Samland force. When launched, the offensive began to make slow but steady progress. On 16 March Vasilevsky produced his plan for the final destruction of Army Group North, signed by himself, Makarov and Pokrovsky, a concise draft order of 800 words under the usual Red Army general staff numbered paragraph sequence, information about the enemy, own aim, grouping, air support, phases, timings, and reinforcements and equipment.[33] Within twenty-four hours the *Stavka* confirmed the order, except that it required that the operations in the south of the Frisches Haff should be concluded by not later than 22 March so that the offensive against Königsberg might start on 28 March.

Vasilevsky said that on the night of 18 March he told Stalin by telephone that the amended *Stavka* timings were unrealistic (*nerealen*) and he asked that the offensive against Königsberg should be delayed until April, the air and artillery assault beginning during the first four days of that month. This time he met with no difficulties for Stalin immediately agreed his proposal and, on reflection, said that 3 Belorussian Front should have the additional air support of a long range air army and the air armies of the Baltic Fleet and 2 Belorussian Front; he would dispatch Novikov and Golovanov to East Prussia immediately.[34] Königsberg fell on 9 April, amid scenes of fearful barbarity.

With the evacuation of the enemy Samland group on 16 April, East Prussia had been finally cleared of the enemy, after a bitter and bloody campaign lasting 105 days. Soviet historians give the credit for the German success in prolonging the struggle to the fact that the enemy was able to make good use of its sea communications uninterrupted by the Baltic Fleet or Red Air Force.

---

On the far southern wing a fierce struggle was being waged by Timoshenko's force in Hungary. By the end of the year Malinovsky and Tolbukhin had entrapped four German divisions and a Hungarian division in Budapest and had successfully beaten off enemy attacks to relieve the capital. On 11 February the Axis garrison was finally destroyed when trying to break out to the west.

At the end of the Budapest fighting, Timoshenko was ordered to give his recommendations on a projected advance to Vienna. Small planning staffs from 3 and 4 Ukrainian Fronts set to work on the problem, but a dispute immediately arose as to which of the fronts was to make the main thrust. Since each of the two front commanders considered this to be his duty, alternative plans were sent to Moscow. The *Stavka* decided in favour of Malinovsky and on 17 February put out a directive on the lines of his proposal. Meanwhile Tolbukhin, remaining convinced of the soundness of his own plan, pressed his views on Timoshenko, who demanded new facts and figures, which, when produced, eventually persuaded him that the offensive should be mounted by Tolbukhin. Timoshenko reported his opinion to Stalin, who ordered the plans to be re-examined. The *Stavka* then reversed its earlier decision and issued a revised directive on 9 March in favour of Tolbukhin.[35]

By the end of February, however, Tolbukhin had become aware that a German offensive was imminent against his front and, when this was reported to Moscow, the *Stavka* decided to delay the launching of the Vienna operation until after the enemy's effort was spent. Tolbukhin's troops were defending low lying ground interlaced by a network of rivers and canals. In the forward area the ground favoured the defence but to the rear it made movement and supply difficult; moreover, the Danube to the east formed a great obstacle across the front's lines of communications, since the ice floes threatened the pontoon bridges and ferry points.

The main German offensive began on 5 March when Wöhler's Army Group South, reinforced by Dietrich's 6 SS Panzer Army, recently arrived from the Ardennes, attacked to the north and south of Lake Balaton and advanced about sixteen miles in four days. When Tolbukhin informed Moscow of the presence of 6 SS Panzer Army, a disbelieving Antonov asked the front commander whether he really thought that Hitler would move such a formation to Lake Balaton at a time when Berlin was threatened with destruction. Ivanov, who was the front chief of staff, has said that the arrival of this panzer force apparently worried Stalin, for during a telephone discussion with Tolbukhin he wanted to know whether it would be feasible to withdraw 3 Ukrainian Front eastwards behind the Danube. The question surprised Tolbukhin but he and his council recommended that they remain where they were.[36]

Shtemenko has a very different version of the incident. On 6 March the Germans attacked with 'exceptional ferocity', and, on 9 March, Tolbukhin, who, according to Shtemenko, enjoyed indifferent health and lacked the resolution and ruthlessness of the other marshals, asked that 3 Ukrainian Front should be permitted, in case of necessity, to withdraw behind the Danube. The matter was referred to Stalin. Antonov and Shtemenko were present in Stalin's office when Tolbukhin telephoned the dictator. Stalin reflected for a moment and then, said Shtemenko, without anger or emotion, replied in an even and calm voice:

Comrade Tolbukhin! If you are thinking of extending the war by five or six months then please do withdraw your troops

behind the Danube. It will of course be quieter there. But I
doubt whether that is your intention. Therefore you must defend
the right bank and stay there yourself with your headquarters.
I am sure that the troops will do their duty and fulfil their difficult task. All that is necessary is that they should be commanded
properly.³⁷

By 16 March Tolbukhin knew that he had won the defensive
battle without Malinovsky's forces or the *Stavka* reserve army
coming to his assistance. When that evening Tolbukhin asked for a
tank army to be transferred to him from 2 Ukrainian Front for use
in accordance with the counter-offensive directive of 9 March,
Stalin agreed and immediately telephoned Malinovsky, ordering
him to concentrate the army the next day.³⁸ The reserve army,
which had been previously refused to Tolbukhin, was ordered to
move across the Danube to join the tank army in the thrust which
was to outflank Army Group South and reach Vienna by the middle
of April.

Meanwhile, to the north of Malinovsky's 2 Ukrainian Front,
Petrov's 4 Ukrainian Front had left Cracow behind it and had
begun the thrust on Moravska-Ostrava. Progress was slow. On or
about 15 March, Moskalenko, one of Petrov's army commanders,
had been called to the front headquarters where he was invited to
sit at his ease and drink tea with Petrov and Mekhlis, 'unofficially'
discussing the reasons for the lack of success. Moskalenko gave as
his opinion that the main thrust was being made in the wrong
sector; he would have preferred to have seen the axis further to the
north where the going was better. Moskalenko said that, as he
spoke, he noted that Mekhlis was scribbling on a pad, and he dis-
covered afterwards that the political member was writing up the
conversation on signal sheets for telegraphing to Moscow.

At 0300 hours the next morning Moskalenko was awakened by a
telephone call from Antonov, who, said Moskalenko, first talked
about trivialities in order to allow him sufficient time to shake off
the effects of sleep and compose himself. The Supreme Commander, said Antonov, wanted to know more about Moskalenko's
views on the lack of success of the operation, and, when Moskalenko answered that he could hardly talk behind the commander's
back, Antonov told him that Stalin already knew of the conversa-

tion from Mekhlis's signalled report; Stalin just wanted a little more detail. Following this conversation, Petrov was ordered to explain himself, which he did by an answering signal on 17 March. That evening, at 1830 hours, Stalin and Antonov signed a personal signal to both Petrov and Mekhlis, saying that the Supreme Commander considered the explanation of General of the Army Petrov dated 17 March as unconvincing. If General Petrov had been of the opinion that his command was not yet ready for battle he should have told the *Stavka* so and have asked for more time; this would not have been refused. The member of the military council, Colonel-General Mekhlis, had informed the Central Committee of the shortcomings in the preparations only after the failure of the operation. The message ended 'The *Stavka* warns (*preduprezhdaet*) General of the Army Petrov for the last time'. Petrov and Korzhenevich were removed from their posts on that day but Mekhlis was allowed to remain.[39] Eremenko and Sandalov arrived from the old 2 Baltic Front to replace the outgoing commander and chief of staff.

---

By 4 April the enemy's main East Pomeranian grouping had been destroyed except that an isolated pocket of German troops remained near the mouth of the Vistula. The occupation of Pomerania finally removed, as Shtemenko said, any danger of the Soviet offensive against Berlin being wrecked by attacks from the flank or rear, and 'for this reason the postponement could not have been avoided'. On 23 March Montgomery's 21 Army Group had established a firm foothold over the lower Rhine and started to move eastwards, while further to the south Bradley's 12 Army Group extended its bridgeheads at Remagen and Mainz. Two United States armies then began the double envelopment which ended on 1 April with the encirclement of Model's 325,000 strong Army Group B in the Ruhr; Stalin was surprised by the scale and speed of the operation.

On 28 March, when the Anglo-American troops were already advancing into Germany, Eisenhower, without consulting the Combined Chiefs of Staff or his British deputy, sent a telegram directly to Deane in Moscow for handing to Stalin. Eisenhower explained that his primary mission, after he had destroyed the Ruhr pocket, would be to split the enemy forces by making a junction with the Soviet armies in the east, and that the main axis to be taken by the Anglo-American forces would be from west to south-east in the direction of Erfurt, Leipzig and Dresden.[40]

Although Germany and Europe had been politically dissected at Yalta there had been no agreement on the co-ordination of military strategy between the Red Army and the Anglo-American forces. In the previous September Eisenhower and Montgomery had been in accord that the main political and military objective was the capture of Berlin. Even as late as 27 March, the day before Eisenhower had sent his telegram to Moscow, Montgomery had informed Churchill that he was thrusting for the Elbe and Berlin, and Churchill intended that he should do so.[41] Eisenhower's military objectives were apparently unrelated to post-war political strategy since, in Pogue's view, the President and the United States Chiefs of Staff left the final stages of the war to their military commander.[42]

Stalin told Deane that Eisenhower's plan fitted with that of the Red Army; he agreed with Eisenhower 'that Berlin no longer had its former strategic significance' and said that henceforth the main effort of the Red Army would be in the direction of Dresden to form a junction with the United States forces.[43] The Soviet offensive, said Stalin, would begin in the second half of May, although this date might be subject to alteration.[44]

Immediately after the western delegation had gone Stalin sent for Zhukov, who arrived in the capital on 29 March from 1 Belorussian Front. Stalin told him that although the Red Army had serious fighting ahead of it, the enemy defence in western Germany had collapsed; Zhukov thought that he could be ready to start an offensive against Berlin in a fortnight and imagined that Konev could too; Rokossovsky, however, was likely to be delayed as the larger part of his troops were still in East Pomerania. Stalin concluded that the offensive would have to start without Rokossovsky.[45] Stalin told Zhukov that he had been informed by telegram that the enemy had made overtures to the western allies and in consequence the possibility could not be dismissed that the Germans would let the Anglo-Americans through to Berlin; 'as for Churchill', said Stalin, 'he might do anything'. Although Zhukov has misrepresented the content of Eisenhower's message and omitted Stalin's reply, it is not improbable that Stalin expressed himself in these terms.[46]

Zhukov and Antonov were ordered to continue planning the offensive until Konev should arrive from 2 Ukrainian Front, and Zhukov makes the point that, before 30 March, the strategic plan involving fronts other than his own was unknown to him.[47] On 31 March they were joined by Konev, 'who became very excited (*ochen' razvolnovalsia*)' over the inter-front boundary between himself and Zhukov; but since this was Stalin's work, no one in the general staff, Shtemenko drily commented, could do anything about it.[48] Konev has told how the concept of the 1 Ukrainian Front plan originated from his front staff and, when approved in Moscow, was incorporated in the *Stavka* directive. On this particular occasion Stalin had ordered that the front commanders were not to leave Moscow without having the directives, agreed and signed, in their hands.[49]

On 1 April Zhukov, Konev, Antonov and Shtemenko were summoned to a GKO meeting. Antonov first gave a strategic introduction presenting the situation on all the German fronts both in the west and in the east. The need, said Stalin, was to take Berlin before the western allies, and the offensive would have to start not later than 16 April and be completed within fifteen days. Zhukov and Konev in turn presented their plans based on a frontal offensive by 1 Belorussian Front on the Küstrin-Berlin axis, its two tank armies outflanking the city from the north, while 1 Ukrainian Front advanced on the axis Spremberg-Beelitz (immediately south of Potsdam) making only subsidiary thrusts in the direction of Dresden and Leipzig. Antonov again drew Stalin's attention to the inter-front boundary, which ran from Gross Gastrose on the Oder to Gross Michendorf twenty miles south of the capital and thence to Brandenburg, since this demarcation line prevented Konev from entering the Berlin suburbs. Konev, whose orders with regard to his right flank had up to this time been by no means clear, also spoke in favour of directing his tank armies into Berlin from the south-west.

Stalin would not abandon his original idea that Zhukov should take Berlin. Nor, on the other hand, would he accept the general staff's and Konev's view. So, taking a pencil, he silently crossed out the inter-front boundary leaving only that part which ran from Gross Gastrose to Lübben, a distance of about twenty-five miles from the start line. Stalin gave no explanation for his action and made no further comment, but Konev believed that the dictator deliberately introduced an element of competition between the two fronts; and this view is confirmed by Shtemenko, for Stalin later told the general staff that Berlin should be taken by whoever broke in first.[50]

The directives to the two fronts were signed by Stalin on 1 and 3 April. The mission paragraph of the directive to Zhukov instructed him 'to conduct an offensive and capture Berlin, and, not later than the twelfth–fifteenth day of the operation, reach the Elbe'. The mission given to Konev read 'to destroy the enemy grouping in the area of Cottbus and the south of Berlin and, not later than the twelfth–fifteenth day of the operation, reach the line Beelitz–Wittenberg exploiting towards Dresden'. The tank and reserve armies intended for the break-out battles were not to be committed until the enemy defences had been pierced. No mention was made in the confirmatory directive of the possibility that 1 Ukrainian Front would be called upon to turn its tank armies into Berlin. Although the directives were specific in covering the break-in battles, the break-out and exploitation phases were left open; Konev, in particular, has emphasized that there was no pre-determined or centralized plan covering the Berlin operation; as the battle developed orders were passed according to the changing situation, and the hour by hour control of the fronts was exercised from Moscow.[51]

Konev saw Stalin again on 3 April and asked for two more armies to form the reserve for the break-out operations. Stalin consulted his pad and allotted two armies from the Baltic area. The problem immediately arose as to whether these troops could arrive with Konev by 15 April, and Stalin wanted to know the answer from the general staff there and then. The rail movement authority could not guarantee their arrival until after the offensive had started, but this was apparently acceptable to Konev.

On 6 April, two days after Zhukov and Konev had returned to their fronts, Rokossovsky was called to Moscow for briefing on his part in the new offensive, the advance into Mecklenburg to cover Zhukov's right flank. The troops of 2 Belorussian Front were still 150 miles away, having, only a few days before, cleared the enemy in the areas of Gdynia and Danzig. Rokossovsky was to close up to the lower Oder and take over the sector held by a single army, the right hand formation of 1 Belorussian Front. But whereas Zhukov has said that Stalin had accepted that Rokossovsky's offensive could not begin until 20 April, Rokossovsky has maintained that the postponement of four days was given grudgingly by Stalin, and then only after he had heard an explanation of the difficulties to be overcome.

When Rokossovsky was given his written directive on 6 April, his men were already on the march and the army commanders and staffs had begun their reconnoitring of the banks of the Oder. But Rokossovsky's offensive differed from those of Zhukov and Konev in that no front plans were in existence to form the outline of the *Stavka* directive, and much of the planning had, of necessity, to be done from the military council's reading of the map. When the troops did arrive many of them were ordered piecemeal into the attack, with little or no time for preparation. However that may be, on 19 April Rokossovsky reported to Stalin by telephone that his front was ready to begin the offensive at the time appointed by the *Stavka*.[52]

The 1 Belorussian Front plan agreed in Moscow envisaged the committal of two tank armies north of Berlin as soon as the enemy defences had been overcome and there was sufficient room for manoeuvre. But Zhukov became apprehensive about the strength of the enemy Seelow defences facing the Küstrin bridgeheads and recommended, in the second week in April, that Katukov's tank army be moved further to the south in support of Chuikov's army in the break-out battle against Seelow. Stalin told Zhukov to act as he thought fit since he was best able to see the local situation.[53] In the event, Zhukov was, quite rightly, to bear the blame.

In the first week in April Stalin had decided to strengthen the command of 1 Belorussian Front by allotting Sokolovsky to Zhukov as a front deputy commander, and in this way, only seven days before the opening of the offensive, Konev lost his chief of staff, who had been with the front for nearly a year. Stalin had telephoned Konev to offer Petrov, by way of replacement, and, whether willingly or not, Konev had accepted him. Not surprisingly, he found that Petrov was more at his ease commanding troops than sorting paper, and Konev was later to send him as his representative to where the battle was in doubt, to put what Konev calls some heart into the troops.

By 15 April the western allies had become aware of the imminence of the Soviet offensive through monitoring the German radio
and, in answer to a direct question from the United States Embassy
in Moscow, the information was given that the offensive would
begin on the morrow, Stalin still insisting, even at that late hour,
that the main thrust was to be made on Leipzig.[54]

Zhukov's overall frontage had been reduced from 200 to 120
miles by the arrival of 2 Belorussian Front, but the actual assault
frontage of the main offensive was only twenty-eight miles, so that
each of the four first echelon armies in the area of the breakthrough
had a sector of little more than 12,000 yards. The three Soviet
fronts are said to have numbered two and a half million men,
41,000 guns and mortars, 6,200 tanks and 7,500 aircraft, with an
artillery density of up to 400 gun and mortar barrels to the mile in
the area of the main assault.[55] Figures by themselves, however,
tend to be misleading due to the Soviet practice of counting all
aircraft as warplanes and including even 82mm infantry mortars
as artillery. The war diary entry of Busse's 9 Army, after the first
day of Zhukov's offensive, estimated that it had been under the
fire of only 2,500 guns and 450 tanks.[56]

Zhukov was beset with difficulties. His decision to blind the
enemy defenders by the direct illumination of searchlights and to
move Katukov's tank army forward on to the bridgehead had not
been a happy one. The marshy and broken ground restricted
deployment so that the roads and tracks became jammed with
vehicles, and the lights confused the Red Army troops. The enemy
resistance was bitter. At two-thirty on the afternoon of 16 April,
when, after nine hours fighting the attacking troops had moved
forward only four miles, Zhukov decided to commit both of his
tank armies, although the infantry formations had not yet broken
out and the Seelow defences were still intact in front of him. Half
an hour later when he telephoned a description of the position to
Stalin, the dictator listened quietly, merely ordering him to reinforce the strike of the tank armies with bomber aircraft. Konev,
Stalin said, had found matters easier and was already across the
Neisse. Zhukov was to call again that night and report the situation.

That evening, when Zhukov made his second call, Stalin spoke
'somewhat less calmly'. The dictator blamed Zhukov for having
altered the axis of Katukov's tank army to a sector where the enemy

defences were so strong, and he asked if he could have an assurance that the Seelow would be taken the next day. Zhukov believed that it would be taken by the next night and he justified the changing of the axis by claiming that he was drawing enemy troops out of Berlin 'where they could be more easily defeated in the open'. Stalin's reply, that he was 'thinking of taking the capital using Konev from the south and Rokossovsky from the north', made it clear that he had lost confidence in Zhukov's handling of his front. Nor was he prepared to listen to Zhukov's long-winded objections that Rokossovsky would have difficulty in advancing from the Oder before 23 April, for the dictator merely cut him off with, as Zhukov expressed it, 'a dry good-bye in lieu of reply', and hung up.[57]

On the evening of 17 April Konev was about to cross the Spree when he was telephoned by Stalin who explained that Zhukov was having difficulty in penetrating the enemy defences; then he fell silent, obviously weighing up the situation. Konev remained waiting for the dictator to take up the thread of the conversation. When Stalin began again he asked whether Konev thought it would be possible to pass Zhukov's motorized troops through the 1 Ukrainian Front gap in the area of Spremberg. Konev was against this solution, as it would take time and cause confusion; in any case, he said, it was unnecessary, as his own tank armies were already there and in a favourable position to take Berlin from the south. When Konev outlined how he could direct his armour on Zossen, fifteen miles south of Berlin, Stalin was obviously having difficulty in following place names, for he asked the scale of the map which Konev was using. After a short pause, he spoke again, agreeing that Konev should direct Rybalko and Leliushenko on Berlin.[58] That night the military council issued its directive requiring that Potsdam and south-west Berlin be taken by 21 April.[59] In the three days from 18 to 21 April, during which time 1 Ukrainian Front broke into Zossen, Konev spoke only once to Moscow, although detailed situation reports were sent regularly from his headquarters to the general staff. Virtually no queries were raised on these reports and, as Konev said, 'there was no interference from above on those days'.[60]

Whereas Konev's remarkable success could hardly have been improved, Zhukov was to come in for much criticism. Looking at the problem in retrospect, he thought that 1 Belorussian Front should have been concentrated on closer assault frontages. But, said Zhukov, such a proposal would have been out of the question at the time, since Stalin favoured only the offensive on the broad front.[61] As an alternative, said Zhukov, all the troops deployed in the taking of Berlin could have been entrusted to 1 Belorussian Front alone, since this would have avoided the friction between the fronts, particularly during the fighting in the capital.

Meanwhile, in the middle of April, Eisenhower had sent another message to Deane for delivery to the Red Army general staff, suggesting that all the allies, whether in the east or west, should be free to advance until contact was imminent. This proposal alarmed Antonov. Agreement was eventually reached, but when, on 4 May, Eisenhower said that he proposed to advance deeper into Czecho-Slovakia to the west banks of the Elbe and Vitava rivers, this brought such a violent protest from Antonov that the Supreme Allied Commander in the west acceded to Moscow's wishes.[62]

By 21 April Zhukov's right wing had at last gained operative depth and began to penetrate the northern outskirts of Berlin. Four days later Leliushenko's tank army joined with Perkhorovich's troops of 1 Belorussian Front to the west of the capital, so encircling the city, and that same day United States and Red Army patrols met at Torgau on the Elbe. Konev's and Zhukov's troops were fighting their way against bitter resistance towards the centre of Berlin, 1 Belorussian Front from the east and north and 1 Ukrainian Front from the south and west, and the difficulties of observation and control resulted in the supporting front air forces bombing their own troops and those of the adjoining fronts. On 25 April Konev and Zhukov appealed to Stalin to lay down a firm inter-front boundary.[63] Up to this time both Zhukov and Konev had been striving to occupy the city centre, the suspicious Zhukov (the description used by Chuikov) sending out reconnaissance patrols to seek information, not about the enemy but about Konev's troops, in case these should penetrate into the heart of Berlin before him.[64]

On 29 April Stalin telephoned Konev asking for his opinion as to who should clear and occupy Prague. American troops had already arrived in the western Czech territories, while Malinovsky's 2 Ukrainian Front had overrun Slovakia in the east and south; the northern Czecho-Slovakian border was, as Konev described it, overhung by the 1 Ukrainian Front. When Konev told Stalin that his front would be able to take Prague, Stalin altered his right front boundary in Berlin further to the west. This allowed Zhukov to complete the overrunning and occupation of the Berlin city centre.[65]

On the afternoon of 30 April Hitler had committed suicide and, early the next morning, Krebs, the last Chief of German General Staff, arrived at the command post of Chuikov's army with a written proposal from Goebbels for peace negotiations. The text of the letter was telephoned to Zhukov who, having sent Sokolovsky to represent him at Chuikov's headquarters, called up Moscow to report to Stalin. When Stalin, who was at Kuntsevo, was awakened, he ordered that there should be no negotiations or talks, only unconditional surrender. Fighting in the capital continued for a further two days, until the German surrender on 2 May. Elsewhere the war in Europe was virtually at an end, and, on 7 May, the emissaries sent by Doenitz, the new head of the German government, signed the surrender at Rheims, a document on which Susloparov, the representative to Eisenhower's headquarters, obligingly added his signature.

That day Stalin telephoned Voronov, asking angrily who was 'this celebrated general of artillery Susloparov' who, without even telling the Soviet government and certainly without its authority, had dared to sign a document of such tremendous international importance. Stalin vented his anger on Voronov, who as a marshal of artillery, 'had failed to educate his artillery officers'. Susloparov, said Stalin, would be recalled to Moscow immediately and harshly punished.[66] That same day Stalin telephoned Zhukov in Berlin to say that he disagreed with the signing of the document in Rheims, for it was the Soviet people who had borne the main brunt of the war, not the allies. Stalin demanded a second signing of a surrender document, this time before the Supreme Command of all the countries of the coalition, and not just before the Anglo-American Supreme Commander. Zhukov was to represent the *Stavka* at the ceremony. Thereafter Zhukov was to remain as the head of the Soviet zone of occupation and the commander of the Soviet troops in Germany, and Vyshinsky would join him as the deputy commander for political affairs.[67]

Werth has described the press conference which Zhukov and Vyshinsky gave a little later. Zhukov described how *he* (Werth's italics) had attacked along the whole front and at night, and 'very soon' had broken the German defences; the main point, emphasized Zhukov, was that the Germans were smashed on the Oder, for Berlin itself was just one immense mopping-up operation. It was, added Zhukov, very, *very* (Werth's repetition and italics) different from the battle of Moscow, for out of more than half a million German soldiers who had taken part in the Berlin operation, 300,000 were taken prisoner even before the capitulation, about 150,000 had been killed and the rest had fled. Werth was to note later that Zhukov had mentioned nothing of the part played by Rokossovsky's or Konev's forces, or of the 2,000 Soviet tanks destroyed and the 300,000 Red Army casualties. Werth commented that the tenor of Zhukov's account had little in common with the official Soviet history which described German resistance as fanatical, fighting continuing to the end, even in the corridors of the Reichstag in the heart of the city. Zhukov had added a tribute to Comrade Stalin 'and to his great understanding of military affairs', but this had come almost as an afterthought. None of the other Soviet marshals had been mentioned. Zhukov, said Werth, had a very high opinion of himself, and with a curious mixture of modesty and almost boyish boastfulness he had tended to take the credit for nearly all the decisive victories the Red Army had won. Vyshinsky outwardly treated Zhukov with admiration, almost obsequiousness, but in reality the political supervision was always in evidence, and Werth had the vague feeling that Zhukov resented it.[68]

Berzarin, the first military commandant in Berlin, perished on 16 June 'in the performance of his duties', either in a car accident or, according to the current Russian rumour in Berlin, at the hands of Nazi terrorists. He was replaced by Gorbatov.

When Prague had been taken, Konev was surprised to witness an altercation between Rybalko and Leliushenko as to who had arrived in the city first and who, by right, should be its first military governor; Konev solved the problem by selecting Gordov to be the chief of the Prague garrison. When he reported his decision to Stalin by telephone that evening, he at first met with an unexpected objection over the title of the post, and a long hair-splitting discussion followed as to the designation and duties of district commanders, governors, city commandants and town majors. The dictator finally ruled that Gordov should be styled 'commandant', since, said Konev, the sound of the name pleased Stalin better.[69]

---

Throughout the duration of the war in Europe there were five armies in the Far East, but whereas the order of battle had been increased in terms of front and army headquarters, the real fighting strength sank to about thirty divisions.[70] In the spring of 1942 Zhigarev, who had previously commanded the air forces of 2 Independent Red Banner Army, was returned from Moscow to command the Far East air forces, and, in April 1943, Purkaev replaced Apanasenko as the commander of the Far East Front. The most important staff change was that of Shevchenko, formerly head of the Far East section of the general staff operations department in Moscow, who was exchanged for Lomov, the deputy chief of staff of the Far East Front. Shevchenko was later promoted and became the front chief of staff.

On 4 October 1944, when Harriman raised the question of allied military staff talks covering the war against Japan, Stalin said that he had sent for Shevchenko and Zhigarev to come from the Far East to brief him on the constantly changing situation there. The primary reason for the summons to Moscow was connected with the instructions Stalin had given to the general staff a few days earlier, when, at the conclusion of a routine *Stavka* briefing, he told Shtemenko, 'almost casually', to begin work on drawing up plans and estimates for the new war, since, as Stalin worded it, 'it looked as if they would soon be needed'. These figures, produced within a fortnight, were those used by Antonov and Shevchenko when Stalin briefed Churchill and Eden in the second half of the month.[71] In February 1945 Stalin's political conditions for entering the war, three months after the end of the war in Europe, had been agreed with his allies, and on 5 April the Soviet government renounced its non-aggression pact with Japan.

On 26 March Vasilevsky was withdrawn from 3 Belorussian Front to begin his task of co-ordinating the fronts which were to destroy the Japanese Kwantung Group of Armies in Manchuria.[72] Stalin had ruled that the existing Far East field organization should not be altered and that full use should be made of the local knowledge of the commanders and staffs already there. On the other hand he wanted battle-experienced headquarters and troops brought from Europe as complete formations, these to be fitted into the Far East order of battle with a minimum of dislocation, so that the newly arrived 'westerners' were in command, with the 'easterners' as their deputies.[73] The strategic and operative plan put forward for Stalin's approval appears to have been drafted by Lomov and Shevchenko, working under Antonov's and Shtemenko's supervision.

The Transbaikal Front, on the right, had the main role, since this was to involve the rapid movement of large armoured forces over a great distance, from Transbaikal and Outer Mongolia south-eastwards towards Tsitsihar, Changchun, Mukden and Chinwangtao. At Vasilevsky's suggestion the command of this front was given to Malinovsky, an officer who had much experience in handling mobile troops, and whose calm, thoroughness and judgement were highly regarded. Kovalev was to remain as Malinovsky's deputy, with Zakharov as the new chief of staff. In the centre, the battle-experienced Purkaev was left in command of the Far East Front, later to be redesignated as 2 Far East Front, his task being to cross the Amur and advance on Tsitsihar. On the extreme left, the maritime group in the area of Vladivostok, recently under Purkaev, but now subordinated directly to Stalin, was to be redesignated as 1 Far East Front, this command being given to Meretskov, who was waiting at Yaroslavl with the former Karelian Front headquarters in *Stavka* reserve; the former maritime group commander, Parusinov, was to remain with the group as Meretskov's deputy. Stalin rated Meretskov's ability to overcome fortified areas highly, for, in making this appointment he gave as his opinion that 'the wily man from Yaroslavl' would soon smash the Japanese. Meretskov's task was to provide the left wing of the double envelopment which would move from the maritime provinces north of Vladivostok to Harbin, Changchun and into North Korea, joining with Malinovsky's armoured columns coming from the Transbaikal. Three armies were on their way from Europe to the Transbaikal Front, while a further army joined the maritime group. In addition a number of experienced army commanders were transferred from the west to take over the armies already in the theatre.

The Japanese were poorly prepared to withstand an offensive from the Transbaikal area and Outer Mongolia; this, and geo-

**31** Leliushenko, a tsarist cavalry NCO and Red Army cavalry leader who qualified as a commissar in 1925. In 1933 he went to the armoured forces as a commander.

**32** The military council of the Leningrad Front in 1943 showing its commander Govorov with Zhdanov his commissar.

**33** At 3 Belorussian Front July 1944; from the left, Makarov the commissar, Vasilevsky the Chief of General Staff, and Cherniakhovsky the front commander (killed 1945).

**34** In the Far-East August 1945; Meretskov *(left)* commanding 1 Far East Front, Malinovsky commanding the Transbaikal Front and Vasilevsky, the C in C Far East.

graphy, dictated the Soviet strategy, since the open country, without fortified areas, water obstacles or taiga, favoured the use of motorized forces by the Transbaikal Front, although the Hingan mountain range would eventually have to be overcome. Meretskov's 1 Far East Front on the other hand would have to penetrate the wire and concrete static defences built up long before the war on the old Russo-Japanese frontier; Purkaev had yet a different problem in that he had to cross the broad Amur. The area of operations extended over 1,000 miles, and since the three widely separated fronts were to converge from the outer circumference on to a central point, co-ordination and timing of the initial offensives were to present a difficult problem. Stalin ruled that plans should be prepared in detail covering a number of variations, since it would be easier to know which to choose nearer the time.[74]

Meretskov, having arrived at Vladivostok, took over from Parusinov and set to work on his plans, reconnoitring selected points of the frontier dressed in the uniform of a private soldier of NKVD border troops. He and Parusinov were well acquainted from the time of the Finnish Winter War, but, as they were unable to work together, Stalin withdrew Parusinov to the *Stavka* reserve.[75]

All front and army commanders were to attend the Moscow victory parade celebrations in the last week in June, and Stalin had ordered that Malinovsky and Zakharov should come earlier in order to work on an outline plan. They were given the mission to destroy the enemy Kwantung force within a space of eight weeks from the beginning of the offensive on 20–25 August. At the end of five days work in the general staff, they produced a plan which Malinovsky presented to Stalin on 18 June. But the general staff was unable to agree that Malinovsky should keep his tank army in reserve as part of his second echelon of armies, for it believed that such a course would tie the rate of advance of the tank formations to that of infantry. Moreover, the tanks would be unable to seize the mountain passes by a *coup de main*, or indeed be in the forward area to support the forward infantry. Stalin told Malinovsky to reconsider his own plan when he had arrived in the Transbaikal area, and then make the final decision. Malinovsky's decision, when eventually made, conformed to the plan of the general staff. In reality Malinovsky appears to have had little choice, nor did

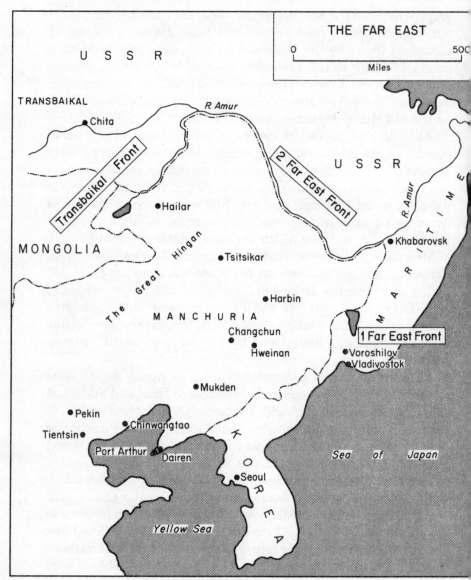

THE FAR EAST

0                                         500
                    Miles

U S S R

TRANSBAIKAL

Chita

R. Amur

2 Far East Front

U S S R

Transbaikal Front

MONGOLIA

Hailar

Hingan

Tsitsikar

Khabarovsk

M A R I T I M E

R. Amur

The Great

Harbin

M A N C H U R I A

Changchun

Hweinan

1 Far East Front

Voroshilov

Vladivostok

Mukden

Pekin

Chinwangtao

Tientsin

Port Arthur

Dairen

K O R E A

Sea   of   Japan

Seoul

Yellow Sea

Stalin intend that there should be any doubt on the matter, for when he came to sign the directive to the Transbaikal Front he had the following paragraph inserted:

6 Guards Tank Army, operating in the main sector in the general direction of Changchun, shall by the tenth day of the operation force the Great Hingan, seize the passes and seal the area off from the enemy reserves from Central and Southern Manchuria until the arrival of the main infantry forces.[76]

The war in the Far East raised a new problem, however, since it was likely to be a fast moving campaign in a remote theatre involving a million and a half men in three converging and possibly simultaneous offensives from widely separated start lines. It would be impossible to control operations from Moscow, and for this reason, so Stalin is said to have told Vasilevsky in Antonov's and Shtemenko's presence, a Commander-in-Chief was essential to the theatre, to command the three fronts and the supporting air and naval forces. Vasilevsky was to set up his headquarters at Khabarovsk, with arms advisers and staff, fifty-two officers in all, detached to him from the Commissariat of Defence. Novikov was to control the air forces; Shikin was to be the political member of the military council and Stalin recommended that Zakharov should be Vasilevsky's chief of staff. In the event however, Zakharov asked to be allowed to remain with Malinovsky; the post was offered to Kurasov, but he, too, asked to be excused; finally Ivanov was selected.

At the time, Deane was certain that Stalin would retain operational control in Moscow, notwithstanding the distances involved. Deane wanted to establish a link between Vasilevsky and MacArthur and Nimits, and he proposed to Antonov that there should be an exchange of liaison staffs and the provision of radio teleprint equipment from United States resources. Deane suggested that the Soviet answer should be given at the time of the Potsdam conference.

At the Potsdam conference Stalin's military attendants included Zhukov, Kuznetsov, Antonov, Gryzlov and Slavin. Leahy gave Antonov an *aide-mémoire*, listing five requests from the United States chiefs of staff concerning the forthcoming operations in the

Far East. The answers came by hand of Stalin to Truman. The request for weather stations at Khabarovsk and Petropavlovsk was agreed, after some quibbling, and modifications were required to the United States' suggestions concerning naval and air operational boundaries. In answer to the fourth American point, a request for information, Deane was surprised to hear that Vasilevsky 'would have complete control of all Soviet operations in the Far East, without supervision from Moscow'.[77] Stalin had already informed Truman, and Antonov afterwards told the assembled chiefs of staff, that Soviet operations against the Japanese in the Far East would begin in the latter half of August.

Stalin had rejected a Japanese approach asking that the Soviet Union mediate between Tokyo and the western allies, and had informed Hopkins earlier, on 28 May, that the Soviet Union preferred to go through with the war until unconditional surrender and the occupation of the Japanese mainland were achieved. An undefeated Japan would, Stalin thought, start to plan a war of revenge. Stalin admitted that insistence on unconditional surrender would mean that the Japanese would go on fighting until the end, and he hinted that milder terms could be offered provided that these involved the occupation of the Japanese homeland by the victorious allies. Then, once the allies were in occupation, Stalin saw no reason why, in Hopkins's words, the Japanese should not 'be given the works' and the same results thus obtained as under unconditional surrender.[78] In the event, the Potsdam declaration, promulgated with Stalin's concurrence although the Soviet Union was not a party, demanded unconditional surrender.

On 22 July, after a consultation with Churchill and Eden, Truman and Byrnes had decided that an atom bomb would be dropped on Japan if it did not accept immediate surrender. Stalin was to be told of the intention without giving him the details of the new weapon or how it was to be used, and he was in fact informed in these terms by Truman at the conclusion of a meeting on 24 July. His response, according to Eden, was a nod of the head and a brief 'Thank you'. He made no other comment.[79] Stalin told Antonov of this conversation, but according to Shtemenko he had little idea of the potential of the bomb.[80] Vasilevsky has recounted how Stalin telephoned him at Chita from Potsdam, and asked whether the Japanese War could not be brought forward by about ten days.

But Vasilevsky has given the date of this conversation as 16 July, roughly the date, he said, of the successful atomic explosion at Los Alamos; Vasilevsky added that he did not know 'to what extent Truman had informed Stalin of this trial but later it became obvious that Stalin's 16 July telephone conversation had a direct bearing on that event'.[81]

The first atom bomb was dropped on Hiroshima on 6 August and the second on Nagasaki three days afterwards. On the afternoon of 8 August the head of the United States and British military missions in Moscow were sent for by Antonov and given a copy of a note sent to the Japanese Government declaring war as from midnight that same day. When the Soviet Ambassador in Tokyo handed the Japanese Foreign Minister this declaration of war, the minister had replied that Japan was prepared to accept the Potsdam declaration subject only to certain reservations about retaining the Emperor as the sovereign ruler. According to Deane's view of the situation, although the Hiroshima atomic bomb received scant notice in the Soviet press, it must have been given the greatest attention in the inner councils, for 'Russia had to buy her ticket to the Pacific peace conference, but she had to hurry or the show would have started and the seats would all be taken'.[82]

Soviet historians portray what they call the rout of the Kwantung Army as a mighty campaign involving a Red Army force of one and a half million men, 5,500 tanks and 4,000 combat aircraft. The atom bomb, they say, did not influence Japan's ability to continue the fight; even after 14 August, when the Japanese government finally capitulated, the Kwantung Army continued to resist 'for a further three days'.

Stalin had told Truman at Potsdam that the new Japanese war would begin in the latter half of August and Malinovsky had been given from six to eight weeks to accomplish his mission. According to the present Soviet account, when Vasilevsky made his report to the Supreme Commander in Moscow on 3 August, he pressed that the war might be brought forward, basing his argument on the intelligence that the number of Japanese divisions in Manchuria and Korea had been increased in June (*sic*) from nineteen to twenty-three.[83] This factor seems scarcely pertinent. If the bringing forward of the war by two to three weeks was, as Soviet writers affirm, entirely unconnected with the use of the atomic bomb or the readiness of the Japanese to surrender, the real reason for the haste to rush into a campaign before the end of the rains, remains obscure.

In spite of what had been said at Potsdam, it was somewhat doubtful whether it was really intended that Vasilevsky should command the Far East forces without supervision from Moscow. On 3 August he had proposed to Stalin that the main body of Meretskov's 1 Far East Front should go over to the offensive five to seven days after Malinovsky's Transbaikal Front. Stalin had the timings 'checked mathematically' by the general staff before rejecting the idea, and decided that the offensive should start simultaneously on all fronts. The *Stavka* decision was immediately transmitted to Vasilevsky, but the final directive confirming the tasks already given to the fronts, and including dates and timings, was not signed by Stalin until 1630 hours on 7 August. Operations began at 0010 hours in the early morning of 9 August, and the war took on the character of an exercise in movement.

On 11 August, Molotov called Harriman and Clark-Kerr to his office to discuss the appointment of a Supreme Commander to whom the Japanese Emperor and Government were to be subordinated 'in case the Japanese decided to surrender'. To Harriman's suggestion that this might be MacArthur, Molotov replied that there might have to be two Supreme Commanders, MacArthur and Vasilevsky. Harriman did not think so; the United States had carried the main burden of the war in the Pacific for four years 'and kept the Japanese off Russia's back'; the Soviet Union had been in the war only two days. Molotov, too, became heated, and said that he did not wish to reply as he would have to refer to the war in Europe. He would consult with Stalin. Antonov's Potsdam statement that Marshal Vasilevsky would have complete control, without supervision from Moscow, of all Soviet operations in the Far East, should probably be viewed against this political background.

The Soviet military representative Lieutenant-General Derevianko, who was a co-signatory to the final surrender document signed on the *Missouri* at Manila, was nominated for this duty by Stalin in a personal communication to Truman. The lesson of Susloparov had not been forgotten.

# 12
# *Epilogue*

Trotsky said of Stalin that his ambition had acquired an untutored Asiatic cast of mind, intensified by European techniques, so that he had to have the press extol him extravagantly every day, publish his portraits, refer to him on the slightest pretext, and print his name in large type. Everything had to revolve around Stalin.[1] At a later period Khrushchev said much the same.

With the partial rehabilitation of Stalin, however, the military men have been constrained to voice a qualified view. Zhukov in his 1968 memoirs has glossed over the pre-war purges in a passing reference of a few lines; in Vasilevsky's 1974 autobiography they are not even mentioned. Zhukov and Shtemenko maintain that Stalin 'did not decide and, in the main, did not want to decide important military questions personally, for he well understood the necessity for collective work in these complicated spheres', notwithstanding that their own memoirs are brimming with descriptions of Stalin taking capricious and wrongful decisions of great moment, without consulting anyone.[2] It is clear that the dictator continued to do so until the time of his death. In 1946, for example, following a chance conversation with Voronov immediately after the May day parade, he decided, on the spur of the moment, to create a special academy of artillery sciences, for he had always had an admiration for that arm which he called 'the God of War'. The general staff and Commissariat of Defence were against the decision, but, as Shtemenko said, 'no one could point out to Stalin that the project was illogical and in truth did not try to do so'. The academy was formed in the following September, only to be disbanded shortly afterwards.[3]

Numbers of present day Soviet writers have attempted to explain Stalin's character against the background of the infallibility of the Communist Party. Shtemenko wrote, in 1973, that Stalin had enormous power and that it was fitting to regard this as the recognition of his services to the Communist Party, at the head of which he stood. Stalin's authority and the respect in which he was held by the people were, continued Shtemenko, created by the party, although they were strengthened by the man's own personal qualities; indeed 'in the latter years of his life' the ugly pattern of the cult of the individual emerged, and although Stalin made some efforts to protest against the glorification of his person, these were not convincing.[4] Yet at a 1946 meeting of the Supreme Military Council (VVS) which was presided over by Stalin, all present had to listen to a long harangue by the chairman, directed against 'one of our most important soldiers [presumably Zhukov]', on the subject of immodesty, unjustified conceit and megalomania.[5] Vasilevsky has included a number of paragraphs in his memoirs which appear to have been written by a hand other than his own, since they contradict the conclusions to be drawn from the body of his book. These paragraphs emphasize that the credit for the successful leadership of the armed forces and the people lay with the Communist Party, 'for all principal questions concerning the war were decided by the Central Committee – the Politburo, Orgburo, and Secretariat'. This point is accepted and re-emphasized by his literary reviewers.[6]

Soviet historians writing in the period of Khrushchev's ascendancy have blamed the Stalin personality cult for the slowness of the Soviet armed forces between 1946 and 1953 to adapt to the likely conditions of rocket and nuclear warfare.[7] At the time, Stalin said that 'the artificially sustained hullabaloo about the danger of a third world war' was meant for people with weak nerves, and he refused to be frightened 'by their atomic blackmail'.[8] Yet he wasted neither opportunity nor effort in launching a massive atomic and rocket research programme and, in the event, although probably by good fortune rather than by sound judgement, he lost nothing by leaving his ground forces equipped and trained in the fashion of the great armoured battles of 1945.

In 1942 Stalin had produced his own principles of war, based on permanently operating and transitory and fortuitous factors.[9]

Three of the constantly operating factors, quantity and quality of divisions, equipment, and the organizing ability of the commanders, being based on substance rather than theory, certainly reflected Stalin's cast of mind and were in contradistinction to the military principles accepted by the other great powers. In Soviet terminology 'morale' became 'morale of the army' and the fifth factor, stability of the rear, was adopted directly from Lenin.[10] By 1949 Stalin had become 'the greatest man on our planet' and Soviet military science, which embraced not only the purely military elements of the military art, strategy, operations, tactics and the organization and training of troops, but also social-political, economic and home-morale factors, was known as 'Stalin military science'. The dictator's infallible pronouncements assumed the style of oracles so that, according to the 1964 military textbooks, the principles enunciated by Stalin blocked further research and development in the military field. Yet the principles of war promulgated in 1964 differed little, except in their manner of presentation, from those originally formulated by Stalin.[11]

In the summer of 1949 Stalin was lecturing the Politburo that 'Hitler's generals, raised on the dogma of Clausewitz and Moltke, could not understand that war is won in the factories'. Out of a population of eighty million, continued Stalin, the German adventurists maintained armed forces totalling thirteen million, whereas 'history tells us that no single state could maintain such an effort'. Stalin contrasted this with the 194 million population of the Soviet Union at the beginning of the war and the maximum size of the Red Army – which he put at eleven and a half million men.[12] Stalin's statement was not entirely correct, for Hitler's generals had as little effect on the outcome of the Russo-German War as Stalin's generals, and Stalin does not take into account many other pertinent factors which contributed to the Soviet victory. But what does emerge from these pronouncements is Stalin's insistence on a firm home economic base, together with the stability of the Soviet military rear. Lenin once said that 'the unstable rear of Denikin, Kolchak, Wrangel and the imperialist agents, predetermined their defeat'. In the Second World War the Soviet rear was safeguarded by the party and by NKVD troops; and Stalin, as the chairman of the *Tsentral'nyi Shtab*, which was outside the *Stavka*, controlled partisan activities aimed at destroying the authority of the occupying power and the security of the enemy lines of communication.

Stalin was unresolved as to the relative position of the Soviet Navy within the High Command and, in February 1946, he joined the Commissariats for Defence and for the Navy into a single Ministry of the Armed Forces. Four years later this was split again into separate Ministries of Defence and of the Navy. There was, in addition, other re-organization, for within the Ministry of Defence Stalin had created a Headquarters Ground Forces responsible for doctrine and training, which was later redesignated as the Headquarters of the Soviet Army. In 1947 Stalin formally relinquished the post of Commissar for Defence to Bulganin.

Most of Stalin's senior generals continued to hold high appointments, some for a decade or more after his death. There were, however, some changes. Vasilevsky was one of the ablest and best educated of the marshals belonging, like Shaposhnikov, to a bygone age; his writings show that he stood intellectually head and shoulders above Zhukov. Vasilevsky replaced Antonov as Chief of General Staff in November 1948 and then, four months later, became Minister of Defence in place of Bulganin. Zhukov's education was largely self-acquired, but he was a decisive and hard character of genius who willingly accepted, or took, responsibility for the conduct of operations. According to Vasilevsky, Zhukov had marked originality and creative ability, particularly in the operative field, and Stalin frequently called on him for advice; Zhukov was, concluded Vasilevsky, 'one of the most brilliant of the military leaders of the Second World War'.[13] Zhukov was removed from his post as Deputy Supreme Commander in March 1946 and sent to relatively subordinate appointments, the command of the Odessa and then the Ural Military Districts, and disappeared, at least from public notice, for several years. At about this time Gordov was arrested when in command of the Volga Military District and became, according to Konev, 'a victim of the repression'. Novikov and Kuznetsov were soon under a cloud and Stalin took a dislike to Antonov, who was sent off to the Caucasus. When Montgomery visited Moscow in 1948, he noted that all the ministers and marshals stood in the greatest awe of Stalin 'and shut up like an oyster in his presence'.[14]

Konev held a special position among the marshals because he was favoured by Stalin as a counter-weight to Zhukov. He was a strong, somewhat brutal character, a man of limited education but great energy, unable to express himself well on paper; but he realized his own limitations and sorted out operative and tactical problems on the spot with the forward troops, leaving all other matters to his staff. Konev became the Commander-in-Chief of the Ground Forces from June 1946 until March 1950 when he was appointed as Inspector-General. Rokossovsky was particularly talented militarily, for he had the ability, rarely met in the Red Army, of using, and relying on, his subordinates, and he had an excellent relationship with Malinin, his chief of staff. Rokossovsky became Soviet Commander-in-Chief in Poland and then the Polish Minister for Defence. No one could use their staffs better than the gloomy and taciturn Govorov, whose powers of organization were the envy of all; he was persistent and demanding, and, according to Vasilevsky, no officer in his headquarters found that time hung heavily on his hands. Govorov knew staff work well, though he took good care never to do it. From 1947 Govorov became the first Inspector-General of the Armed Forces. Meretskov, Malinovsky, Tolbukhin and Bagramian went to internal military districts. Vasilevsky has agreed with Stalin's evaluation of Meretskov, who was distinguished for cunning, circumspection and thoroughness; when working out solutions, Meretskov tried to agree his decisions with the general staff by 'first finding out the opinion of the highest power in the land'. Malinovsky and Tolbukhin had worked on the staff and they took a prominent part in their own staff planning, often doing the work of the chiefs of staff, a failing which Vatutin had shared. But whereas Malinovsky was a hard character, Tolbukhin was of a particularly mild disposition. Tolbukhin's control did not suffer on this account as he was most ably supported by his chief of staff Biriuzov, a practical man of strong views. Bagramian was a man of education, of clear sight and lucid expression, and in Vasilevsky's view, a hard and single-minded commander.[15] Stalin used his marshals in accordance with their capabilities, but owed no great debt to any one of them. The higher their rank and the more popular their fame, the less they enjoyed his trust, so that the command of by far the largest and most experienced front in the Soviet Army held on a war footing, the Group of Soviet Forces in Germany, was to be given to Chuikov, a general of no great importance who had commanded only an army throughout most of the war and who was not on close terms with his more illustrious fellows.

Later in life Stalin became a glutton, but his mind was never confused by strong drink although he encouraged that failing in others; for his own drinking was a pretence, and the special carafe of colourless vodka, from which he drank his many toasts, was in fact water.[16] Stalin was always sober. Yet once during a Kuntsevo supper in 1944, the dictator got up, hitched up his trousers as though he was about to wrestle or to box, and cried out: 'The war will soon be over. We shall recover in fifteen or twenty years and then we will have another go at it!'.[17] In this was revealed the mentality of the man. By 1948 his intellect was already declining but his control over the affairs of state was as tight as ever. He became even more suspicious and quicker to take offence. A foreigner, Djilas, could discern tension between the dictator and Molotov, and, according to Khrushchev, Stalin had formed the notion 'to finish off' both Molotov and Mikoian. Voroshilov, too, was in some danger, for Stalin, toying with the suspicion that Voroshilov was an English agent, had for several years past forbidden Voroshilov to attend Politburo sessions or receive documents.[18] Voznesensky, another Politburo member, had been shot and, as a result of the Leningrad affair, Stalin had purged Zhdanov's associates and protégés. At home a new terror began to gather momentum, while abroad the former western allies were deliberately provoked by the Berlin blockade. The Soviet armed forces were rapidly increased by a partial mobilization so that the 1948 strength of 2,874,000 rose to near the six million mark.[19]

A woman doctor, one Timashuk, wrote a private letter to Stalin criticizing the treatment prescribed by eminent Soviet medical specialists, and this was enough to cause Stalin to believe, so he said, that the doctors were conspiring to murder prominent leaders loyal to himself. Vasilevsky, Konev, Govorov and Shtemenko were the military names among the so-called plot victims. The doctors' plot, according to Khrushchev, was a fabrication from beginning to end, the whole case having been set up by Stalin, 'who did not, however, have the time to bring the matter to the end which he had mapped out'.[20] Stalin's sudden death was a temporary reprieve for his courtiers and henchmen, and perhaps for the populations of the Soviet Union and the rest of the world. For so died one, whom Djilas, a fellow communist, called 'the greatest criminal in history'.

———————

Stalin's military qualities were not conspicuous during his stay at Tsaritsyn and Petrograd in 1918 and 1919, for, like Trotsky, he was without training or experience, a political figure who wanted to shine militarily. His judgement was clouded not by political prejudice but by personal ambition, envy and rancour. Yet the Perm and Polish War correspondence shows that he had organizational ability which was, in due course, to stand him well in the military field. There is little doubt that, at the time, Stalin was highly regarded, both by Lenin and by Trotsky, as a political and military worker of outstanding force of character; and Voroshilov was correct when he said that from 1919 onwards Stalin was moved from theatre to theatre, being sent by the Politburo to those fronts where the threat was most dangerous. Although his personal achievements may be questioned, his experience during the Civil and Polish Wars was later put to good use. Stalin learned much from Lenin.

The subversion and demoralization of the Imperial Russian Army led directly to the destruction of the last of the Romanovs; this was a lesson which Stalin was not likely to forget. During the period between the two world wars he quickly gained control of the police and of the Red Army and, from 1926 onwards, he interested himself closely in military affairs. The political controls over the armed forces, introduced by Trotsky in what was probably intended as a temporary expedient, were never to be loosened, notwithstanding the occasional experiments with unified command; the NKVD para-military organization was created to form a counterweight to the Red Army. Although the collegiate and commissar system and the secret police organization within the armed forces detracted from military efficiency, they effectively served their purpose in safeguarding Stalin against further revolution. The purges and terror were two of the measures used to destroy or deter possible opposition.

During Stalin's dictatorship it had been obligatory for the Soviet press to denigrate all capitalist states, the tsars, the Russian Empire, and the old army. Whether Stalin believed his own propaganda organs is perhaps doubtful, for he was a strange revolutionary with complexes of inferiority unexpected in such a man; he admired the Great Russian and the old tsarist army, with its centuries of tradition and its imposing imperial names. Like the Russian, he had a healthy respect for German efficiency and for French military *élan*.

During the late twenties and the thirties Stalin, in the final outcome, controlled senior Soviet military appointments, and approved or directed military theory, training, organization, equipment and deployment. Stalin alone was responsible for the purges which destroyed the larger part of the senior command of the Red Army. Stalin's principal positive contribution at this time was the creation of a well-developed home industrial base, responsible for the production of a great quantity of military equipment, much of it of modern design and good quality at the time it was taken into service. But by 1941 the Red Army was already paying the penalty for over-production and was using a large variety of weapons, diverse in model and pattern, many of them obsolete or obsolescent. Although Soviet small-arms and artillery were generally of high quality, tanks and aircraft were much inferior to those of German design, an inferiority which was only partially redressed when some of the post 1940 production became available. The fighting efficiency of aircraft, tanks and guns and of air and ground formations, depends largely, however, on the associated fire-control, communication and auxiliary equipment, and this was woefully lacking in the Soviet Union in 1941. All in all, however, Russia went to war immeasurably better prepared and equipped than it had ever done in tsarist times and, in quantitative terms, took the field with the greatest army in the world. Qualitatively, however, it was, at the time, hardly to be compared with the German Army.

Stalin's failure in the opening days of the war was political rather than military, for it was the direct consequence of his own political misjudgement. It is doubtful whether a military commander of genius could have saved the Soviet Union from a series of defeats and an enormous loss of territory in the first few months of the war, so great were the effects of surprise and the superiority of the *Wehrmacht*. According to the account said to have originated from the Soviet Chief of General Staff, Stalin was aware of this truth, even before the outbreak of war. If this was in fact the case, Stalin's fault becomes even more grievous, for he would have been wiser to have adopted a mobile defence, following the example of Barclay de Tolly, withdrawing his armies eastwards to the outskirts of Moscow and Rostov in preparation for a winter campaign. For the winter, not Kutuzov, destroyed Bonaparte. Stalin's insistence on the holding of ground was responsible for the loss in the first nine months of the war of three and a half million Red Army men as prisoners, in addition to the heavy casualties in killed and wounded. Stalin repeated his error in May 1942, when, buoyed by his successes during the winter fighting, he tried to enter the western Ukraine.

The Stalingrad battle on the other hand was fought deep in the interior of Russia, near what was once Sarai, the Tatar capital of the Golden Horde, at the gateway to Asia. The Axis troops, badly clothed and poorly supplied, were extended to their limit and the hard weather was approaching. In the previous winter the enemy Army Groups Centre and South had retreated up to distances of 200 miles, often in defiance of the Führer's standstill orders, and so saved themselves from destruction. In Stalingrad, however, 6 German Army had a commander who implicitly obeyed his orders to remain on the Volga.

Stalin alone was responsible for the heavy losses of 1941 and 1942. But if he is to bear the blame for the defeats of the first two years of war, he must be allowed the credit for the amazing successes of 1944, the *annus mirabilis*, when whole German army groups were virtually obliterated with lightning blows in Belorussia, Galicia, Rumania and the Baltic, in battles fought not on the wintry steppes, but in midsummer in Central Europe. Some of these victories must be reckoned as among the most outstanding in the world's military history.

The reasons for the improvement in the Soviet leadership and High Command during the course of the war will be obvious to the reader. Yet a comprehensive analysis of the factors which brought victory to the Soviet Union can only be undertaken with a concomitant study of the reasons for the German military defeats, a subject outside the scope of this work. Hitler's failure in the winter of 1942 was due to an over-ambitious strategy based on inadequate resources and a wilful underestimate of enemy potential; as he himself told Goebbels, he had been unable to overcome the problem of movement and supply in Russia, and he had done what once he had said he would never do, entrusted the security of German troops to his allies. Moreover the Stalingrad victory has to be seen against the world background of war as the first major landmark along the road to victory; not as a cause of German defeat in the Second World War but as an effect of the heavy preponderance of allied resources over those of the Axis powers. By the end of 1942 the balance was already weighted against Germany, and from then onwards this was to show itself in a series of disasters for the Axis, not only in Russia but in the Far East, the Atlantic, the Mediterranean and in Europe. During 1943 it was apparent to the world that Germany's fortunes were on the wane. Air superiority had been lost even in daylight over the Reich, and the Axis allies were ready to capitulate. Not only had the German Army lost its old offensive power, but it no longer disposed sufficient troops to defend and garrison occupied Europe for German manpower was to prove inadequate to maintain the number of field formations in existence. German industry was still not on a war footing and, through failing to recognize the seriousness of the position until it was too late, Hitler lost three years which might have been better used to equip the German forces.

As military commanders Stalin and Hitler had much in common. By 1944, however, the situation had been reversed, so that Axis troops were fighting under conditions of air inferiority, lacking fire support and mobility. Hitler's military strategy became rapidly bankrupt in that he was determined to hold territory by a rigid defence, and he assumed the role acted out by Stalin in 1941. No withdrawal, however limited, could be undertaken without his express permission. Those generals who disagreed with him were dismissed, for the halcyon days of the brilliant panzer envelopments were long passed. So the German formations fell into the Red Army maw, an easy prey to the fast moving Soviet tank armies. The wheel of fortune had turned full circle.

# Appendix
# The Russian and Red Armies

Before 1870 the French were regarded as the prominent military thinkers and the most competent soldiers in the world, so that Napoleon Bonaparte's army organization continued to serve as a model for all the great powers, including Prussia and Russia. After the Franco-Prussian War military interest became focussed on Prussia and the new army of the German Empire, and from then on followed the German lead. So it came about that the methods, organization and tactics of the armies of France, Germany and Russia were all in accordance with a common European continental pattern. The basic field formation devised by the French and still in use over a century and a half later was the infantry division, an all arms grouping, principally of infantry, with artillery and engineer supporting troops. Infantry was the main fighting element and all other arms existed merely to assist it. Other than infantry, only cavalry could, in certain phases of war, operate as a main arm, but then solely for very limited periods on ground suitable for mounted action.

The infantry division was said to be basic because it was designed to be capable of operation in isolation on any terrain, and was self-contained and self-supporting; the military might of a nation came to be reckoned in the number of infantry divisions which it could muster. The strength of a division varied from ten to 17 thousand men, of whom about three-quarters were infantry, but its effectiveness depended not so much on its numbers as on its fire power, mobility, training and tactical handling. There was no hard and fast rule for the grouping of infantry divisions into higher formations. Several divisions, usually three, made up a corps, several corps made up an army and several armies were formed into an army group, known in Russian as a front. Army groups were controlled directly by a General Headquarters or High Command, known in tsarist days as the *Stavka*.

According to French military thought *strategy* is regarded as the art of preparing, mobilizing, deploying, concentrating and moving forces between theatres of war or within a theatre, with a view to success in battle. *Tactics* is the art of actually fighting the resultant battles. German thought extended this doctrine by interposing *operations* (sometimes known as the *operative art*) at an intermediate stage between strategy and tactics, since the experience of the Franco-Prussian, Russo-Turkish and Russo-Japanese Wars showed that separate tactical engagements, instead of being restricted in time and space as they were in Napoleonic times, developed by degrees into prolonged battles covering vast areas and involving large numbers of troops. The preparation and conduct of these major battles within a theatre were held, according to the Berlin school, to be within the sphere of operations. This German concept was assumed by the Soviet High Command in 1924. At the risk of over-simplification it may be said that the Russians tend to regard the warlike activities of divisions and corps as tactical, while armies and fronts are usually employed on operative tasks; the co-ordination and control of two or more fronts comes within the definition of strategy. The distinction between strategy, operations and tactics is admitted to be very fine on occasions since this depends not only on the size of the forces engaged but on frontages, depth, the time element and the nature of the task; for example, tactical formations can perform roles which have an operative significance, particularly when they receive independent missions at critical moments of an action.

The 1914 Russian Army was a short term conscript force organized on the Prussian pattern. The Russian infantry division had two infantry brigades each of two infantry regiments, making four regiments in all, together with a divisional artillery brigade and attached Cossack squadrons. The division was usually commanded by a lieutenant-general, a brigade by a major-general, and a regiment by a colonel; at full strength it totalled 16,000 men, 36 guns, 27 machine-guns and about 200 sabres. An infantry

regiment normally had three battalions, commanded by lieu-
tenant-colonels or majors, each battalion having three or four
rifle companies. A cavalry or Cossack division usually comprised
two brigades each of two cavalry regiments, together with horse
artillery batteries; it rarely mustered more than 4,000 sabres. These
tsarist organizations were used, with some variations, both by the
White forces and by the Red Army; equipment, words of command, uniform (except for the identifying scrap of white or red
cloth) were common to both sides.

During the Civil and Polish Wars the Bolsheviks dispensed with
the corps headquarters so that infantry divisions were grouped
directly under armies, and, in 1918, they experimented by increasing the size of certain Red Army infantry divisions, so that
each had three rifle brigades firstly of two and then of three rifle
regiments each, together with nine artillery battalions. This raised
the strength of the division to 60,000 men, 24,000 horses and 116
guns and was found to be impracticable since the division was too
unwieldy. The old tsarist divisional organization was then re-
adopted at a reduced strength of about 10,000 men.

During the 1920s the infantry brigade headquarters were
abolished and infantry divisions henceforth comprised three
infantry and one artillery regiment with an engineer and signals
battalion. During the late 1930s a tank component was added to
the majority of the infantry and cavalry divisions.

Originally tanks had a role something between that of artillery
and engineers in that they were intended to assist infantry to fight
and to move by providing fire power and by overcoming obstacles,
but the military theorists between the two world wars began to
envisage the use of a large number of tanks, supported by infantry
and other arms, exploiting the flexibility of tactical air power and
outflanking and encircling the slow moving infantry armies of the
enemy. In such a role tanks became co-equal with infantry, a main
rather than a supporting arm. Except in Germany, these theorists
were without position or influence. In the Soviet Union there were
repeated changes of policy regarding the employment and organization of its tank forces, as it followed firstly the French and then
the German lead.

Russian built tanks had become available from 1927 onwards,
the first tank brigades of 90 fighting vehicles being formed in 1931.

By 1932 mechanized corps had been raised, each consisting of three tank brigades and a supporting motorized rifle brigade, totalling in all 490 BT and T 26 tanks. These mechanized corps were redesignated in 1938 as tank corps. In November of the following year, however, it was decided that the primary function of the tank was to support infantry, and the large tank formations were disbanded and reformed as 35 light and four heavy tank brigades, each of three or four tank battalions, the light tank brigade totalling 258 tanks while the heavy tank brigade had 156 (T 28 and T 35) tanks. Each of the fifteen motorized divisions retained its complement of 257 tanks and a further 98 independent tank battalions were allocated to the infantry divisions; in addition there were 20 independent tank regiments forming part of the cavalry divisions. From midsummer 1940 Soviet armour was re-organized once more to a close copy of the new German panzer arm, mechanized corps being formed, each consisting of two tank divisions – each of 410 tanks – and one motorized division. The 1940 Soviet mechanized corps at full strength totalled 1,030 tanks, of which 126 were of KV and 420 of T 34 type.

The Red Air Force had always been an integral part of the Red Army, the aviator being a soldier whose main task, together with the artillery, was to provide fire support for the ground forces. He wore army uniform and could only be distinguished by a different headdress and the light blue colour of his arm of service gorget patch. In 1930 the largest air formation within the Red Army was the air brigade of three squadrons, in all 100 aircraft. Three years later the brigades had been grouped into air corps and by 1936 the first air army had been formed. In 1940 this air organization was abolished in favour of the air regiment, usually consisting of 60 aircraft, and the air division of two or three air regiments.

The heavy Soviet losses in men and equipment at the outbreak of the Russo-German War made it necessary to abolish the corps headquarters as a temporary staff economy measure until 1943 when they were restored to the chain of command. Because of the lack of tanks, the large armoured formations were broken up in July 1941 and reformed as independent tank brigades each of 93 tanks, later reduced to a holding of 67 tanks. By 1942, however, new tanks corps were being formed, although on a much reduced establishment of 168 tanks, together with mechanized corps formed in three variants with a tank strength of 175, 204 or 224 fighting vehicles. Tank and mechanized corps had a brigade but not a divisional organization. In addition independent tank brigades continued their separate existence, by 1943 having been reduced to 53 tanks; the independent tank regiment had 39 and the heavy tank regiment only 21 tanks. From 1943 onwards tank and mechanized corps were grouped into tank armies, the fighting strength of which might vary from 400–1,000 tanks, together with a strong motorized infantry component.

The Soviet Union ended the war with its armies organized in a traditional pattern, the line or 'combined arms' armies having the usual corps and divisional organization while the shock armies had an additional artillery element to assist them in their break-through role. Air armies were usually concentrated directly under front command. Towards the end of Stalin's life, however, it became apparent that the corps organization was going to be dropped once more, while the tank armies were to be re-organized on a divisional pattern, without the corps headquarters, very much in the style of the 1941 German panzer corps.

# Notes

**Chapter 1**

1. Cit., Souvarine, pp. 112–4.
2. *Pravda*, 7 Feb 28 and 20 Dec 29; Yaroslavsky, p. 72.
3. *Stalin Kratk. Biogr.*, p. 56.
4. *Prot. Ts. Kom. RSDRP (29)*, p. 124.
5. Trotsky, *Stalin*, p. 232.
6. Ibid., p. 234.
7. Stalin, *Soch.*, Vol. 3, p. 423; *Hist. Civ. War in USSR*, Vol. 2, pp. 174, 195, 201, 221.
8. Trotsky, *Stalin*, p. 243.
9. Cf., *50 Let*, p. 33.
10. *V. Ist. Zh.*, 6/67, p. 79.
11. Littauer, pp. 246–7.
12. Cf., Rotmistrov, Vol. 1, p. 212; Zaionchovsky, *V. Ist. Zh.*, 3/73, pp. 42, 45–7.
13. Shaposhnikov, *V. Ist. Zh.*, 1/67, pp. 77–8.
14. Knox, Vol. 1, p. xxix.
15. Trotsky, *Hist. Russ. Rev.*, Vol. 1, p. 274.
16. Denikin, p. 159.
17. Trotsky, *Stalin*, p. 278; Lenin, *Poln. Sobr. Soch.*, Vol. 39, p. 313.
18. Trotsky, *Kak Voor. Rev.*, Vol. 1, pp. 17, 151; *Trotsky Papers*, Vol. 1, pp. 148, 544.
19. Cf., *Arm. Sov.*, p. 31.
20. *Iz Ist. Grazhd. Voin.*, Vol. 1, p. 473.
21. *Dir. Kom. Front.*, Vol. 1, p. 250.
22. Stalin, *Soch.*, Vol. 4, pp. 419–20 note 21.
23. Ibid., pp. 116–7; *Trotsky Papers*, Vol. 1, p. 46.
24. *Leninsk. Sborn.*, XXXVII pp. 88–90.
25. *Dir. Kom. Front.*, Vol. 1, p. 265.
26. Ibid., p. 269.
27. *Iz Ist. Grazhd. Voin.*, Vol. 1, p. 470.
28. *Hist. Civ. War in USSR*, Vol. 2, p. 41.
29. *Ist. Grazhd. Voin.*, Vol. 1, p. 231.
30. Denikin, p. 165.
31. Stalin, *Soch.*, Vol. 4, pp. 118–9.
32. Ibid., pp. 120–1.
33. Voroshilov, *Stalin i Kr. Arm.*, p. 10.
34. *Iz Ist. Grazhd. Voin.*, Vol. 1, p. 478.
35. Trotsky, *Stalin*, p. 270.
36. Cf., Souvarine, p. 245.

37. *Dir. Glav. Kom.*, p. 74.
38. Budenny, Vol. 1, pp. 80–3.
39. *Dir. Kom. Front.*, Vol. 1, pp. 289–302.
40. Voroshilov, op. cit., p. 13.
41. Ibid., p. 14.
42. *Grazhd. Voin.*, Vol. 1, p. 20.
43. Stalin, *Soch.*, Vol. 4, pp. 122–4.
44. *Stalin Kratk. Biog.*, pp. 72–3.
45. *Trotsky Papers*, Vol. 1, p. 164.
46. *Grazhd. Voin.*, Vol. 3, p. 252.
47. Stalin, *Soch.*, Vol. 4, pp. 122–6.
48. Denikin, p. 45.
49. Cf., Budenny, Vol. 1, pp. 135–6.
50. Denikin, p. 152.
51. *Dir. Kom. Front.*, Vol. 1, pp. 304, 306–7.
52. Ibid., pp. 309, 314, 722 note 77.
53. Stalin, *Soch.*, Vol. 4, pp. 127–8.
54. Ibid., p. 129; *Iz Ist. Grazhd. Voin.*, Vol. 1, p. 491.
55. Lenin, *Voen. Perep.*, p. 78.
56. *Leninsk. Sborn.*, XXXVII, p. 101; *Trotsky Papers*, Vol. 1, pp. 92–6, 106, 116.
57. *Iz Ist. Grazhd. Voin.*, Vol. 1, p. 494.
58. Stalin, *Soch.*, Vol. 4, p. 453.
59. *Dir. Kom. Front.*, Vol. 1, pp. 322–9.
60. Ibid., p. 336.
61. Ibid., p. 343.
62. Ibid., p. 345.
63. Rotmistrov, Vol. 1, p. 386.
64. Genkina, *Prol. Rev.*, 2/39, p. 101.
65. *Trotsky Papers*, Vol. 1, p. 116.
66. *Dir. Kom. Front.*, Vol. 1, p. 348.
67. *Iz Ist. Grazhd. Voin.*, Vol. 1, p. 496.
68. Sverdlov, Vol. 3, p. 28.
69. *Dir. Glav. Kom.*, pp. 82–3.
70. *Trotsky Papers*, Vol. 1, p. 140.
71. Stalin, *Soch.*, Vol. 4, p. 453.
72. *Trotsky Papers*, Vol. 1, p. 135.
73. *Dir. Glav. Kom.*, p. 118.
74. Ibid., pp. 84–5.
75. *Dir. Kom. Front.*, Vol. 1, pp. 353–4, 358.
76. Cf., Efimov, *V. Ist. Zh.*, 1/67, pp. 108–10.
77. *Trotsky Papers*, Vol. 1, pp. 158–60; *Leninsk. Sborn.*, XXXVII, pp. 106–7.
78. *Grazhd. Voin. na Ukr.*, Vol. 1, Bk 1, pp. 386, 449.
79. *Stalin Kratk. Biog.*, p. 73.
80. Stalin, *Soch.*, Vol. 4, pp. 174–6, 422.
81. *Grazhd. Voin. na Ukr.*, Vol. 1, Bk 2, p. 23.

**Chapter 2**
1. Lenin, *Voen. Perep.*, p. 88; *Trotsky Papers*, Vol. 1, pp. 194–6.

2. Ibid., pp. 228, 230;
   Trotsky, *Stalin*, p. 293.
3. Stalin, *Soch.*, Vol. 4,
   pp. 186–8.
4. *Leninsk. Sborn.*, XXXVII,
   p. 120.
5. Voroshilov, *Stalin i Kr.
   Arm.*, pp. 20–3.
6. Stalin, *Soch.*, Vol. 4,
   p. 425 note 50; Lenin,
   *Poln. Sobr. Soch.*, Vol. 50,
   p. 243.
7. Stalin, *Soch.*, Vol. 4,
   p. 211.
8. Ibid., pp. 197–224.
9. Voroshilov, op. cit.,
   pp. 22–3.
10. Cf., Ironside, p. 167 *et seq.*;
    *50 Let*, p. 72.
11. *KPSS v Rez. i Resh.*,
    Pt I, p. 446.
12. *Leninsk. Sborn.*, XXVII,
    pp. 135–40.
13. Trotsky, *Stalin*, p. 307.
14. *50 Let*, p. 88; Stewart,
    p. 217.
15. *50 Let*, p. 89.
16. Kamenev, *Vosp. o Lenine*,
    Vol. 2, pp. 261–2.
17. *Bol'shevik*, 3/47, p. 6.
18. Trotsky, *Stalin*, p. 277.
19. Lenin, *Poln. Sobr. Soch.*,
    Vol. 50, p. 317.
20. Ibid., pp. 325, 331.
21. Ibid., pp. 334–5.
22. *Trotsky Papers*, Vol. 1,
    pp. 542–4, 546, 552;
    Lenin, *Voen. Perep.*,
    pp. 146–7.
23. Stalin, *Soch.*, Vol. 4, p. 431
    note 73; cf., *Arm. Sov.*,
    p. 74.
24. *Iz Ist. Grazhd. Voin*,
    Vol. 2, p. 328.
25. Stalin, *Soch.*, p. 431 note
    74.
26. *Leninsk. Sborn.*, XXXVI,
    p. 77.
27. *Dir. Kom. Front.*, Vol. 2,
    p. 99.
28. Voroshilov, op. cit., p. 25.
29. *Dir. Kom. Front.*, Vol. 2,
    pp. 100–3.
30. *Iz Ist. Grazhd. Voin.*,
    Vol. 2, p. 341.
31. *Trotsky Papers*, Vol. 1,
    p. 520.
32. Lenin, *Poln. Sobr. Soch.*,
    Vol. 50, pp. 334–5.
33. *Trotsky Papers*, Vol. 1,
    p. 520.
34. Trotsky, *Stalin*, p. 308.
35. *Ist. Grazhd. Voin.*, Vol. 4,
    p. 335.
36. *Dir. Glav. Kom.*, p. 384.
37. *Leninsk. Sborn.*, XXXVII,
    p. 161.
38. Stalin, *Soch.*, Vol. 4,
    pp. 272–4.
39. Kameneva, *Nov. Mir*, 3/69,
    p. 169.
40. Ibid., pp. 173–7;
    Kamenev, op. cit., p. 255.
41. *Trotsky Papers*, Vol. 1,
    pp. 442–4.
42. Ibid., p. 482.
43. Ibid., pp. 578–80; Trotsky,
    *Stalin*, pp. 313–4.
44. *Trotsky Papers*, Vol. 1,
    p. 594.
45. Denikin, pp. 279–80.
46. *Dir. Kom. Front.*, Vol. 2,
    p. 284.
47. Trotsky, *My Life*, p. 387

and *Stalin*, pp. 314, 322–3;
Voroshilov, op. cit., p. 31.
48. Souvarine, p. 242;
Deutscher, p. 211.
49. *Trotsky Papers*, Vol. 1,
p. 604.
50. *Dir. Kom. Front.*, Vol. 2,
p. 284.
51. *Dir. Glav. Kom.*, p. 439.
52. *Trotsky Papers*, Vol. 1,
pp. 610, 664–6.
53. *Iz Ist. Grazhd. Voin.*,
Vol. 2, p. 491.
54. Ibid., p. 499.
55. Ibid., p. 869 note 197.
56. Denikin, p. 283.
57. *Iz Ist. Grazhd. Voin.*,
Vol. 2, p. 521.
58. Ibid., p. 523 note 206.
59. Denikin, p. 159.
60. Lenin, *Poln. Sobr. Soch.*,
Vol. 51, pp. 54–6; cf.,
Rotmistrov, Vol. 1, p. 413.
61. *Trotsky Papers*, Vol. 1,
pp. 686–8.
62. *Stalin Kratk. Biog.*, p. 77.
63. Stalin, *Soch.*, Vol. 4,
pp. 275–7.
64. *Dir. Kom. Front.*, Vol. 2,
pp. 353–6.
65. Kuz'min, *V. Ist. Zh.*, 5/69,
p. 8.
66. *Dir. Kom. Front.*, Vol. 2,
pp. 370, 375.
67. *Trotsky Papers*, Vol. 1,
p. 758.
68. Rotmistrov, Vol. 1, p. 414.
69. *Iz Ist. Grazhd. Voin.*,
Vol. 2, p. 547.
70. *Leninsk. Sborn.*, XXXIV,
p. 239.
71. Voroshilov, op. cit.,

pp. 33–4.
72. Trotsky, *Stalin*, pp. 274–5.
73. Budenny, Vol. 1, pp. 321,
335.
74. Rotmistrov, Vol. 1, p. 422.
75. Budenny, Vol. 1, p. 345.
76. Trotsky, *Stalin*, p. 270.
77. Budenny, Vol. 1, pp.
243–5.
78. Littauer, p. 234.
79. Budenny, op. cit., p. 404.
80. *Trotsky Papers*, Vol. 2,
pp. 24–8.
81. *Iz Ist. Grazhd. Voin.*,
Vol. 2, p. 594.
82. *Trotsky Papers*, Vol. 2,
pp. 61, 66–7.
83. *Iz Ist. Grazhd. Voin.*,
Vol. 2, p. 594.

**Chapter 3**
1. *Trotsky Papers*, Vol. 1,
p. 764.
2. Lenin, *Poln. Sobr. Soch.*,
Vol. 51, p. 158; *Voen.
Perep.*, p. 257.
3. *Trotsky Papers*, Vol. 2,
p. 197.
4. Lenin, *Poln. Sobr. Soch.*,
Vol. 51, p. 205; *Voen.
Perep.*, p. 240.
5. *Trotsky Papers*, Vol. 2,
p. 199.
6. Ibid., p. 206; Lenin, *Poln.
Sobr. Soch.*, Vol. 51, pp.
206–7, 428–9, note 228.
7. *Trotsky Papers*, Vol. 2,
p. 215.
8. *Grazhd. Voin. na Ukr.*,
Vol. 3, p. 166; *Dir. Glav.
Kom.*, p. 687.
9. Ibid., pp. 689–93.

10. Ibid., p. 693.
11. *Grazhd. Voin. na Ukr.*, Vol. 3, p. 306.
12. Budenny, Vol. 2, p. 226.
13. *Leninsk. Sborn.*, XXIV, pp. 333–4.
14. *Iz Ist. Grazhd. Voin.*, Vol. 3, p. 329; *Trotsky Papers*, Vol. 2, p. 240.
15. Lenin, *Poln. Sobr. Soch.*, Vol. 51, pp. 247–8, 441 note 280.
16. *Iz Ist. Grazhd. Voin.*, Vol. 3, p. 336.
17. Ibid., p. 338.
18. Ibid., pp. 339, 341.
19. Ibid., pp. 341, 343.
20. Ibid., p. 342.
21. Budenny, Vol. 2, p. 306.
22. *Iz Ist. Grazhd. Voin.*, Vol. 3, p. 346.
23. Budenny, Vol. 2, pp. 288–9.
24. Lenin, *Poln. Sobr. Soch.*, Vol. 51, pp. 254–5.
25. *Iz Ist. Grazhd. Voin.*, Vol. 3, pp. 348–9; *Dir. Glav. Kom.*, p. 709.
26. Budenny, Vol. 2, p. 308.
27. Golubev, *V. Ist. Zh.*, 8/66, pp. 90–1.
28. *Iz Ist. Grazhd. Voin.*, Vol. 3, p. 350.
29. Ibid., p. 351; *Dir. Glav. Kom.*, p. 711.
30. *Iz Ist. Grazhd. Voin.*, Vol. 3, p. 352.
31. No. 0361/SEK of 15 August; Budenny, Vol. 2, pp. 309–11.
32. *Iz Ist. Grazhd. Voin.*, Vol. 3, p. 355.

33. Ibid., pp. 361–2.
34. *Trotsky Papers*, Vol. 2, p. 260.
35. Lenin, *Poln. Sobr. Soch.*, Vol. 32, p. 149 and Vol. 51, p. 258.
36. Trotsky, *Stalin*, pp. 296, 329.
37. Tukhachevsky, *Izb. Proizved.*, p. 162.
38. Shaposhnikov, *Na Visle*, p. 200.
39. Todorsky, p. 66; Rotmistrov, Vol. 1, p. 426; *V. Ist. Zh.*, 9/62, p. 62.
40. *Trotsky Papers*, Vol. 2, pp. 21, 279.

**Chapter 4**

1. Bazhanov, pp. 29–30.
2. Ibid., pp. 17–22.
3. Ibid., pp. 22–5.
4. Svetlana, p. 27.
5. Bazhanov, pp. 27, 32–4, 94–5.
6. Ibid., pp. 48, 55, 61.
7. Ibid., pp. 40, 45, 91–2, 133–4.
8. Trotsky, *Stalin*, p. 374; Rigby, p. 27.
9. *Ross. Komm. Part. IX S'ezd*, pp. 351 et seq.
10. *KPSS v Rez. i Resh.*, p. 569.
11. Trotsky, *Mil. Writ.*, pp. 28, 54, 59, 63–9, 70–93.
12. Voroshilov, *Stat. i Rech.*, pp. 281, 563.
13. *Arm. Sov.*, p. 105.
14. Ibid., p. 106.
15. Bazhanov, p. 72; Voroshilov, op. cit., p. 8.

16. *Docs Germ. For. Policy*, C, Vol. 2, p. 333.
17. Stalin, *Soch.*, Vol. 7, p. 11.
18. Barmine, p. 219.
19. Voroshilov, op. cit., p. 601.
20. Cit., White, p. 277.
21. Von Manstein, pp. 140–3.
22. Cf., *O Sov. Voen. Nauk.*, pp. 170–8; Kolganov, p. 9.
23. Sokolovsky, *Voen. Strat.*, p. 147.
24. Shaposhnikov, *V. Ist. Zh.*, 8/66, p. 75; 9/66, p. 73.
25. Hilger, p. 207.
26. *Nazi-Sov. Rels*, p. 74.
27. Stalin, *Leninism*, p. 541.
28. *50 Let*, pp. 195–200.
29. *Sobr. Zakon. R. K.*, 27/5, No. 34.
30. Kuznetsov, *Oktiabr'*, 9/63, p. 174.
31. Hilger, pp. 290, 301–3.
32. Meretskov, pp. 168–9.
33. Grabin, *Oktiabr'*, 11/73, p. 151; 12/73, p. 123.
34. Voronov, p. 45.
35. Ibid., pp. 115–6; Samsonov, *V. Ist. Zh.*, 5/69, pp. 52–4.
36. Zhukov, pp. 214, 217, 307.
37. Vannikov, *V. Ist. Zh.*, 2/62, pp. 78–86.
38. *V. Ist. Zh.*, 6/73, p. 79; Kolganov, p. 320.
39. Sherwood, Vol. 1, p. 329.
40. Emelianov, *Nov. Mir*, 2/67, p. 85.
41. *Pravda*, 18 Jul 48.
42. Iakovlev, p. 192.
43. Rotmistrov, Vol. 1, pp. 377, 479–81.
44. Zakharov, *V. Ist. Zh.*, 2/71, p. 40.
45. *Izvestiia*, 28 Feb 38.
46. Meretskov, p. 179; Vasilevsky, p. 100.
47. Rotmistrov, Vol. 1, p. 499.
48. Shtemenko, Vol. 1, p. 18.
49. *Ist. Vel. Ot. Voin.*, Vol. 1, p. 277.
50. *KPSS o Voor. Sil.*, p. 298; *Sots. Vest.*, 25 Feb 41, p. 47.
51. Zhukov, pp. 181–3.
52. Krupchenko, *V. Ist. Zh.*, 5/68, p. 42.
53. Rotmistrov, Vol. 1, p. 479.
54. Vasilevsky, p. 106.
55. Ibid., p. 107.
56. Meretskov, p. 195.
57. Vasilevsky, p. 110.
58. Golikov, *V. Ist. Zh.*, 5/66, p. 65.
59. Knox, Vol. 1, pp. 107, 137.
60. Vasilevsky, p. 110.
61. Meretskov, p. 196.
62. Ibid., pp. 198–200; Zhukov, p. 197; Kazakov, p. 56; Eremenko, *V Nach. Voin.*, p. 45.
63. *Nazi-Sov. Rels*, p. 252.
64. Kuznetsov, *V. Ist. Zh.*, 9/65, p. 73.
65. Zhukov, pp. 233, 244, 245.
66. Ibid., p. 249.
67. Rigby, p. 55; Tiulenev, p. 42; Voronov, p. 171.
68. Kuznetsov, *V. Ist. Zh.*, 9/65, p. 73; *Oktiabr'*, 11/65, pp. 146–7, 162–71.
69. Zhukov, p. 247; Voronov, p. 175; Rigby, p. 53.
70. *50 Let*, p. 235; Zhukov, p. 250.

71. Ibid., p. 212.
72. Ibid., p. 228.
73. Ibid., p. 272.
74. Ibid., p. 232; Vasilevsky, p. 112.
75. Rigby, p. 55.
76. Bagramian, *So Begann der Krieg*, p. 50.
77. *Nazi-Sov. Rels*, p. 326; *Docs Germ. For. Policy*, D. Vol. 12, p. 873.
78. Bagramian, *V. Ist. Zh.*, 1/67, p. 56.
79. Maisky, p. 148.
80. Teske, pp. 304–19.
81. Voronov, p. 171.
82. Bagramian, *So Begann der Krieg*, pp. 61, 82.
83. Maisky, p. 156; Tiulenev, p. 137.
84. Zhukov, pp. 251–3.
85. *Fremde Heere Ost (OKH)* apprec. 20 May 41; Halder, Vol. 2, pp. 351–3.

**Chapter 5**
1. Kuznetsov, *V. Ist. Zh.*, 9/65, p. 73.
2. Zhukov, p. 255.
3. *Ist. Vel. Ot. Voin.*, Vol. 2, p. 17; Halder, Vol. 3, p. 4.
4. Tiulenev, p. 137.
5. Zhukov, p. 257.
6. Vasilevsky, p. 122.
7. Zhukov, p. 259.
8. Peresypkin, *V. Ist. Zh.*, 4/71, p. 19.
9. Vasilevsky, *V. Ist. Zh.*, 6/74, p. 124.
10. Zhukov, p. 283.
11. Rigby, p. 57.
12. Voronov, p. 178.

13. Bagramian, *V. Ist. Zh.*, 3/66, p. 64.
14. Boldin, *V. Ist. Zh.*, 4/61, p. 67; Zhukov, p. 273.
15. Bagramian, *So Begann der Krieg*, p. 140.
16. Zhukov, p. 277.
17. Eremenko, *V Nach. Voin.*, p. 78.
18. Starinov, p. 210.
19. Biriuzov, *Kogda Grem. Pushk.*, p. 10.
20. Zhukov, p. 201.
21. Shtemenko, Vol. 1, p. 31.
22. *KPSS o Voor. Sil.*, p. 305.
23. Von Bock, *Tagebuch*, 8 Jul 41.
24. *Pravda*, 1 Jul 41.
25. Cf., Stalin, *On Great Patriotic War*, p. 50; Kuznetsov, *V. Ist. Zh.*, 9/55, p. 65.
26. *Ist. Vel. Ot. Voin.*, Vol. 2, p. 70.
27. Ibid., p. 62.
28. Von Bock, *Tagebuch*, 5 Aug 41.
29. Zhukov, p. 299.
30. Hubatsch, pp. 145, 148–9.
31. Zhukov, p. 310.
32. *KTB des OKW*, Vol. 1, p. 1062; Halder, Vol. 3, p. 192.
33. Khrulev, *V. Ist. Zh.*, 6/61, p. 64.
34. Sherwood, Vol. 1, pp. 328–47.
35. Vasilevsky, p. 140.
36. Guderian, p. 202; Halder, Vol. 3, pp. 194–5.
37. Zhukov, p. 318; Vasilevsky, p. 141;

Platonov, p. 318.
38. Bagramian, *So Begann der Krieg*, p. 274.
39. *Ist. Vel. Ot. Voin.*, Vol. 2, p. 104.
40. Vasilevsky, p. 139.
41. Ibid., p. 145.
42. Ibid., p. 147.
43. Bagramian, *Gorod-voin na Dnepre*, p. 120.
44. Bagramian, *So Begann der Krieg*, p. 317.
45. *Ist. Vel. Ot. Voin.*, Vol. 2, p. 107.
46. Zhukov, pp. 320–1.
47. Fediuninsky, p. 41.
48. Kuznetsov, *Vopros. Ist.*, 8/65, p. 114.
49. Zhukov, pp. 321–3; Vasilevsky, p. 148; Bagramian, *So Begann der Krieg*, pp. 319–22.
50. Ibid., p. 326; *Ist. Vel. Ot. Voin.*, Vol. 2, p. 108.
51. Vasilevsky, p. 150.
52. Gwyer, Vol. 3, Pt 1, p. 200.
53. Bagramian, *So Begann der Krieg*, pp. 326–34.
54. *Ist. Vel. Ot. Voin.*, Vol. 2, p. 108.
55. *KTB des OKW*, Vol. 1, p. 661.
56. Bychevsky, pp. 92–100.
57. Kuznetsov, *V. Ist. Zh.*, 9/66, pp. 65–6.
58. Hubatsch, p. 150.
59. Konev, *V. Ist. Zh.*, 10/66, p. 56.
60. Rokossovsky, *Sold. Dolg*, pp. 49–50.
61. Sokolovsky, *Raz. Nemets. Voisk pod Moskv.*, p. 30;

*V. Ist. Zh.*, 3/67, p. 70.
62. Gwyer, pp. 155–61.
63. Ismay, p. 233.
64. Leliushenko, *Zar. Pobed.*, p. 43.
65. Livshits, p. 34.
66. Telegin, *Vopros. Ist.*, 9/66, p. 101.
67. Rokossovsky, op. cit., pp. 52–61.
68. *KTB des OKW*, Vol. 1, p. 702.
69. Ibid., p. 531.
70. Sbytov, *Bit. za Moskv.*, pp. 402–4.
71. Zhukov, p. 344.

**Chapter 6**
1. Halder, Vol. 3, p. 295.
2. Zhukov, pp. 345–52.
3. Konev, *V. Ist. Zh.*, 10/66, p. 65.
4. Leliushenko, *Moskv.-Prag.*, pp. 48–9.
5. Werth, p. 234; Birse, p. 79.
6. Pronin, *Bit. za Moskv.*, p. 465; Telegin, *Vopros. Ist.*, 9/66, p. 104.
7. Zhukov, pp. 362–6.
8. Vasilevsky, *Bit. za Moskv.*, p. 23.
9. Vasilevsky, p. 163.
10. *Ist. Vel. Ot. Voin.*, Vol. 2, pp. 271–4.
11. Shelakhov, *V. Ist. Zh.*, 3/69, pp. 56–9.
12. Shtemenko, Vol. 1, pp. 30–2.
13. Shtemenko, Vol. 2, p. 7; Vasilevsky, p. 125.
14. Ibid., p. 124.
15. Ibid., p. 126.

16. Shtemenko, Vol. 2, p. 39; Zhukov, pp. 305–8.
17. Ibid., p. 289.
18. Rotmistrov, Vol. 2, pp. 52, 57, 104.
18. Gorbatov, pp. 104–7, 169.
20. Shtemenko, Vol. 1, pp. 47–8.
21. Voronov, p. 180.
22. Shtemenko, Vol. 1, p. 44.
23. Ibid., pp. 138–9.
24. Ibid., pp. 34–5.
25. Peresypkin, *V. Ist. Zh.*, 6/70, p. 12; 4/71, p. 21.
26. Shtemenko, Vol. 1, pp. 113–8.
27. Voronov, p. 178; *Ist. SSSR*, 4/65, p. 3.
28. Iakovlev, p. 317.
29. Vasilevsky, p. 160.
30. Werth, pp. 897–901; Sherwood, Vol. 2, p. 904; Tedder, p. 685.
31. Voronov, p. 202.
32. Vasilevsky, p. 165.
33. Zhukov, p. 364; Rokossovsky, *Sold. Dolg.*, p. 75.
34. Leliushenko, *Zar. Pobed.*, pp. 82, 88–9.
35. Zhukov, pp. 369–70.
36. Rokossovsky, op. cit., p. 91.
37. Rokossovsky, *V. Ist. Zh.*, 11/66. p. 52.
38. Cf., Iakovlev, p. 202.
39. Rokossovsky, op. cit., p. 93.
40. Zhukov, p. 375.
41. Vasilevsky, p. 167.
42. Ibid., p. 168.
43. Ibid., p. 172.

44. Rotmistrov, Vol. 2, p. 130.
45. Sokolovsky, *Raz. Nemets. Voisk pod Moskv.*, p. 318.
46. Anders, p. 83.
47. Eden, pp. 289–99.
48. Ibid., p. 320.
49. *Ist. Vel. Ot. Voin.*, Vol. 2, p. 213, note 2.
50. Meretskov, pp. 251–75.
51. P. Egorov, *V. Ist. Zh.*, 6/69, p. 96.
52. Zhukov, pp. 379–81; *Bit. za Moskv.*, p. 77.
53. Vasilevsky, pp. 173–9.
54. Zhukov, *Bit. za Moskv.*, p. 89.
55. *Ist. Vel. Ot. Voin.*, Vol. 2, p. 359.
56. Khozin, *V. Ist. Zh.*, 2/66, pp. 35–45.
57. Meretskov, p. 290.

**Chapter 7**

1. Hubatsch, p. 186.
2. Vasilevsky, pp. 184–5; *Stalingrad. Ep.*, pp. 74–5.
3. Vasilevsky, p. 190.
4. Zhukov, p. 396.
5. Vasilevsky, *Stalingrad. Ep.*, p. 75.
6. Vasilevsky, pp. 190–1.
7. Vasilevsky, *V. Ist. Zh.*, 8/65, p. 3.
8. Timoshenko, *Bit. za Moskv.*, p. 97.
9. Vasilevsky, p. 191.
10. Ibid., p. 192.
11. Rigby, p. 58; cf. Eremenko, *Stalingrad*, p. 46 footnote.
12. Djilas, p. 113.
13. Vasilevsky, p. 234.

14. Shtemenko, Vol. 1, p. 49.
15. Ibid., p. 50; Vasilevsky, p. 187.
16. Samsonov, *Stalingrad. Bit.*, pp. 63-4.
17. Ibid., pp. 72-3.
18. Halder, Vol. 3, pp. 470-6; Hubatsch, pp. 183-8.
19. Vasilevsky, *Stalingrad. Ep.*, p. 76.
20. Samsonov, op. cit., p. 74.
21. Rotmistrov, Vol. 2, p. 160; Vasilevsky, *V. Ist. Zh.*, 8/65, p. 7.
22. Kazakov, *V. Ist. Zh.*, 10/64, p. 39; Vasilevsky, *Stalingrad. Ep.*, pp. 76-7.
23. Rotmistrov, Vol. 2, pp. 160-1; *Stalingrad. Ep.*, pp. 605-7.
24. *Ist. Vel. Ot. Voin.*, Vol. 2, pp. 420-1.
25. Kazakov, p. 130.
26. Rokossovsky, *Sold. Dolg.*, pp. 128-30.
27. Vasilevsky, p. 200.
28. *Ist. Vel. Ot. Voin.*, Vol. 2, p. 422.
29. Vasilevsky, *Stalingrad. Ep.*, p. 79; *V. Ist. Zh.*, 10/65, p. 14.
30. Eremenko, *Stalingrad*, pp. 36-9.
31. Zhukov, p. 418.
32. Vasilevsky, *V. Ist. Zh.*, 10/65, p. 17; Moskalenko, *Stalingrad. Ep.*, p. 219.
33. Eremenko, *Stalingrad*, pp. 89-91.

**Chapter 8**
1. Churchill, Vol. 4, p. 429.

2. Sherwood, Vol. 2, pp. 616-8.
3. Cit. Bryant, *Turn of the Tide*, p. 380.
4. Birse, p. 95; Deane, pp. 31-5.
5. Bryant, op. cit., p. 388.
6. Svetlana, p. 183.
7. Vasilevsky, *V. Ist. Zh.*, 10/65, p. 18.
8. Eremenko, *Stalingrad*, pp. 133-6.
9. Ibid., pp. 138-40.
10. Samsonov, *Stalingrad. Bit.*, p. 140.
11. Eremenko, op. cit., p. 325.
12. Zhukov, p. 410; Moskalenko, *Stalingrad. Ep.*, pp. 222-3.
13. Zhukov, p. 407.
14. *Ist. Vel. Ot. Voin.*, Vol. 3, p. 17; Rokossovsky, *Sold. Dolg.*, pp. 139-42.
15. Zhukov, pp. 413-4.
16. Vasilevsky, *Stalingrad. Ep.*, p. 83.
17. Zhukov, pp. 416-7.
18. *Stalin – Kratk. Biog.*, p. 197.
19. Rotmistrov, Vol. 2, p. 197.
20. *Ist. Vel. Ot. Voin.*, Vol. 3, p. 18.
21. Eremenko, op. cit., pp. 326, 329.
22. Vasilevsky, *Stalingrad. Ep.*, p. 85.
23. Zhukov, pp. 433-4.
24. Greiner, pp. 401-2.
25. *KTB des OKW*, Vol. 2, pp. 1305-7.
26. Samsonov, op. cit., pp. 526, 528 and footnotes;

Rokossovsky, *Velik. Pobed. na Volge*, pp. 254–6.
27. Leliushenko, *Stalingrad. Ep.*, p. 685.
28. Zhukov, pp. 438–9.
29. Kolganov, p. 364.
30. Kozhevnikov, *V. Ist. Zh.*, 2/74, pp. 31–5.
31. Nikitin, *V. Ist. Zh.*, 5/74, pp. 55–9.
32. Zhukov, p. 441.
33. Lugansky, p. 83.
34. Tiulenev, pp. 196–7.
35. Vasilevsky, *V. Ist. Zh.*, 10/65, p. 25.
36. Eremenko, op. cit., pp. 347, 354.
37. Vasilevsky, *Stalingrad. Ep.*, p. 92.
38. Ibid., pp. 94–5.
39. Samsonov, op. cit., pp. 436–7.
40. Rokossovsky, *Sold. Dolg*, p. 162.
41. Vasilevsky, *Stalingrad. Ep.*, p. 101.
42. Zhukov, pp. 446–7.
43. Rotmistrov, *Stalingrad. Ep.*, pp. 611–3.
44. Krasovsky, *Stalingrad. Ep.*, pp. 577–8.
45. Eremenko, op. cit., pp. 393–4.
46. Ibid., p. 400.
47. Vasilevsky, *Stalingrad. Ep.*, pp. 103–5.
48. Vasilevsky, *V. Ist. Zh.*, 3/66, pp. 26–7.
49. Vasilevsky, *Stalingrad. Ep.*, p. 102.
50. Rokossovsky, *Stalingrad. Ep.*, p. 173; *Sold. Dolg.*, p. 167.
51. Vasilevsky, *Stalingrad. Ep.*, pp. 107–8.
52. Ibid., pp. 112–3; *V. Ist. Zh.*, 3/66, p. 35; Eremenko, op. cit., p. 411, maps 20, 21.
53. Vasilevsky, *Stalingrad. Ep.*, p. 116.
54. Zhukov, pp. 453–4; Samsonov, op. cit., p. 484.
55. Zhukov, pp. 456–7; Eremenko, *Stalingrad*, p. 426.
56. Meretskov, pp. 319–20.
57. Rokossovsky, *Sold. Dolg*, pp. 175–6.
58. Ibid., p. 179; Voronov, *Stalingrad. Ep.*, pp. 200–1.
59. Rokossovsky, *Sold. Dolg*, p. 192.
60. Shtemenko, Vol. 1, p. 60.
61. Grechko, *Bit. za Kavk.*, pp. 154–5.
62. Ibid., pp. 158–9.
63. Ibid., pp. 161–2; Shtemenko, Vol. 1, p. 64.
64. Ibid., p. 65.
65. Tiulenev, pp. 247–9.
66. Grechko, op. cit., pp. 243–4.
67. Shtemenko, Vol. 1, pp. 68–9.
68. Ibid., p. 72; Grechko, op. cit., p. 232.
69. Vasilevsky, p. 236 footnote.
70. Shtemenko, Vol. 1, p. 75.
71. Zhukov, p. 477.
72. Shtemenko, Vol. 1, p. 91.
73. Kuznetsov, *V. Ist. Zh.*, 9/66, pp. 65–7.
74. Kuznetsov, *Stalingrad. Ep.*, pp. 414–5.
75. Samsonov, op. cit., pp.

164–7.

76. Vasilevsky, p. 127.
77. Shtemenko, Vol. 2, pp. 293–4.
78. Vasilevsky, p. 273.
79. Ibid., pp. 247, 280.
80. Ibid., pp. 281–2.

**Chapter 9**
 1. Golikov, *V. Ist. Zh.*, 1/73, pp. 62–7; Shtemenko, Vol. 1, p. 97.
 2. Ibid., p. 104.
 3. Stalin, *On Great Patriotic War*, p. 49.
 4. Rokossovsky, *Sold. Dolg*, pp. 193–4.
 5. Shtemenko, Vol. 1, p. 107.
 6. Rokossovsky, op. cit., pp. 196–7.
 7. *Geschichte des Grossen Vaterländischen Krieges*, Vol. 3, p. 142. (not in the Russian original).
 8. Vasilevsky, p. 300.
 9. Zhukov, pp. 465–6.
10. Rokossovsky, op. cit., p. 202.
11. Zhukov, pp. 469–70.
12. Vasilevsky, p. 309.
13. Zhukov, pp. 471–3.
14. Shtemenko, Vol. 1, pp. 151–2.
15. Vasilevsky, pp. 309–10.
16. Konev, p. 9.
17. Shtemenko, Vol. 1, p. 156.
18. Zhukov, p. 483.
19. Rokossovsky, op. cit., p. 203; *Ist. Vel. Ot. Voin.*, Vol. 3, pp. 246–7.
20. Vasilevsky, pp. 316–8.
21. Shtemenko, Vol. 1, p. 167.

22. Iakovlev, pp. 330–2.
23. Shtemenko, Vol. 1, pp. 161–2.
24. Bagramian, *V. Ist. Zh.*, 11/67, p. 42.
25. Rokossovsky, op. cit., p. 212.
26. Peresypkin, *V. Ist. Zh.*, 7/73, pp. 51–9.
27. Konev, pp. 11–3.
28. *V. Ist. Zh.*, 6/68, p. 61; 7/68, p. 79.
29. Rokossovsky, op. cit., p. 219.
30. *Ist. Vel. Ot. Voin.*, Vol. 3, pp. 268–9.
31. Ivanov, *V. Ist. Zh.*, 8/73, pp. 11–20.
32. Rotmistrov, Vol. 2, p. 246.
33. Shtemenko, Vol. 1, p. 155.
34. Zhukov, pp. 198–9.
35. Ibid., p. 505.
36. Ibid., pp. 518, 523.
37. Shtemenko, Vol. 1, pp. 172, 182–4; Vasilevsky, p. 336.
38. Ibid., p. 335.
39. Ibid., p. 338.
40. Konev, p. 37.
41. Rokossovsky, op. cit., p. 235.
42. Shtemenko, Vol. 1, pp. 178–9.
43. Zhukov, p. 523.
44. Ibid., pp. 524–5.
45. Shtemenko, Vol. 2, p. 314.
46. Rigby, p. 57; Voronov, p. 384.
47. Ibid., pp. 391–7.
48. Shtemenko, Vol. 1, pp. 187–8.
49. Moskalenko, pp. 150–3.
50. Shtemenko, Vol. 1, p. 116.

51. Moskalenko, pp. 180–2.
52. Rokossovsky, op. cit., p. 240.
53. Konev, pp. 77–8.
54. Rokossovsky, op. cit., pp. 251–3; Batov, *V. Ist. Zh.*, 10/74, p. 65.
55. Vasilevsky, p. 371.
56. Leliushenko, *Moskva-Praga*, pp. 196–8.
57. Konev, p. 120; *V. Ist. Zh.*, 2/69, pp. 57–64.
58. Zhukov, pp. 553–5.
59. Novikov, *Nov. Mir*, 3/70, pp. 169–85.
60. Djilas, pp. 51–4.
61. Shtemenko, Vol. 1, p. 203.
62. Ibid., p. 206.
63. Ibid., pp. 206–21; Vasilevsky, *V. Ist. Zh.*, 5/71, p. 70.
64. Ismay, p. 325.
65. Eden, p. 411.
66. Ibid., p. 415.
67. Ismay, p. 327.
68. Shtemenko, Vol. 1, pp. 190–4.
69. Birse, p. 156.
70. Ismay, p. 338.
71. Deane, p. 43.
72. Ibid., p. 44.
73. Bryant, *Triumph in the West*, p. 90.
74. Sherwood, Vol. 2, p. 775.
75. Bryant, op. cit., pp. 91–4.
76. Eden, p. 413; Sherwood, Vol. 2, p. 777.
77. Ibid., pp. 784, 787.
78. Deane, pp. 145–7.

**Chapter 10**

1. *Ist. Vel. Ot. Voin.*, Vol. 3, pp. 372, 374 note 3; Vol. 4, pp. 46, 123.
2. Sandalov, pp. 3–10.
3. Shtemenko, Vol. 1, p. 269.
4. Meretskov, pp. 365–7.
5. Vasilevsky, *V. Ist. Zh.*, 9/69, p. 50.
6. Shtemenko, Vol. 2, pp. 152–3.
7. Shtemenko, Vol. 1, pp. 271–7.
8. Ibid., pp. 224–7.
9. Rokossovsky, *Sold. Dolg*, pp. 257–8.
10. Shtemenko, Vol. 1, pp. 231–2.
11. Kiseev, *V. Ist. Zh.*, 6/66, p. 36.
12. Shtemenko, Vol. 1, pp. 227–30.
13. Zhukov, pp. 564–5.
14. Vasilevsky, p. 408.
15. Vasilevsky, *V. Ist. Zh.*, 9/69, pp. 47–51.
16. Shtemenko, Vol. 1, pp. 232–5.
17. Shtemenko, Vol. 2, p. 373.
18. Shtemenko, *V. Ist. Zh.*, 6/72, pp. 64–5.
19. Shtemenko, *V. Ist. Zh.*, 7/72, p. 64.
20. Shtemenko, Vol. 1, pp. 280–1; Meretskov, p. 377.
21. Ibid., p. 379.
22. Vasilevsky, *V. Ist. Zh.*, 9/69, p. 55.
23. Meretskov, pp. 380–1.
24. Novikov, *Nov. Mir*, 3/70, pp. 168–9; *V. Ist. Zh.*, 7/69, p. 62.
25. Nepomniashchy, pp. 238–40.
26. Batov, *V. Ist. Zh.*, 12/66, p. 41; Rokossovsky, op. cit., pp. 260–1.

27. Zhukov, p. 570.
28. Telegin, *V. Ist. Zh.*, 9/69, p. 84.
29. Zhukov, pp. 570–1; Shtemenko, Vol. 1, p. 257.
30. Ibid., p. 239.
31. Ibid., p. 250.
32. Ibid., pp. 239–42.
33. Vasilevsky, p. 362.
34. Vasilevsky, *V. Ist. Zh.*, 9/69, pp. 47–52.
35. Simonov, *V. Ist. Zh.*, 9/66, p. 49; Shtemenko, Vol. 1, pp. 245–6.
36. Batov, p. 274.
37. Zhukov, pp. 574–6; *V. Ist. Zh.*, 2/69, p. 72.
38. Shtemenko, Vol. 1, p. 254.
39. Ibid., pp. 243, 252.
40. Vasilevsky, *V. Ist. Zh.*, 9/69, pp. 55–7.
41. Peresypkin, *V. Ist. Zh.*, 6/69, p. 70.
42. Konev, p. 274.
43. Ibid., pp. 233–4; Krainiukov, *V. Ist. Zh.*, 7/69, p. 77.
44. *Ist. Vel. Ot. Voin.*, Vol. 4, pp. 158–67.
45. *OKH Schem. Kriegsgliederung*, 15 June 44.
46. *KTB des OKW*, Vol. 4, p. 858.
47. Burrows, *PRO file WO/106/3273*.
48. Zhukov, pp. 583–6.
49. Rokossovsky, op. cit., p. 265.
50. Zhukov, pp. 591–2.
51. Shtemenko, Vol. 2, pp. 69–70.
52. Konev, p. 268.
53. Shtemenko, Vol. 2, pp.
54. Churchill, Vol. 6, pp. 118–20.
55. Ibid., p. 114; Bor-Komorowski, pp. 212, 342–6; Feis, p. 380.
56. Rokossovsky, op. cit., pp. 284–91.
57. *Trotsky Papers*, Vol. 2, 279.
58. Zhukov, pp. 601–3.
59. Rokossovsky, op. cit., pp. 297–8; *V. Ist. Zh.*, 2/65, p. 25.
60. Shtemenko, Vol. 2, pp. 34–5.
61. Shtemenko, Vol. 1, p. 282.
62. Cf., *Ist. Vel. Ot. Voin.*, Vol. 4, p. 347.
63. Ibid., p. 345.
64. Ibid., p. 356.
65. Shtemenko, Vol. 1, p. 297.
66. Kazakov, *V. Ist. Zh.*, 2/67, pp. 37, 71.
67. Shtemenko, Vol. 2, pp. 19–20.
68. *Ist. Vel. Ot. Voin.*, Vol. 4, pp. 260–6.
69. Shtemenko, Vol. 2, pp. 125–33.
70. Cf., Matsulenko, p. 103; Biriuzov, *Surov. God.*, p. 423.
71. *Ist. Vel. Ot. Voin.*, Vol. 4, pp. 293–4.
72. Zhukov, pp. 596–8.
73. Grechko, *Cher. Karp.*, p. 15.
74. Shtemenko, Vol. 2, p. 253.
75. *Ist. Vel. Ot. Voin.*, Vol. 4, p. 390.
76. Malinovsky, *Budapesht-Vena-Praga*, pp. 81–3.

77. Shtemenko, Vol. 2, pp. 255–6.

**Chapter 11**
1. Shtemenko, Vol. 2, pp. 250–1.
2. Bryant, *Triumph in the West*, p. 304.
3. Eden, p. 488.
4. Deane, p. 155.
5. Ismay, p. 378.
6. Deane, pp. 245–7.
7. Bryant, op. cit., pp. 307–8.
8. Deane, pp. 248–51.
9. Shtemenko, Vol. 1, pp. 306–14.
10. Zhukov, pp. 608–12.
11. Rokossovsky, *Sold. Dolg*, p. 299.
12. Vasilevsky, *V. Ist. Zh.*, 3/69, pp. 35–9.
13. Rokossovsky, op. cit., p. 313.
14. *Dir. Glav. Kom.* 1455 of 8 Feb 45 signed by Stalin and Vasilevsky (when Stalin was still in the Crimea).
15. Konev, *Nov. Mir*, 5/65, p. 3.
16. *KTB des OKW*, Vol. 4, p. 993.
17. Ibid., p. 1002.
18. Churchill, Vol. 6, p. 243.
19. Deane, pp. 156–7; Birse, pp. 176–7.
20. Vasilevsky, p. 481.
21. Shtemenko, Vol. 2, p. 251.
22. Sherwood, Vol. 2, pp. 843–4; Bryant, op. cit., pp. 402–6.
23. Zhukov, p. 618.
24. Shtemenko, Vol. 1, p. 317.

25. Zhukov, p. 622.
26. Chuikov, *Oktiabr'*, 4/64, pp. 128–31; *Nov. i Noveish. Ist.*, 2/65, p. 6.
27. Telegin, *V. Ist. Zh.*, 4/65, pp. 62–4.
28. Shtemenko, Vol. 1, pp. 317–23.
29. Ibid., pp. 325–7.
30. Rokossovsky, op. cit., p. 326.
31. Ibid., pp. 334, 339.
32. Vasilevsky, *V. Ist. Zh.*, 3/69, pp. 41–3.
33. No 215/K of 16 March.
34. Vasilevsky, *V. Ist. Zh.*, 3/69, pp. 46–50.
35. Ivanov, *V. Ist. Zh.*, 6/69, p. 25.
36. Ibid., 3/69, pp. 14–18.
37. Shtemenko, Vol. 2, p. 275.
38. Ivanov, *V. Ist. Zh.*, 6/69, p. 28.
39. Moskalenko, pp. 569–70.
40. FWD – 18264 (SCAF 252).
41. *Command Decisions*, pp. 377–8; Churchill, Vol. 6, pp. 399–409; Eisenhower, pp. 433–40.
42. Pogue, p. 440.
43. Deane, p. 158.
44. *Ist. Vel. Ot. Voin.*, Vol. 5, p. 257.
45. Zhukov, pp. 640–2.
46. Cf., Djilas, pp. 70, 106.
47. Zhukov, p. 642.
48. Shtemenko, Vol. 1, p. 329.
49. Konev, *Nov. Mir*, 5/65, pp. 38–40.
50. Shtemenko, Vol. 1, pp. 329–31; Zhukov, p. 643.
51. Konev, *Nov. Mir*, 5/65,

pp. 44–7.
52. Rokossovsky, op. cit., pp. 351–2.
53. Zhukov, p. 648.
54. *KTB des OKW*, Vol. 4, pp. 1240–2.
55. Zhukov, p. 660.
56. *KTB des OKW*, Vol. 4, p. 1249.
57. Zhukov, p. 660.
58. Konev, *Nov. Mir*, 5/65, pp. 58–60.
59. 00215 of 17 April issued at 0247 hrs on 18 April.
60. Konev, *Nov. Mir*, 6/65, pp. 14–5.
61. Zhukov, p. 663.
62. Deane, p. 159.
63. Konev, *Nov. Mir*, 6/65, p. 47.
64. Chuikov, *Oktiabr'*, 4/64, p. 156.
65. Konev, *Nov. Mir*, 6/65, p. 59; 7/65, pp. 100–1.
66. Voronov, *Ist. SSSR*, 4/65, p. 24; Shtemenko subsequently denied that Susloparov was brought to account; Vol. 2, pp. 432–4.
67. Zhukov, p. 682.
68. Werth, p. 901; cf. also Sherwood, Vol. 2, p. 904.
69. Konev, *Nov. Mir*, 7/65, p. 134.
70. Shelakhov, *V. Ist. Zh.*, 3/69, pp. 56–9.
71. Shtemenko, Vol. 1, p. 334.
72. Vasilevsky, *V. Ist. Zh.*, 6/67, pp. 82–3.
73. Shtemenko, Vol. 1, pp. 336–7.
74. Ibid., p. 347.

75. Meretskov, pp. 411–2.
76. Shtemenko, Vol. 1, p. 354.
77. Deane, pp. 272–4.
78. Sherwood, Vol. 2, pp. 892–3.
79. Eden, pp. 547–8.
80. Shtemenko, Vol. 1, p. 359.
81. Vasilevsky, *V. Ist. Zh.*, 6/67, p. 86.
82. Deane, pp. 275–6.
83. Shtemenko, Vol. 1, pp. 359–61.

**Chapter 12**

1. Trotsky, *Stalin*, pp. 393–4.
2. Shtemenko, Vol. 2, p. 279.
3. Ibid., p. 300.
4. Ibid., p. 499.
5. Ibid., p. 500.
6. Cf., Matsulenko, *V. Ist. Zh.*, 5/74, p. 110.
7. *O Sov. Voen. Nauk.*, pp. 200–2.
8. Voroshilov, *Stalin and Armed Forces*, p. 144.
9. Ibid., pp. 105–114.
10. Lenin, *Poln. Sobr. Soch.*, Vol. 24, p. 544.
11. *O Sov. Voen. Nauk.*, pp. 292, 296.
12. Shtemenko, Vol. 2, p. 505.
13. Vasilevsky, p. 529.
14. Montgomery, p. 415.
15. Vasilevsky, pp. 530–1.
16. Shtemenko, Vol. 2, p. 77.
17. Djilas, p. 106.
18. Rigby, p. 81.
19. *O Sov. Voen. Nauk.*, pp. 201–2. In 1955 its strength was 5,763,000.
20. Rigby, p. 67.

# Select Bibliography

This list is not a comprehensive bibliography but indicates the principal works to which reference has been made in the writing of this study.

## I. Books

Anders, W. *An Army in Exile*. Macmillan, London 1949.

Bagramian, I. Kh. *Gorod-Voin na Dnepre*. Moscow 1965.
*So Begann der Krieg*. Militärverlag, Berlin 1972.

Barmine, A. *Memoirs of a Soviet Diplomat*. Lovat Dickson, London 1938.

Batov, P. I. *V Pokhodakh i Boiakh*. Moscow 1962.

Bazhanov, B. *Stalin – Der Rote Diktator*. Aretz, Berlin 1931.

Birse, A. H. *Memoirs of an Interpreter*. Michael Joseph, London 1967.

Biriuzov, S. S. *Surovye Gody*. Moscow 1966.
*Kogda Gremeli Pushki*. Moscow 1961.

Blumenthal, F. *Politicheskaia Rabota v Voennoe Vremia*. Moscow 1929.

Bor-Komorowski, T. *The Secret Army*. Gollancz, London 1950.

Bryant, A. *The Turn of the Tide*. Collins, London 1957.
*Triumph in the West*. Collins, London 1959.

Budenny, S. M. *Proidennyi Put'*. (Two Vols). Moscow 1958–65.

Butler, J. R. M. *Grand Strategy*. (Vol. 3, Pt II). HMSO 1964.

Bychevsky, B. V. *Gorod-Front*. Moscow 1963.

Chamberlin, W. H. *The Russian Revolution 1917–21*. (Two Vols). Macmillan, London 1935.

Churchill, W. S. *The Second World War*. (Six Vols). Cassell, London.

Danilevsky, A. F. *V. I. Lenin i Voprosy Voennogo Stroitel'stva na VIII S'ezde RKP(b)*. Moscow 1964.

Deane, J. R. *The Strange Alliance*. Murray, London 1947.

Denikin, A. I. *The White Army*. Cape, London 1930.

Deutscher, I. *Stalin – A Political Biography*. OUP, London 1967.
Djilas, M. *Conversations with Stalin*. Rupert Hart-Davis, London 1962.
Eden, A. *Memoirs – The Reckoning*. Cassell, London 1965.
Egorov, A. I. *Razgrom Denikina*. Moscow 1936.
Eisenhower, D. D. *Crusade in Europe*. Heinemann, London 1948.
Eremenko, A. I. *Stalingrad*. Moscow 1961.
*V Nachale Voiny*. Moscow 1964.
*Pomni Voinu*. Donbass 1971.
Fediuninsky, I. I. *Podniatye po Trevoge*. Moscow 1964.
Feis, H. *Churchill, Roosevelt, Stalin*. Princeton UP, 1966.
Frunze, M. V. *Sobranie Sochinenii*. (Three Vols). Moscow 1929.
*Izbrannye Proizvedeniia*. (Two Vols). Moscow 1957.
Golikov, F. I. *V Moskovskoi Bitve*. Moscow 1967.
Golikov, S. *Vydaiushchiesia Pobedy Sovetskoi Armii v Velikoi Otechestvennoi Voine*. Moscow 1954.
Golovin, N. N. *The Russian Army in the World War*. OUP, London 1931.
Gorbatov, A. V. *Years off my Life*. Constable, London 1964.
Grechko, A. A. *Bitva za Kavkaz*. Moscow 1967.
*Cherez Karpaty*. Moscow 1970.
*Osvodobitel'naia Missiia Sovetskikh Vooruzhennykh Sil vo Vtoroi Mirovoi Voine*. Moscow 1971.
Greiner, H. *Die Oberste Wehrmachtführung*. Limes Verlag, Wiesbaden 1951.
Guderian, H. *Panzer Leader*. Michael Joseph, London 1952.
Gwyer, J. M. A. *Grand Strategy*. (Vol. 3, Pt I). HMSO 1964.
Halder, F. *Kriegstagebuch*. (Three Vols). Kohlhammer, Stuttgart 1962.
Hilger, G. *The Incompatible Allies*. Macmillan, New York 1953.
Hodgson, J. E. *With Denikin's Armies*. Lincoln Williams, London 1932.
Hubatsch, W. *Hitlers Weisungen für die Kriegführung 1939–1945*. Bernard u. Graefe, Frankfurt a.M. 1962.
Iakovlev, A. S. *Tsel' Zhizni*. Moscow 1966.
Ironside, E. *Archangel 1918–19*. Constable, London 1953.
Ismay, H. L. *The Memoirs of General the Lord Ismay*. Heinemann, London 1960.
Kamenev, S. S. *Vospominaniia o V. I. Lenine*. Moscow 1957.
*Zapiski o Grazhdanskoi Voine i Voennom Stroitel'stve*. Moscow 1963.

Kazakov, M. I. *Nad Kartoi Bylykh Srazhenii.* Moscow 1965.

Knox, A. *With the Russian Army 1914–17.* (Two Vols). Hutchinson, London 1921.

Kolganov, K. S. *Razvitie Taktiki Sovetskoi Armii v Gody Velikoi Otechestvennoi Voiny (1941–5).* Moscow 1958.

Konev, I. S. *Zapiski Komanduiushchego Frontom 1943–4.* Moscow 1972.

Korolivsky, S. M. *Grazhdanskaia Voina na Ukraine 1918–20.* Moscow 1968.

Kravchenko, G. S. *Voennaia Ekonomika SSSR 1941–45.* Moscow 1963.

Krivitsky, W. G. *I was Stalin's Agent.* Hamish Hamilton, London 1939.

Kurochkin, P. M. *Pozyvnye Fronta.* Moscow 1969.

Kuznetsov, N. G. *Nakanune.* Moscow 1966.

Leliushenko, D. D. *Zaria Pobedy.* Moscow 1966.
*Moskva-Stalingrad-Berlin-Praga.* Moscow 1970.

Lenin, V. I. *Leninskii Sbornik.* Moscow XXXIV (1942), XXXV (1945), XXXVI (1959), XXXVII (1970).
*Voennaia Perepiska (1917–20).* Moscow 1956.
*Polnoe Sobranie Sochinenii.* (5th Ed.) Vols 8, 24, 29, 30, 32, 35–7, 39, 40, 50–1, 54–5.

Littauer, V. S. *Russian Hussar.* Allen, London 1965.

Livshits, Ia. L. *Pervaia Gvardeiskaia Tankovaia Brigada v Boiakh za Moskvu.* Moscow 1948.

Löbell. *Jahresberichte 1908–14.*

Lugansky, S. D. *Na Glubokikh Virazhakh.* Alma-Ata 1966.

Lunacharsky, A. V. *Revoliutsionnye Siluety.* Moscow 1923.

Maisky, I. *Memoirs of a Soviet Ambassador.* Hutchinson, London 1967.

Malinovsky, R. Ia. *Final.* Moscow 1966.
*Budapesht-Vena-Praga.* Moscow 1969.

Manstein, E. von. *Aus einem Soldatenleben.* Athenäum, Bonn 1958.

Martel, G. *The Russian Outlook.* Michael Joseph, London 1947.

Mazulenko, W. A. *Die Zerschlagung der Heeresgruppe Südukraine.* Berlin 1959.

McNeal, R. H. *Stalin's Works (Bibliography).* Stamford University 1967.

Melikov, V. A. *Geroicheskaia Oborona Tsaritsyna 1918.* Moscow 1938.

Meretskov, K. A. *Na Sluzhbe Narodu.* Moscow 1970.

Miliukov, P. *Rossiia na Perelome*. Paris 1927.

Molotov, V. *Stalin and Stalin's Leadership*. Moscow 1950.

Montgomery, B. L. *Memoirs*. Collins, London 1958.

Moskalenko, K. S. *Na Iugo-Zapadnom Napravlenii 1943–45*. Moscow 1972.

Nepomniashchy, K. *Polki Idyt na Zapad*. Moscow 1964.

Novikov, A. A. *V Nebe Leningrada*. Moscow 1970.

Peresypkin, I. T. *Radio-Moguchee Sredstvo Oborony Strany*. Moscow 1948.

*Sviaz' v Velikoi Otechestvennoi Voine*. Moscow 1973.

Petrov, Iu. P. *Partiinoe Stroitel'stvo v Sovetskoi Armii i Flote*. Moscow 1964.

*Stroitel'stvo Politorganov, Partiinykh i Komsomol'skikh Organizatsii Armii i Flota (1918–1968)*. Moscow 1968.

Petrovsky, D. A. *Voennaia Shkola v Gody Revoliutsii*. Moscow 1924.

Pilsudski, J. *Year 1920*. Pilsudski Institute 1972.

Platonov, S. P. *Vtoraia Mirovaia Voina*. Moscow 1958.

Pokrovsky, M. *Ocherki po Istorii Oktiabr'skoi Revoliutsii*. (Two Vols). Moscow 1927.

Reznichenko, V. G. *Taktika*. Moscow 1966.

Rigby, T. H. (ed.) *The Stalin Dictatorship*. Sydney UP, Sydney 1968.

Rokossovsky, K. K. *Velikaia Pobeda na Volge*. Moscow 1965.

*Soldatskii Dolg*. Moscow 1968.

Rotmistrov, P. A. *Istoriia Voennogo Iskusstva*. (Two Vols). Moscow 1963.

Sandalov, L. M. *Perezhitoe*. Moscow 1961.

Samsonov, A. M. *Die Grosse Schlacht vor Moskau*. Militärverlag, Berlin 1959.

*Stalingradskaia Bitva*. Moscow 1968.

Seaton, A. *The Russo-German War 1941–45*. Arthur Barker, London 1971.

Shaposhnikov, B. M. *Na Visle*. Moscow 1924.

*Mozg Armii*. Moscow 1927.

Sherwood, R. E. *The White House Papers of Harry Hopkins*. (Two Vols). Eyre and Spottiswoode, London 1948–9.

Shtemenko, S. M. *General'nyi Shtab v Gody Voiny*. (Two Vols). Moscow 1968–73.

Sokolovsky, V. D. *Voennaia Strategiia*. Moscow 1963.

*Razgrom Nemetsko-Fashistkikh Voisk pod Moskvoi*. Moscow 1964.

Souvarine, B. *Stalin.* Secker & Warburg, London 1939.
Stalin, J. V. *Na Putiakh k Oktiabru.* Leningrad 1925.
*Leninism.* Lawrence & Wishart, London 1940.
*On the Great Patriotic War.* Hutchinson, London 1947.
*Sochineniia.* (13 Vols). Moscow 1946–51.
*Stanford Sochineniia.* (3 Vols). Ed. R. H. McNeal. Stanford UP, 1967.
*Economic Problems of Socialism in the USSR.* Moscow 1952.
*Stalin – Kratkaia Biografiia.* Moscow 1950.
Starinov, I. T. *Miny Zhdut Svoego Chasa.* Moscow 1964.
Stewart, G. *The White Armies of Russia.* Macmillan, New York 1933.
Sukhanov, N. N. *Zapiski o Revoliutsii.* Moscow 1922.
*The Russian Revolution 1917.* OUP 1955.
Svechin, A. A. *Strategiia.* Moscow 1927.
Sverdlov, Ia. M. *Izbrannye Proizvedeniia.* Moscow 1960.
Svetlana Alliluyeva. *Twenty Letters to a Friend.* Hutchinson, London 1967.
Tedder, A. *With Prejudice.* Cassell, London 1966.
Teske, H. *General Ernst Köstring.* Mittler, Frankfurt a.M. 1966.
Tiulenev, I. V. *Cherez Tri Voiny.* Moscow 1960.
Todorsky, A. I. *Marshal Tukhachevskii.* Moscow 1963.
Trotsky, L. D. *Kak Vooruzhalas' Revoliutsiia.* Moscow 1924.
*My Life.* Butterworth, London 1930.
*The History of the Russian Revolution.* (Three Vols). Gollancz, London 1932–3.
*Stalin.* Harper, London 1946.
*Military Writings.* (Ed. Breitman). Merit, New York 1969.
Tukhachevsky, M. N. *Voina Klassov.* Moscow 1921.
*Manevr i Artilleriia.* Moscow 1924.
*Izbrannye Proizvedeniia.* (Two Vols). Moscow 1964.
Vasilevsky, A. M. *Delo Vsei Zhizni.* Moscow 1974.
Vorob'ev, F. D. and Kravtsov, V. M. *Pobedy Sovetskikh Vooruzhennykh Sil v Velikoi Otechestvennoi Voine.* Moscow 1953.
Voronov, N. N. *Na Sluzhbe Voennoi.* Moscow 1963.
Voroshilov, K. E. *Stat'i i Rechi.* Moscow 1937.
*Stalin i Krasnaia Armiia.* Moscow 1938.
*Stalin and the Armed Forces of the USSR.* Moscow 1951.
Werth, A. *Russia at War.* Barrie and Rockcliff, London 1964.
White, D. *The Growth of the Red Army.* Princeton UP 1944.

Yaroslavsky, E. *Landmarks in the Life of Stalin.* Lawrence & Wishart, London 1942.
Zakharov, M. V. *Osvobozhdenie Iugo-Vostochnoi i Tsentral'noi Evropy Voiskami 2go i 3go Ukrainskikh Frontov.* Moscow 1970.
Zhukov, G. K. *Vospominaniia i Razmyshleniia.* Macdonald, London 1969.

## II Anthologies, Edited Works, Printed Documents, Official Publications and Reference Books

*Armiia Sovetskaia.* Moscow 1969.
*Bitva za Moskvu.* Moscow 1968.
*Bitva za Stalingrad.* Volgograd 1973.
*Bol'shaia Sovetskaia Entsiklopediia.* (Three Eds). Moscow 1926–70.
*Command Decisions.* Harcourt Brace, New York 1959.
*Dekrety Sovetskoi Vlasti.* (Five Vols). Moscow 1957–71.
*Direktivy Glavnogo Komandovaniia Krasnoi Armii (1917–1920).* Moscow 1969.
*Direktivy Komandovaniia Frontov Krasnoi Armii (1917–1920).* (Two Vols). Moscow 1971–2.
*Documents of German Foreign Policy.* HMSO, London.
*Dokumenty o Geroicheskoi Oborone Petrograda v 1919 g.* Moscow 1941.
*Dokumenty o Geroicheskoi Oborone Tsaritsyna v 1918 g.* Moscow 1942.
*Geschichte des Grossen Vaterländischen Krieges der Sowjet Union.* (Five Vols). Militärverlag, Berlin.
*Grazhdanskaia Voina.* (Vols 2 and 3). Moscow 1928–30.
*Grazhdanskaia Voina.* (2nd Ed. Four Vols). Moscow 1953–9.
*Grazhdanskaia Voina na Ukraine.* (Four Vols). Kiev 1967.
*Istoriia Kommunisticheskoi Partii Sovetskogo Soiuza.* (Vol. 3). Moscow 1968.
*Istoriia Velikoi Otechestvennoi Voiny Sovetskogo Soiuza.* (Six Vols). Moscow 1961–5.
*Iz Istorii Grazhdanskoi Voiny v SSSR.* (Three Vols). Moscow 1960–1.
*KPSS v Rezoliutsiiakh i Resheniiakh.* (Vol. 2). Moscow 1970.
*KPSS o Vooruzhennykh Silakh Sovetskogo Soiuza (Dokumenty 1917–68).* Moscow 1969.
*Kriegstagebuch des Oberkommandos der Wehrmacht.* (Four Vols). Bernard u. Graefe, Frankfurt a.M.
*Malaia Sovetskaia Entsiklopediia.* (3rd Ed). Moscow 1958.

*Nastavlenie po Postoiannym Liniiam Sviazi 1943 g.* Moscow 1945.
*Nazi-Soviet Relations 1939–41.* Department of State
   Publication 3023.
*O Sovetskoi Voennoi Nauke.* Moscow 1964.
*Osnovy Sovetskogo Voennogo Zakonodatel'stva.* Moscow 1966.
*Pogranichnye Voiska v Gody Velikoi Otechestvennoi Voiny.*
   Moscow 1968.
*Protokoly Tsentral'nogo Komiteta RSDRP (1929).*
*Sluzbba Sviazi. (uchebnik dlia shkol RKKA).* Moscow 1935.
*Sobranie Zakonov i Rasporiazhenii R.K. Pravitel'stva SSSR,*
   27/5 1937, No. 31.
*Spisok General'nago Shtaba.* St Petersburg 1913.
*SSSR v Velikoi Otechestvennoi Voine (1941–1945) (Kratkaia
   Khronika).* Moscow 1964.
*Stalingradskaia Epopeia.* Moscow 1968.
*Supreme Command.* The United States in WW II. (Pogue).
   Department of the Army 1954.
*The History of the Civil War in the USSR.* (Vol. 2). Lawrence &
   Wishart, London 1947.
*The Red Army Today.* Moscow 1939.
*The Trotsky Papers (1917–21).* (Ed. Meijer – Two Vols).
   Mouton, The Hague 1964–71.
*Ukrains'ka Radians'ka Entsiklopediia.* Kiev 1959.
*Velikaia Otechestvennaia Voina Sovetskogo Soiuza 1941–1945
   (Kratkaia Istoriia).* Moscow 1965.
*Voprosy Strategii i Operativnogo Iskusstva v Sovetskikh Voennykh
   Trudakh (1917–1940).* Moscow 1965.
*50 Let Vooruzhennykh Sil SSSR.* Moscow 1968.

## III Periodicals

*Bol'shevik.*
*Istoriia SSSR.*
*Kommunist.*
*Kommunist Vooruzhennykh Sil.*
*Novaia i Noveishaia Istoriia.*
*Novyi Mir.*
*Oktiabr'.*
*Proletarskaia Revoliutsiia.*
*Sotsialisticheskii Vestnik.*
*Soviet Military Review.*
*Voenno-Istoricheskii Zhurnal.*
*Voprosy Istorii.*

# Index